The King's Men

The Sandringham Company and the Norfolk Regiment Territorial Battalions 1914-1918

Neil R. Storey

First published in Great Britain in 2020 by
Pen & Sword Military
an imprint of
Pen & Sword Books Ltd
Yorkshire – Philadelphia

ISBN 978 1 52676 511 6

A CIP catalogue record for this book is
available from the British Library.

Printed and bound in the UK
by TJ International Ltd, Padstow, Cornwall.

Typeset in Times New Roman
by IMPEC eSolutions

Pen & Sword Books Limited incorporates the imprints of
Atlas, Archaeology, Aviation, Discovery, Family History, Fiction, History, Maritime, Military, Military Classics, Politics, Select, Transport, True Crime, Air World, Frontline Publishing, Leo Cooper, Remember When, Seaforth Publishing, The Praetorian Press, Wharncliffe Local History, Wharncliffe Transport, Wharncliffe True Crime and White Owl.

For a complete list of Pen & Sword titles please contact
PEN & SWORD BOOKS LIMITED
47 Church Street, Barnsley, South Yorkshire, S70 2AS, England
E-mail: enquiries@pen-and-sword.co.uk
Website: www.pen-and-sword.co.uk

Or

PEN AND SWORD BOOKS
1950 Lawrence Rd, Havertown, PA 19083, USA
E-mail: Uspen-and-sword@casematepublishers.com
Website: www.penandswordbooks.com

This book is dedicated to the memory of my Great Grandfather Frederick Griffin, 5th Battalion, The Norfolk Regiment, all those who served in the Norfolk Territorial Battalions during the First World War and their families.

Frederick Griffin (1890 - 1965).

Contents

The soldiers of the Downham Detachment, B Company, 5th Battalion, The Norfolk Regiment (T.F.) parade for the camera as their home town of Downham Market bids them farewell on 5 August 1914.

Introduction

Greater love hath no man than this that a man lay down his life for his friends.
(John 15.13)
Inscribed upon the headstone of Captain Evelyn Beck MC,
1/5th Norfolk Regiment, Gaza War Cemetery

The notion of 'Pals' battalions by name was very much a phenomenon of the First World War but it should not be forgotten that battalions made up of friends, brothers, extended family members, in-laws, neighbours and workmates from a particular locality were nothing new. Whenever Britain has been threatened, units of volunteer soldiers have been mustered in local areas to defend our shores but were disbanded when the emergency passed. In 1859 the first units of Volunteers were raised, trained and retained in peace-time. The Territorial Force, created in 1908, was the latest generation of this part-time soldiery; never intended to serve abroad, their duty was purely to defend the British homeland in the event of Regular Army forces being sent abroad in a war situation as a British Expeditionary Force.

In the days before television, joining the Territorials was seen as much a pastime for any young man as joining a local football team or the Boy Scouts. But what came with being part of this new Territorial Force, probably because it was better organised, equipped, uniformed and trained than its predecessors and because the men who were joining had been raised and educated in the patriotic ethos, was a very real sense of it being an honour to serve king and country as a Territorial soldier. This sense of belonging and comradeship that seems, especially as time passes, distinct to the generations raised in the Victorian and Edwardian eras, has never really been seen again after the carnage of the First World War. In their day, there were no prouder Territorials than those of the Norfolk Regiment. They were not only part of a good old British regiment with a distinguished history dating back to 1685, but the 5th Battalion, The Norfolk Regiment, contained the only company in the entire Territorial Force to be raised on a royal estate – The Sandringham Company.

Each and every company would have its own local identity and pride and together they gave each battalion its character. It should not be forgotten the 5th Battalion had companies based in a number of towns along the coast in North Norfolk between King's Lynn and Great Yarmouth; the 4th Battalion was raised in the city of Norwich and had companies in the south of the county. Both battalions were reorganized and their identities changed somewhat during training and when they were deployed; both battalions remained in the same infantry brigade and division throughout the war and they *all* did their bit.

The problem occurred when, after the action of 12 August 1915, the losses were severe but the exact fate of the fallen soldiers of the 5th Battalion was unclear because the enemy had closed in over the area and General Ian Hamilton in his despatch, published in January 1916, used unwise prose stating…

> '*the Colonel, with sixteen officers and 250 men, still kept pushing on, driving the enemy before him. Amongst these ardent souls was part of a fine company enlisting from the King's Sandringham estates. Nothing more was ever seen or heard of any of them. They charged into the forest and were lost to sight or sound. Not one of them ever came back.*'

The press latched onto the 'mystery' and the involvement of the 'King's Company'; the concern of King George V himself intensified media interest and very soon the story of the 'Vanished Battalion' spread across newspapers and magazines, totally ignoring the numerous letters published in the local press by survivors. The 'mystery' has been revived in a variety of publications and TV documentaries ever since. In some ways this a good thing because it has renewed interest in the story for new generations; in other ways it is both frustrating and tiresome that the mystery has overshadowed the remarkable stories of comradeship, endurance and courage demonstrated by the 4th and 5th Battalions, The Norfolk Regiment as a whole during the war, as they saw out the rest of the campaign in Gallipoli, manned defences in Egypt, marched across the Sinai to Palestine and fought in the battles for Gaza, Jerusalem and beyond.

My great-grandfather Frederick Griffin served in the 5th Battalion, The Norfolk Regiment during the First World War. Sadly he passed away before I was born, but his daughter, my grandmother, my mother and great uncles all shared their affectionate memories of him with me, as well as telling of his great sadness at having survived the 'War to End All Wars' only to have one of his sons killed serving in the 5th Battalion in the Second World War.

I was fortunate to have the chance to meet the last survivors of the Norfolk Territorial Battalions who served in the First World War; the last of them, Fred Frostick, lived in my home town of North Walsham. I remember him well for his kindness towards my pal Tim and I, his cap badge, identity tag and the copy of his memoirs that he gave to us all those years ago are treasured to this day and feature in this book. I remember Fred always had a ready smile but when we discussed the war he did feel that he and his pals were 'forgotten men from a forgotten war'. His parting words to me were 'Don't forget us, boy'. I never have.

Over the past 35 years it has also been my pleasure and a privilege to meet the descendants of many other Norfolk Territorials who have shared their precious family photographs, letters and memorabilia with me. Over the First World War centenary years I have had the chance to meet more descendants through some very special projects, exhibitions and commemoration services. It has proved to me again and again the memories of our ancestors in the Norfolk Territorial battalions are treasured to this day. Told, as often as possible, in their own words, this is their story.

Neil R. Storey
Norfolk 2019

Chapter 1

Norfolk Before the Great War

In the two decades or so before the outbreak of what soon became known as The Great War in August 1914, Norfolk was still very much an agricultural county and there were thousands of men employed on its many farms as agricultural labourers. The problem was, however, that work on the land was becoming increasingly mechanised with the likes of horse-drawn reaper binders and steam-driven threshing machines. These slashed the amount of manual labour that had been traditionally required to help with the harvest, previously a labour-intensive process where fields of corn, wheat and barley were mown by teams of men wielding scythes. Consequently, the population of the countryside was changing, and many men and their families were migrating to the towns and Norwich city, moving to more industrial areas or even starting new lives abroad.

Billy Dan Boldero scaring crows near Castle Acre. This is how many Norfolk children began their working lives on the land, earning a penny a day.

All was not lost though, there were still plenty of farms that had not mechanised and there was a growing need for cattlemen, dairy herdsmen and stockmen because the railways that came to Norfolk in the late nineteenth century gave access to a great livestock trade in London and the industrial areas of the Midlands and the North. The growing demand for fruits such as apples for cider and soft fruits for jams, popular among the people in industrial areas, also saw new orchards and fruit farms established around the county and fruit was despatched by the trainload from our stations. There were also numerous wealthy estates where employment could be sought in a host of roles such as gardeners, grooms, gamekeepers, foresters, shepherds, saw mill workers and general labourers. Being in the regular employment of 'the big house' also carried a bit more status than that of a regular farm labourer and often came with perks such as well-maintained tied cottages.

Harvestmen sharpening their scythes at Houghton St Giles c1890.

Gamekeepers and brushers, Ketteringham c1910. Employment on a country estate was seen as quite a step up from being an agricultural labourer on a farm.

Fishing Drifters being towed out by steam tug from the harbour mouth at Gorleston c1910 when over 9,000 men were working on the fishing boats and drifters that operated out of Great Yarmouth.

The West Cliff with its smart new hotels, beach, bathing machines and pier at the popular Norfolk coastal resort of Cromer c1909.

All along the Norfolk coastline, very much as there had been for centuries before, there were still fishing communities in every coastal village and town. Some, such as Great Yarmouth, famed for its cured herring industry, Cromer, Sheringham and Hunstanton, had grown beyond all recognition over the past two decades. Thanks to the railways they had become popular seaside resorts for both day-trippers and holiday makers. The new-found wealth generated through advances in agriculture and trade and tourism generated by railways saw many county towns prosper and grow as they developed their own agricultural machinery manufacturers and engineering works. As more people had better, more stable incomes, savings banks and building societies were created and ordinary people were able to buy their own homes for the first time.

Norwich had massive boot and shoe factories. There were engineering foundries, breweries and Colman's mustard works that required thousands of employees and the city had rapidly developed suburbs of long rows of terraces beyond the city walls. Many county towns also had expanding workforces that needed homes, so numerous rows of houses or whole areas of properties were built to provide homes for the workers. These new roads would often be named after members of the royal family or notable military leaders, battles, politicians and industrialists that had all helped to build the British Empire. The downside of the great demand for affordable housing was the emergence of the 'jerry-builders' who put up rows of poor-quality terraced houses prone to damp, which often ended up being bought up by landlords who rented them out to less affluent families.

Old shops with new painted frontages and colourful signage on St. Augustine's Street, Norwich c1911.

The International Stores and staff, Holt c1910. Shops with smart frontages, well-stocked window displays and staff in clean white aprons were to be found in every Norfolk town by the early twentieth century.

Shops smartened themselves up with well-painted, or even new, frontages, smart glass signage and more shop windows were glazed than ever before. There were jewellers and watchmakers, ironmongers that sold fittings, fireplaces and beautiful oil lamps to brighten any home, cruet sets and cutlery to make any dinner table a decent one, gentlemen's outfitters, off-the-peg women's dress shops, small department stores offering clothes, underwear, millinery and drapery. Grocery shops selling tea and tinned foods served by smartly turned out staff became a common feature on the high streets of our growing county towns.

Post offices, bright red post boxes and smart, uniformed postmen provided a service second to none, with many towns enjoying the benefit of around ten postal deliveries and collections every day. The streets regularly heard the horses' hooves of the roundsmen delivering milk, bread and meat and they were lit by gas lamps fuelled from the many local gas works that also sprang up around the county. That said, many Norfolk towns and even Norwich city parishes still had to wait another decade or so before their roads were metalled and they could enjoy such modern wonders as clean piped water available at the turn of a tap, toilets, bathrooms and electricity in their homes.

Sadly, not everyone succeeded in life and there were some still living in biting poverty, but there were far more charities than ever before to help them and the average child growing up in the early years of the twentieth century had the benefit of an education provided for them, by law, under the 1870 Education Act. Admittedly there was little room for creativity in the system that taught children the three 'R's

Postmaster, Post Office staff and uniformed postmen, Fakenham c1910.

of Reading, wRiting and aRithmetic; they simply had enough learning to fulfil the requirements of many modern jobs. They were also given physical education, usually in the form of drill exercises, and living, as they were, at the height of the British Empire, they were taught about their monarch as its head, what it meant to be a world power and to be thankful for it!

The Ffolkes Arms Inn, Hillington c1910. Pubs were the hub of many rural communities where men could socialise, take part in sporting activities and hold meetings for fraternal organisations.

Lads from a village near King's Lynn ready for a run out on their bicycles c1910.

In the days of quiet roads with next to no motorised vehicles, and before the advent of television, children would play in the street and in the fields around their homes; but they would be expected to do useful things too, such as attending Sunday school, joining the church or chapel choir, Salvation Army Young People's bands or youth groups such as Church Lads' Brigade and Boys Scouts. For those who had reached their maturity there were numerous fraternal men's groups such as the Ancient Order of Foresters, Independent Order of Rechabites or Manchester Unity Oddfellows that often met in the 'club room' of the local pub in many villages and towns. Membership of such societies and the subscriptions each member paid provided benefits, such as payments for those off sick from work, those suffering hardship or towards funeral costs. There were also regular informal outings of groups for those who owned or could borrow a bicycle, local sports teams for quoits, bowls and football were particularly popular. There were numerous leagues, including a Wednesdays league for shop staff who had Wednesdays as their half day off. All of these were avidly supported as teams in the Premier League are supported today and train-loads of supporters would regularly follow their local teams for their away matches.

The Norfolk boy or girl growing to maturity in the years before 1914 would probably have their participation in a parade for Queen Victoria's Diamond Jubilee in June 1897 as one of their earliest memories. They would also have celebrated the coronation of Edward VII in 1901, marked the end of the South African War in 1902, marched alongside and cheered their local volunteer infantry in their red jackets at their public parades, celebrated Empire Day every year, popped over to the Lynn Mart or the Tombland Fair, cheered King Edward on his visit to Norwich in 1910 or maybe they were one of the 10,000 children who gathered on Mousehold Heath to sing to him as he drove past in his carriage.

Happisburgh village football team, season 1910-11. Country people avidly supported their local teams, watched them play and talked of players and matches much as people follow premiership matches today.

Well-wishers walking and cycling alongside their local company of Norfolk Volunteers in their smart red jackets on their return from Church Parade, Harleston 1905.

North Walsham Market Place packed with tables and diners celebrating the Coronation of King George V in 1911.

Magdalen Street, Norwich during the floods of August 1912. No one who lived through the floods would forget seeing the city streets under water.

Nineteen-year-old Joe Bentley of South Lynn with his sweetheart in 1914. Joe was killed in action along with over 150 of his comrades in the 1/5th Norfolks on 12 August 1915.

They would have celebrated the coronation of King George V in 1911, probably with a street party followed by sports, fireworks and bonfires in the evening. They would also have lived through 1912 when Bentfield C. Hucks became the first man to fly over Norwich in an aeroplane. They would have witnessed, and maybe suffered as a result of, the extensive flooding in Norwich and across the county, and would have seen the columns of marching troops along our country lanes during the great manoeuvres of the British Army that were staged across the county that year.

The years leading up the First World War were exciting and vibrant for many in Norfolk; yes, work was hard, but the remarkable events and the simple pleasures of life seemed to be fulfilling in equal measure. In many ways it was still an age of innocence. The world had never seen a war like the Great War, for the people of Britain wars had been distant affairs fought on foreign shores and the consequences of war had never been seen first-hand by the British public as they would soon be seen when wounded began to return by the trainload from France and Flanders.

The men who went to war in 1914 could not have predicted the horrors they were to see nor, in the case of our lads, imagined where they would end up serving. Every Norfolk veteran I had the chance to interview who recalled the atmosphere of August 1914 spoke of feeling they were embarking on a great adventure and most lads didn't want to miss being part of it. Those a little too young to join up or a little above the upper age limit were not above telling a fib or two so they did not miss out and more than one veteran I knew would then pause when recalling these times, shake his head sadly and say...never again.

Chapter 2

The Creation of the Territorial Force in Norfolk

'...the basis of our whole military fabric must be the development of the idea of a real national army, formed by the people'.

Richard Burdon Haldane

In 1908 Richard Burdon Haldane, the new Liberal Government's War Secretary was entrusted with the most radical reforms the British Army had seen to date. Much had been learned from the South African War (1899-1902) and many of the recommendations of these lessons were encapsulated in the Esher Report. Major nations on the world stage addressed the structure, training and equipment of their forces and Britain was not going to be caught out of step. Haldane and his team of advisers were handed the challenge of the complete reorganisation of the Home Field Army and Reserve System. Under this scheme most county regiments would have two regular army battalions,

F Company, 5th Battalion (Cromer), with their trophies and visiting dignitaries just before their memorial parade for HM King Edward VII, May 1910.

one to provide garrison troops for the Empire, the other battalion would be on home service which, in the event of a war emergency, would combine with other regular army battalions to create a six-division-strong British Expeditionary Force. Meanwhile, the part-time soldiers of the Territorial Force would be mobilised to provide troops for the defence of Britain. When the Territorial Force was created there was no intention for it to ever be deployed abroad.

The old system of Volunteers was unsuitable for the new reformed army. Haldane maintained a vision of a nation that could be mobilised for war without resorting to conscription – 'a real national army formed by the people'. The Territorial and Reserve Forces Act of 2 August 1907 created the foundations for a Territorial Force that would be funded and commanded centrally by the War Office and raised, supplied and administered by County Territorial Associations.

The County Associations led by lord lieutenants were formed rapidly and included many of the military elite in every county. The Territorial Force (TF) was established on 1 April 1908. The Norfolk Regiment, which was allocated three battalions in the new Territorial Force, was required to find its quota towards the formation of the East Anglian Division which was to consist of three infantry brigades. Each battalion was to be equal in numbers, each of them made up of eight companies or 1,009 officers and men. These new battalions were initially created out of the old Norfolk Volunteer Battalions (VBs), the 4th Battalion drawing its men from the 1st and 2nd VBs and the 5th Battalion from the 3rd and 4th VBs respectively. The Norfolk Regiment was also granted the honour of raising one of the much heralded eleven Cyclist Battalions (eight English, two Scottish and one Welsh) included in the scheme, thus our final battalion was designated the 6th Battalion (Cyclists) TF.

The individual units that made up each new Territorial division or brigade were administered by County Associations, with the county's Lord Lieutenant as President. In the case of Norfolk it was the Earl of Leicester, the county's biggest private land owner, who resided at Holkham Hall. The other members of the association consisted of military members chosen from the commanding officers of the units, representative members nominated by the county councils and county boroughs and co-opted members, most of whom were retired officers. Associations took over any property vested in the volunteers or yeomanry under their administration and each regiment or battalion had a regular army officer attached as full-time adjutant.

The new Norfolk Territorial Force battalions were made up of eight companies, each of which consisted of about four officers and a hundred men. The allocation of men to each company depended largely upon which part of the county they lived or worked in. This suited most recruits who were more than happy to serve with their brothers, friends and acquaintances and it made the battalion a close-knit society. In fact, amongst all ranks the battalion was riddled with extended family ties of uncles, nephews, cousins and in-laws serving side by side and throughout the various companies. Its rank structure reflected society at the time: the officers were from the local gentry, farmers, solicitors and respected professionals; the NCOs were works foremen and ex-servicemen and the other ranks comprised men from all walks of life.

Members of 5th Battalion, The Norfolk Regiment marching to camp at Aldershot 1909. Serjeant Bland and Second Lieutenant Betts of the Sandringham Company are foreground right.

Headquarters of 4th Battalion, Chapelfield Drill Hall, Norwich c1910.

Recruits had to be aged between 17 and 35, with a minimum chest measurement of 33in, a minimum height of 5ft 2in and would have to enlist for a minimum of four years in the Territorial Force. Upon joining, the recruit was obliged to attend forty parades of one-hour duration in his first year of enlistment. In the battalion one hour on two parade nights each week were set aside for recruit drill. New recruits were also required to pass a course of musketry held on two appointed afternoons throughout the summer months. In the second, third and fourth year of service the recruit became a 'trained man', obliged to perform a minimum of twenty drills in the second year and ten drills in the third and fourth years and, in the trained man's course of musketry, to be passed as 'efficient'. Throughout this period there would be regular parades, competitions, social gatherings and weekend manoeuvres. Tom Williamson of F Company, 5th Norfolks recalled when he first joined:

> *We used to attend our drill hall every Wednesday night under the instruction of a regular Sergeant Major plus our Sergeant Major voluntary and we would do drill... we would go through the practice of shooting on the inside range and later on of course we became efficient to do manoeuvres outside with the rest of my Company... we would go out in Section form to do manoeuvres, night manoeuvres, in the course of our nightly application drill we used to go out in the open air and we would do strict field training as a section and then eventually the whole company would connect and we would do an operation of field training intensively, say, three days where you have to assemble at a spot and take an enemy post at a distance.*
>
> *You were then divided up into sections, each section with its own commander. You had to extend across your front and you would then advance in section rushes until you came involved with the imaginary enemy. You go through all the drill with a blank fire and you would really be in your joy, that you were at battle and then there would have been night operations which would be more difficult for scouting and we realised we had to more or less keep together. We got the instinct of these manoeuvres implanted in us so that it became second nature.*

Such exercises and the occasional weekend camps were often the butt of jokes among the roughs of a town or village and any recruit would soon find membership of the Territorial Force earned him the nickname of a 'Saturday Night Soldier', or in the case of the Territorial Cyclists, 'The Gas Pipe Cavalry'. Names that, particularly after they went to war and saw action, the Terriers took great pride in throwing back at those who had taunted them.

The first time the Norfolk Territorials gathered together for a grand display for the public since their creation, occurred when they mustered on Mousehold Heath to be inspected by King Edward VII on his visit to Norwich on 25 October 1909. Over 3,000 troops were assembled on the cavalry drill ground under the overall command of Brigadier General John H. Campbell, the commander of the East Anglian Division. The 4th and 5th Norfolks were in review order of scarlet jackets with yellow facings and blue cloth helmets with polished brass and gilt fittings, the cyclists and all other Territorials were in khaki.

After a march past and an inspection of the parade, a short religious ceremony was held with prayers led by Bishop John Taylor-Smith, of Thetford, chaplain general to the forces and battalion chaplains. The Colours were then presented to The King's Own Royal Regiment, Norfolk Yeomanry and 4th and 5th Norfolks. Staff officers handed each colour to the king, who touched the gold crown on the head of each lowered colour and it was then handed to the officer selected to receive it, who did so upon bended knee. The colour parties of 4th and 5th Norfolks returned to their respective battalions and this magnificent occasion was concluded with a general march past by all units. This occasion was one of the earliest events ever in Norwich to be captured on moving film. The king then retired for luncheon at the officer's mess at the Chapelfield Drill Hall.

Standard uniform for the English and Welsh Territorials consisted of a service dress uniform of khaki serge jacket, trousers, stiffened peaked hat, puttees and boots, just like the regular soldiers. Along with the basic uniform they also had a greatcoat, waterproof cape and a set of the 1908 pattern webbing. Their Norfolk Territorial's best parade and 'walking out' dress consisted of a blue stiff cap with red piping, red frock tunic with yellow facings and navy-blue trousers with narrow red stripe. Men serving in the Territorial Force often provided their own boots and were granted a small amount of money for wear and tear; many companies even had their own cobbler to effect repairs. The Norfolk Regiment Territorials wore the same cap badge as the soldiers of the Regular battalions, but where the shoulder titles of Regulars would normally simply have their county designation in a semicircle of brass lettering reading 'Norfolk',

Presentation of Colours to the Norfolk Territorial Battalions by King Edward VII on the parade ground, Mousehold Heath, Norwich, 25 October 1909.

HM King Edward VII with the officers of 4th Battalion with their newly presented Colours at The Chapelfield Drill Hall, 25 October 1909.

the Territorials had their battalion designation such as T4, for 4th Norfolks or T5 for 5th Norfolks above the county title. Officers did not wear shoulder titles, instead they wore small a letter 'T' under their Officer's Service Dress collar badges.

A unique badge of the Territorial Force was the five-pointed star worn on the right forearm by other ranks soldiers and NCOs to denote the wearer had been returned as 'qualified' four times. The return of 'qualified' was measured over a period of a year and subsequent stars were awarded for every aggregate of four years. Pay was not bad for other ranks either, a private soldier would draw a shilling a day, corporals 1s 8d, sergeants 2s 4d, up to colour sergeants on 3s 6d per day. Great emphasis was placed on the *espirit de corps* of the unit, always doing your best in all ranks.

On first joining, pay was not exceptional; a young second lieutenant who received 5s 6d a day would be expected to purchase all his uniform, kit and equipment and pay his

Brass shoulder titles of the 4th, 5th and 6th Battalions, The Norfolk Regiment TF.

Members of G Company, 4th Battalion on full dress parade in front of Thetford Guildhall for the proclamation of King George V on 10 May 1910.

The Drums of the 4th Battalion marching under the triumphal arch on London Street on the occasion of King George V's first official visit to Norwich, 1911.

own mess bills. However, most of the subalterns came from families who had money and were given financial assistance or were professionals in their own right. All officers were expected to be able to ride and to follow field sports, indeed belonging to the officer's mess of one of the Territorial Force battalions was just as much a pursuit for young gentlemen in peacetime as playing sport to a high standard and was a much sought after honour. The messes themselves were bedecked with pictures, paintings, swords, weaponry and memorabilia reflecting the long heritage of volunteer soldiery. Regimental silver would be displayed and meals would be eaten with due ceremony off regimentally-marked china and cutlery. Tradition and patriotism were inherent, some would even reflect on it being rather like a membership to a rather good gentleman's club.

There were two highlights of the year for Territorials: one was the Field Day when there would be parades, an inspection, sports and speeches for the wives, sweethearts and family guests, who were able to see their 'soldier boy' put what he had learnt into practice with his comrades. The other event was annual camp. This lasted for fourteen days and every soldier was expected to attend at least eight days unless prevented by illness or for urgent business reasons. The men lived eight to a tent under the supervision of an NCO; these were large white bell tents and soldiers would be expected to lie with their heads to the pole and feet to the walls of the tent when sleeping. Every man attending camp also received an allowance of 3s for wear and tear to boots. The 8,000 men of the entire East Anglian Territorial Division held their first camp together at Thetford Warren during the last week in August 1911.

Norfolk and Suffolk Territorial Force Infantry Brigade Camps 1908-1914:

1908 Yarmouth
1909 Aldershot
1910 Norwich
1911 Thetford
1912 Lowestoft
1913 Diss
1914 Holkham

A contemporary recruiting leaflet stated that Norfolk Territorial camps were '*most pleasant, exhilarating and healthy. No better holiday can be spent than as a Territorial... The work is neither too hard nor too strenuous, the hours of work are not long and the fun is immense. It is by no means a miserable or tiring time*.' Judge for yourself by reading a typical itinerary for the day at 6th Norfolk Cyclists camp in 1912.

Reveille was at 5.30am, coffee and biscuits served at 6am with drill or lectures between 6am and 8am. Breakfast was served at 8.30am followed by field and physical exercises from 9am until 1.30pm. Lunch was served at 2pm and at 3pm sharp there would be an inspection of rifles and tents. And the rest of the day was free – except for those detailed for duties.

There would also be inter-company challenge contests in shooting, boxing, bayonet fencing and running, with handsome cups for the company to display and medallions

Great Yarmouth Company Signallers, Diss Camp. 1913.

or fobs for the men of the winning side to keep. Shooting championship winners were often presented with silver spoons engraved with the regimental badge and the date of the competition. The bicycle riding skills of the men of the 6th Norfolks were also tested with a variety of challenges, including riding correctly in pairs, maintaining the regulation distance and at the end of the ride firing a number of rounds at fixed targets,

Men of the Great Yarmouth Company, 5th Battalion, The Norfolk Regiment, Diss Camp, 1913.

4th Battalion Transport Section, Lowestoft Camp 1912.

the best company winning The Ross Cup presented by Yarmouth detachment supporter Mr Lockhart Ross.

The fare in camp varied from day-to-day; a standard menu would include a breakfast of fried sausages, bread, butter, jam, coffee or tea. Dinner would consist of roast beef, potatoes, fruit pies and mineral waters. Tea was literally bread, butter, jam and tea.

The 6th Norfolk (Cyclists) were not part of the Norfolk and Suffolk Infantry Brigade and did not share their summer camps with the 4th and 5th Norfolks. On the outbreak of war they were deployed to coastal defence duties along the Norfolk coast. As the war progressed many of the A1 men were drawn off for active service battalions of the Norfolk and other regiments. The 1/6th Norfolks were deployed on peace-keeping duties to Ireland during the war but were never sent as a unit to an active theatre of war. This book will now concentrate on the 4th and 5th Norfolks.

4th Battalion Maxim Gun and limber, Diss Camp 1913.

By 1912 the new Territorial Force had settled down and was flourishing. Battalion headquarters, drill halls and companies were established across the county in the following structure, noting senior officers and NCOs for the 4th and 5th Norfolks:

4th BATTALION

Honorary Colonel: The Earl of Leicester CMG, GCVO (Lord Lieutenant)

Members of the 4th Battalion digging trenches during field manoeuvres, Diss Camp 1913.

Headquarters: Drill Hall Chapelfield, Norwich.

Staff: Commanding, Lieutenant Colonel J.R. Harvey DSO; Majors E. Mornement TD and F.G.W. Wood; Instructor of Musketry Captain W.H.M. Andrews; Adjutant Captain F.R. Day (Norfolk Regiment), Quartermaster Hon. Lieutenant R.W. Moore; Medical Officer Lieutenant J.H. Owens RAMC (TF); Chaplains Rev E.W. Hardy and Rev C.U. Manning.

A Company: Captain S.D. Page (Chapelfield Road, Norwich)

B Company: Captain W.H.M. Andrews (Chapelfield Road, Norwich)

C Company: Captain H.R. Rudd (Chapelfield Road, Norwich)

Colour Serjeant Instructor C.E. Medlicott and Serjeant Major Hemmings, Drill Instructors

D Company: Lieutenant S.H.W. Coxon (Denmark Street, Diss); Serjeant Thomas Stubbs, Drill Instructor

E Company: Captain Herbert Charles Long (Attleborough with detachments at East Harling and Hingham); Colour Serjeant Instructor J. Munnings

F Company: Captain Henry R. Fletcher (Drill Hall, Town Green, Wymondham); Serjeant Instructor Alfred Pitcher, Drill Instructor

G Company: Captain H.E. Holmes (Guildhall, Thetford and Brandon); Captain C.W.W. Burrell; Colour Serjeant James William Hall, Drill Instructor

H Company: Captain R.T.E. Gilbert (Thorpe St Andrew)

A Company, 5th Battalion (King's Lynn) 'The Lynn Company' with their company commander Captain Arthur Pattrick seated centre, 1914.

5th BATTALION
Honorary Colonel: The Earl of Albemarle CB KCVO JP DL VD

Headquarters: Quebec Street, East Dereham

Staff: Commanding, Lieutenant Colonel P.J. Petrie; second-in-command Lieutenant Colonel and Honourable Colonel T.P. Angell VD; Major A.W. Thomas VD; Instructor of Musketry Lieutenant E.R. Cubitt; Adjutant Captain A.E.M. Ward (Norfolk Regiment); Quartermaster Hon. Major A. Smith VD, Chaplain Rev A.R.H. Grant

A Company: Captain Edward Milligen Beloe (Nelson Street, King's Lynn); Serjeant Instructor Henry Harwood

B Company: Lieutenant S.A. Coxon (Downham); Serjeant Major W. Ford, Drill Instructor

C Company: Captain Herbert Ellis Rowell (Holt Road, Fakenham and Crown Hotel, Wells Detachment); Colour Serjeant Frank Harris, Drill Instructor; Captain Thomas Woods Purdy (Pound Road, Aylsham Detachment); Serjeant Instructor Thomas Davis

D Company: Captain Walter John Barton (Quebec Street, East Dereham and Castle Acre Street, Swaffham Detachment); Serjeant Instructor W.H. Adcock (East Dereham)

E Company: Captain Frank Reginald Beck MVO (Sandringham)

F Company: Captain Havard Noel Bridgwater (Central Road Cromer with detachments at Sheringham, Holt and Melton Constable); Serjeant Instructor Samuel Parker, Drill Instructor (Cromer); Colour Serjeant Instructor Hall, Drill Instructor (Holt Detachment)

G Company: Captain Leonard Joynson Brown (York Road, Great Yarmouth); Lieutenant W.L. Blake

H Company: Captain T.B. Hall (York Road, Great Yarmouth); Colour Serjeant H. White, Drill Instructor; Lieutenant E.R. Cubitt (North Walsham Detachment); Serjeant J. Coe, Drill Instructor

The last peacetime summer camp of the Norfolk and Suffolk Infantry Brigade took place in July 1914 on Holkham Park, part of the Holkham Estate, seat of the Earl of Leicester, Lord Lieutenant of Norfolk, who was also president of the County Territorial Association. The brigade in camp comprised three Territorial Force Infantry battalions, the 4th and 5th Norfolks, 5th Suffolks, 2nd East Anglian Brigade Royal Army Medical Corps (TF) and a Norfolk and Suffolk company of the Army Service Corps (TF). During the week they worked together in field operations and played in sporting competitions in the evenings. The culmination of the camp was a march past of 2,000 Territorials in extended column of companies, with Colours flying and bayonets fixed. The Earl of Leicester took the salute accompanied by Major General Francis Seymour Inglefield CB DSO, the General Officer Commanding the East Anglian Division.

Members of the 5th Battalion marching to church parade, Holkham Park Camp, July 1914.

Lieutenant Colonel Thomas (centre) accompanied by Captain Tom Purdy (behind) and the Adjutant, Captain Arthur Ward (right) inspecting Aylsham Detachment, C Company, 5th Battalion, Holkham Park Camp, 1914.

Colour Party, 4th Battalion, Holkham Park Camp, July 1914.

The Norfolk and Suffolk Infantry Brigade march past The Earl of Leicester and Major General Inglefield in extended column of companies, with Colours flying and bayonets fixed, Holkham Park Camp 1914.

When the parade had marched past, the troops formed a square and were addressed by the lord lieutenant who expressed his great pleasure at what he had seen, not only on parade but throughout the week's camp stating, '*You marched past well and if each battalion is called upon for more serious work it will do its duty to uphold the honour of its county and country*,' a sentiment later echoed in a brigade order from the brigadier.

Once camp was struck the first to go were the members of the Sandringham Company, who left at 6am to march back the 17 miles to Sandringham. They were greeted at Burnham by Captain Frank Beck, who had not attended the camp. For many men it would seem like they were never out of khaki again because they found OHMS envelopes sent on 29 July 1914 warning of the impending embodiment of the Territorial Force waiting for them when they returned home.

Chapter 3

The Sandringham Company

'Dear old Sandringham, the place I love better than anywhere in the world.'
HM King George V

Sandringham House and Estate
As Albert Edward, Prince of Wales (later King Edward VII), eldest son of Queen Victoria and HRH Albert, the Prince Consort, approached his twenty-first birthday his parents, particularly Prince Albert, felt that upon his coming of age he should move out of the family home and into his own residences. His London home of Marlborough House had already been assigned by Act of Parliament, but he was also to have a country home to escape to when duty permitted and where he could enjoy the benefits of a country life. The search for a suitable property was still ongoing when Prince

The east front of Sandringham House, the much-loved country residence of HM King Edward VII and Queen Alexandra c1910.

Albert died in December 1861 and the queen resolved that her late husband's wishes would be enacted.

The Sandringham Estate, that consisted of the late eighteenth century Sandringham House, 2,800 hectares of agricultural land and wooded escarpment overlooking the Wash, was offered for the sum of £220,000 by Charles Spencer Cowper, stepson of Prime Minister Lord Palmerston, who wished to sell up and move to France. The Prince of Wales visited the estate for the first time on Monday, 3 February 1862 with a small entourage including Sir Charles Phipps, Keeper of the Privy Purse. Phipps sent a favourable report on the residence and estate to the queen and the purchase was completed shortly after.

A scheme of works to improve and make the property habitable for the prince was undertaken and, with the initial works completed, his house staff arrived from late 1862. On 6 January 1863 the Prince of Wales arrived by train at Wolferton Station, proceeding the two miles or so to the hall by private carriage with Lieutenant General Knollys and Captain Grey and followed by a suite of staff, to take possession of his new estate. His new bride followed soon after and the Prince of Wales and Princess Alexandra of Denmark soon made Sandringham their principal home.

Their first child, Prince Albert Victor, the Duke of Clarence was born the following year. Other children followed soon after and it quickly became apparent that the original hall was not large enough for the Prince of Wales's growing family, his household, the ever-growing number of guests and their staff. Thus began a rolling scheme of building, reconstruction, improvement, landscaping and farming on the estate that would continue until the death of King Edward in 1910. The old Sandringham Hall was almost completely demolished and the new, far more impressive Sandringham House, designed by architect A.J. Humbert, was built over the years 1867-70 by Goggs Brothers of Swaffham. Humbert died in 1877 and was succeeded as the prince's architect by Colonel Robert Edis who designed the ballroom which was completed in 1883.

The Prince of Wales redecorated the church of St Mary Magdalene, just to the west of Sandringham House, and installed oak pews in the chancel for the royal family. New properties were built in the grounds, also designed by Edis, such as Park House just beyond the church, Bachelor's Cottage a quarter of a mile away to the south of Sandringham House and the twenty-bedroom Appleton House for family, guests and senior members of royal household was built about a mile away. There were also houses for the land agent, head gamekeeper and head gardener, bothies for the young single gardeners and new lodges and cottages constructed in the local materials of carrstone and flint were built for Sandringham Estate workers. Farm buildings were built new, older ones restored and roads constructed.

Such was the prince's hospitality and love of socialising that Sandringham House was often filled with guests who would usually bring their own personal servants, valets and ladies' maids with them, so further wings and domestic offices were added, along with a vast sixteen-acre kitchen garden and long glasshouses erected to supply the house with its huge demand for vegetables, fruit and flowers.

The Church of St Mary Magdalene, Sandringham c1910.

The Head Gardener's House, Sandringham c1908 home to Mr Thomas Cook, one of the original serjeants of the Sandringham Company.

One glasshouse was dedicated entirely to carnations, the preferred flower worn by the king as his buttonhole. If you were a young, single man employed as one of the sizeable team of gardeners on the Sandringham Estate you would be accommodated in one of the bothies with other young gardeners. This could really seem like you had landed on your feet, every man had his own bedroom with built in wardrobe, dressing table, chair and bed. There was hot and cold running water in the communal bathroom and a woman, Mrs Nurse, was employed to make and change the beds, cook a mid-day meal and make sure the bothies were kept clean and presentable.

The Prince of Wales also pursued his passion for horse racing, breeding many fine racehorses at the two thoroughbred stud farms he established at Sandringham and Wolferton. Notably 'Persimmon' and his brother 'Diamond Jubilee' both won the Derby and a host of notable races for the Prince of Wales. There were also fine Hackneys bred for the royal carriages and the famed Sandringham Shire horses.

The landscape gardener W.B. Thomas was employed to move the ornamental lake further away from the house and create two new lakes to the south. The gardens were beautifully landscaped, and a nine-hole golf course was created. Kennels were built for Princess Alexandra's dogs; there was even a pigeon loft and dove house nearby. About half a mile down the Anmer Road was the Queen's Dairy, tea room and model dairy farm with its milk herds of Irish Dexters and Jersey cows. The Sandringham farms were renowned for their stock; there was a herd of pedigree shorthorns, a flock of Southdown sheep that were reared in pens near Commodore Wood and beef herds

One of the magnificent Shire horses bred on the Sandringham Estate c1908.

of Red Poll and West Highland cattle at Church Farm, all of which regularly won prizes at agricultural shows.

H. Rider Haggard recounted in his introduction to *The King's Homeland* (1904):

> *His Agent, Mr Frank Beck informed me that his Majesty, whose training has been essentially that of an English country gentleman, takes the liveliest personal interest in every detail connected with his land, himself marking trees to be felled and directing where others should be planted, or superintending that choice of stock and all questions that have to do with Home Farm which covers, I believe, about 2,000 acres.*

There were always construction projects going on and the perambulation around these developments led by the prince accompanied by his agent became a regular feature for house guests staying at Sandringham.

Schools were built for the education of the children of the estate workers at West Newton and two technical schools instituted by Princess Alexandra in 1889, one for girls to learn weaving, spinning and needlework, the other for boys to learn cabinet making, carpentry and joinery. For most schools a visit from royalty would be a once in a lifetime occasion but at Sandringham the queen and her daughter Princess Victoria took a personal interest in all the schools and visits were frequent.

As royalty, heads of state and dignitaries became regular visitors to Sandringham more appropriate waiting rooms were required at Wolferton Station and a handsome suite of royal waiting rooms was built and beautifully furnished in 1876. When the line between King's Lynn and Wolferton was doubled, a new station was erected including

Sandringham School children and their headmaster Mr Walter Jones c1892.

Shooting Party, Sandringham 1902. Seated centre is the German Empress with Princess of Wales left and Duchess of York right. Standing just behind the Empress and Duchess is the Prince of Wales (later Edward VII), and standing between the Duchess of York and Princess Charles of Denmark is Kaiser Wilhelm II of Germany, next to him is the Duke of York (later George V).

a further royal suite of elegantly furnished oak panelled rooms on the down side in 1898. Local people would get wind of notable arrivals and would often gather on the banks and verges to watch the guards of honour, look for the king, the royal family and the arrival of the noble guests and wave and cheer as they watched the spectacle of outriders and liveried coachmen driving immaculately-polished carriages pass by.

Throughout the year at Sandringham House there were regular soirées, dinners, parties, dramatic performances by some of the greatest actors of the day such as Sir Henry Irving and Ellen Terry, but it was the game shoots for which the estate became famed. They provided the focus for the house parties in the autumn and winter months and would often include a host of royals from across Europe including the King and Queen of Denmark, King Carlos of Portugal, the King of the Belgians, the Tsarevich of Russia (later Tsar Nicholas II), the King and Queen of Norway, King Alfonso of Spain and even Kaiser Wilhelm II of Germany. The shoots had a sense of occasion with the gamekeepers dressed in green and gold and an army of beaters in smocks wearing hats bound in royal red. The spectacle was described by Louise Cresswell in *Eighteen Years on the Sandringham Estate* (1887):

> *At about eleven o'clock the Royal party arrives in a string of wagonettes, and range themselves in a long line under the fences or behind the shelters put up for the purpose, each sportsman having loaders in attendance with an extra gun or guns*

to hand backwards and forwards, to load and re-load. The boys and the beaters are stationed in a semi-circle some distance off and it is their place to beat up the birds and drive them to the fences, the waving of flags frightening them from flying back. On they come in ever increasing numbers until they burst in a cloud over a fence where the guns are concealed. This is the exciting moment, a terrific fusillade ensues, birds dropping down in all directions, wheeling about in confusion between the flags and the guns, the survivors gathering themselves together and escaping into the fields beyond. The shooters then retire to another line of fencing, making themselves comfortable with campstools and cigars until the birds are driven up as before and so on through the day...

The Prince of Wales and Princess Alexandra raised their five children: Prince Albert Victor, Prince George (later George V), Princess Louise, Princess Victoria and Princess Maud, at Sandringham. At a time when many believed children should be seen but not heard guests were often astonished at the freedom with which the children mingled with the adults. Indeed, the royal children growing up at Sandringham lived a life with little more restriction than if they had been a squire's children in a country village, especially princesses Maud and Victoria who loved to fly around the estate on their bicycles. In 1899 a feature in *Lady's Realm* told of their lifestyle:

The style of living adopted by their Royal Highnesses at Sandringham was of the homely simple kind. The children breakfasted with their parents. Breakfast over all gave themselves up to the delights of out-door life, the Prince, in Norfolk jacket and knickerbockers, followed by his dogs, going the round of the estate and consulting with his agent on matters agricultural, while the Princess wrote letters in her boudoir or accompanied the children in their country rambles...After luncheon the Princess and her daughters would set out for a driving expedition to Castle Rising or King's Lynn or go in the 'Blues' cart drawn by the faithful 'Huffy' to the neighbouring villages of Dersingham or West Newton to visit among the poor and sick. The cottage children were never forgotten in these expeditions and the Princess Victoria and her sisters were provided with bags of sweet-meats and oranges to distribute amongst them.

The Prince of Wales bestowed Bachelor's Cottage on his son Prince George, the Duke of York (later King George V) and his wife, Princess Victoria Mary of Teck, Duchess of York (later Queen Mary), in 1893. Renamed York Cottage, it served as the couple's official residence for thirty-three years. With the only exception of their first child (Prince Edward), all of their children were born at York Cottage and all of the children spent a considerable portion of their young years happily growing up on the Sandringham Estate. There they went out for walks learning about the flora and fauna of the area with Sandringham School headmaster Walter Jones, who arranged for princes and princesses to play group games and team sports with the children who attended the school.

The royal children were not hidden away, the estate workers watched them grow up and they loved the freedom they had at Sandringham. They rode on their bicycles

York Cottage, Sandringham, home of the Prince and Princess of Wales c1906. All bar one of their children were born there and spent a lot of their youth on the estate.

The Prince of Wales (later George V) on a stroll through Sandringham Park with his children in 1902. (left to right) Prince Albert (later George VI), Princess Mary, Prince Edward (later Edward VIII) and Prince Henry.

to West Newton, Castle Acre or Dersingham to buy sweets at Parker's Store and loved to pedal down the steep hill at breakneck speed to Wolferton station, learn about how things worked from the staff there and watch the trains come in. The royal children would play with the daughters of the king's agent Mr Frank Beck, who lived with his wife Mary at Sandringham Cottage, and they would often visit their aunt Princess (later Queen) Maud of Norway and her son Prince Alexander (later King Olav V of Norway) during one of their regular extended stays at Appleton House, which had been given to Maud upon her marriage to Prince Carl of Norway in 1896.

The Sandringham estate was a happy one where loyal and reliable staff could find employment for their entire working lives; indeed, some families worked on the estate for generations. The formal gardens and grounds of the house were absolutely beautiful, the cottages where the estate staff lived were well maintained, their tenants tended their gardens with the same pride that they served their highnesses and were further encouraged in these endeavours by the chance to exhibit their prize blooms at an annual Sandringham Flower Show founded by the Prince of Wales in 1881.

In 1884 the Sandringham Club at West Newton was built as a recreation centre with a medical surgery attached. The club itself was for estate workmen over 14 years old and they would pay a subscription of one shilling a quarter for membership. On any night of the week the estate workers from gardens, stables, coverts and farms would gather here to warm themselves by the fires in the winter time, smoke their pipes, read the newspapers, magazines or illustrated weeklies it held, play chess, draughts or dominoes, have a yarn and a pint or two. Originally beer consumption had been limited to a pint a day but the king, who considered such a measure to 'belong to a most

Alexandra Cottages, West Newton built by Edward VII when he was Prince of Wales as homes for employees on the Sandringham Estate c1910.

unworkable class of regulation', abolished the restriction, instead he made it incumbent upon each man to judge what was good for himself, in the knowledge that any that showed intemperance would be suspended for a month. If found so a second time a suspension of six months would be imposed and a third would result in expulsion. In the first eighteen years of the club only one member was suspended for a month and he did not repeat the offence. Other clubs followed soon after rather than there being any pubs in the seven villages encompassed by the estate.

The Sandringham Estate, its villages and farms were, and remain to this day, set in a landscape that was nothing short of a rural idyll, consisting of gentle rolling fields of swaying wheat and barley or the green of vegetables and grasses, the fruit farm, fields of cattle, a deer park, salt marsh, woods, spinneys and hedgerows. Life on the estate was punctuated by regular visits from both British and foreign nobility and the associated preparations that surrounded them. There were frequent teas, concerts and special events, such as an annual treat for children and a Christmas party. Every Christmas the estate staff, some 300 of them, or their wives, would line up in the stable yard outside the Coach House from where they would collect a side of beef for their festive table and King Edward, Queen Alexandra and their family would wish each one of them a Merry Christmas. There were also many on the estate who could proudly relate how they had received not only personal gifts, but gifts made by the hands of Queen Alexandra or her three daughters as thanks for loyal service or to mark weddings, anniversaries, births and significant birthdays.

On the occasion of the marriage of the Prince of Wales and Mary of Teck in 1893 over a thousand of the Sandringham tenantry dined in a marquee under the presidency of the agent, Mr Frank Beck. There were sports all afternoon and, when the couple arrived at Wolferton in the evening and were driven to the estate, their route was lined by cheering estate workers. The trees and the lake around York Cottage were illuminated with fairy lamps and there was a firework display to complete the welcome.

There were also a variety of regular organised sports for the estate workers including the hotly competed Sandringham and District Cricket League and bowls tournaments. In the spirit of Sandringham being a 'model' estate it had, since 1865 its own volunteer fire brigade. A company of 3rd Volunteer Battalion, the Norfolk Regiment was founded in 1906 and a Voluntary Aid Detachment of the British Red Cross Society, recruited from the women of the estate, was established before the outbreak of the First World War.

Captain Frank Beck MVO, Sandringham Company Commander

Frank Reginald Beck was remembered by the Rev A. Rowland Grant, the Rector of Sandringham as *'so splendidly wholesome, with the laughter light dancing in his eye with nothing mean or petty about his character, he was a man whom it was good to meet and good to know...endowed with gifts of leadership, capable of inspiring others in a high degree, flinging himself into everything wholeheartedly, he made things go.'*

Born at Oxwick in Norfolk on 3 May 1861, Frank was the third of six children of Edmund Beck, farmer, land agent and auctioneer who had been appointed by the Prince of Wales as his agent to run the Sandringham estate in 1865. During Edmund's tenure as

The Sandringham Fire Brigade and the fire engine in front of the East Front of Sandringham House c1912. Several members of the Fire Brigade were also members of The Sandringham Company.

agent he oversaw much of the building of the new Sandringham House, estate buildings and projects that established the estate we know today. He also acted as farm manager of the estate and stud farms. Well known and well liked, Edmund Beck was respected as one of the best agriculturalists and stock breeders in the country. His son Frank, educated at the Norfolk County School, North Elmham, joined his father working at the estate office in 1880 and assisted the management of the royal stud.

Mr Frank Reginald Beck MVO, The King's Estate Agent, Sandringham, 1915.

Frank married Mary Plumpton Wilson of West Newton in 1891; tragically Frank's father died the same year as a result of a carriage accident at the gates to York Cottage. Frank succeeded his father as agent to the Prince of Wales at the age of 30. Frank and Mary Beck had six children, five daughters – Alexandra, Phyllis, May and Victoria – and one son, Edmund Edward Jack, who died in infancy in 1895. He is buried in Sandringham churchyard a short distance from the Prince of Wales's youngest son, Prince

Alexander John of Wales who lived for barely twenty-four hours after being born prematurely at Sandringham House in April 1871. It is not without some terribly sad irony that in the same cemetery lies Prince John, the youngest son of King George V who died as the result of an epileptic seizure aged 13 in 1919.

Frank worked closely with General Sir Dighton Probyn, the Prince of Wales's household comptroller and the two men became great friends. In the 1901 Coronation honours, the newly crowned King Edward VII rewarded his land agent by making him a Member of the Royal Victorian Order. As agent Frank had to walk a tightrope of diplomacy at times to accommodate the impatience of the king. King Edward's assistant private secretary Sir Frederick 'Fritz' Ponsonby recalled one incident on the Sandringham golf links. The putting greens were good, though small, and the fairways were properly mown, but there were no bunkers. To remedy this the agent Frank Beck had asked the head gardener to place wicker hurdles to indicate the places where the bunkers would eventually be dug. The problem was His Majesty kept hitting the hurdles at every hole and the king got louder and louder in his denunciation of the stupidity of the person who had placed the hurdles. Frank came over and took copious notes from the king as he directed exactly where the hurdles should be placed. The following day the hurdles had been moved but the king continued to drive into them. The monarch thundered his disapproval and demanded to know who had placed the hurdles there. When Beck replied by reading his notes showing the king's directions had been complied with to the letter, the king exploded with rage and ordered the hurdles to be removed immediately. There were only ever two bunkers on the nine holes and, as 'Fritz' commented, they were 'made like fortifications'.

In addition to his duties running the estate, Frank Beck personally attended numerous monarchs during their visits, among them, King Alfonso of Spain, Kaiser Wilhelm of Germany and King Haakon of Norway. The prerogative of some monarchs to express their thanks by bestowing honours upon those who served them well saw Frank gratefully receive the Order of St Olav from King Haakon in 1906. However, he declined a German order offered to him by the Kaiser after his visit, but then that occasion had been neither a social or political success for cousin Willi, even King Edward was heard to remark upon his departure, 'Thank God he's gone.'

His Majesty King Edward VII.

The Sandringham Company

From shortly after settling into his country home The Prince of Wales took an interest in the military forces of Norfolk. In 1872, while still Prince of Wales, Edward consented to become honorary colonel of the Norfolk Artillery Militia, a prestigious unit that counted members of many of the local elite families among its officers. With the blessing of the prince, the unit was officially styled the Prince of Wales's Own Norfolk Artillery Militia from 1875. They would often parade for special occasions and their band played for some of the balls and entertainments at Sandringham House.

Learning during the South African War that Norfolk did not have its own county yeomanry, the Prince of Wales soon set about changing that after his accession when he asked former regular cavalry officer Colonel Henry Barclay of Hanworth Hall to raise The King's Own Royal Regiment Norfolk Imperial Yeomanry in 1901. King Edward became their honorary colonel and took a personal interest in the design of their uniforms. The regiment wore the royal cypher as its badge and His Majesty even granted them his racing colours.

In 1906 King Edward VII asked his faithful agent Frank Beck to raise a company of Volunteers from workers on the estate. Frank carefully selected a team to create the firm foundations of a successful company befitting the King's Sandringham Estate. He chose Anthony 'Tony' Knight, the manager of the royal estate farm at West Newton to be his second-in-command. Born at Castle Rising where his family had been well-to-do farmers since the mid-nineteenth century, Tony was Haileybury educated, amiable and a good organiser; he was the ideal man for the job. He took his position seriously, attending military 'school' at Chelsea Barracks in 1907 and was made a Member of the Royal Victorian Order (MVO) the same year as a mark of thanks for his work establishing the Sandringham Company. He passed out at the School of Musketry at Hythe in 1908 and was on detached duty to the 1st Norfolks in 1912, during which time he was attached to the 1st Guards Brigade for six weeks field training at Aldershot in February and March, returning to take part in the 'Great Manoeuvres' across East Anglia in September. In 1913 Anthony became musketry officer and took on the role of assistant adjutant on the outbreak of war (until 20 April 1915) and was promoted to captain in November 1914.

Frank Beck chose his senior non-commissioned officers from the men he both knew well and who already held management positions with staff responsibility on the royal estate. His colour serjeant was Walter Jones, the head teacher of Sandringham School and the manager of the king's pigeon loft. The serjeants were Frederick Bland, the head keeper, Thomas Cook, the head gardener, and Harry Saward, the station master at Wolferton. The other ranks were made up from Sandringham gardeners, gamekeepers, grooms, dairymen, woodsmen, estate office clerks, farm workers and engineers department employees, many of them had been known by Frank Beck since they were born; some were brothers, some were cousins, in-laws, friends, neighbours or work colleagues. Raised with a sense of duty, proud to be members of the Sandringham Company they were truly 'the King's Men'.

Frank was also grateful to have experienced officer Lieutenant Stephen Coxon of the 3rd Volunteer Battalion, The Norfolk Regiment assigned to help him. Coxon received the following letter on Buckingham Palace headed notepaper dated 6 May 1906 from the King's Comptroller, General Sir Dighton Probyn VC:

Dear Sir,

I must apologise for not having written one letter to thank you for the valuable assistance which Capt Beck tells me you have rendered him in work connected with the raising of the Volunteer Company at Sandringham.

I am sure it will have pleased you to see how readily the Estate answered to the call for 'a Sandringham Company'.

I remain dear Sir

D.M. Probyn

Frank Beck wrote to Lieutenant Coxon in a letter of 9 June 1906:

Dear Mr Coxon

This morning I hear officially that this is now the E Company and to make us efficient we are to act on our own with the exception of Sergt. Hodgkins whom you kindly lent.

I feel like one did in the old days at school and thrown into deep water to learn to swim. This letter is written in haste for early post and I am not going to try to express my gratitude to you now though it is very heartfelt. Please wait for this till Friday. Monday, Tuesday, Wednesday we will drill and with the help of Hodgkins and 2 Norwich men.

On Friday next I want you please to let us have your three company sergeants at West Newton for drill at 7 o'clock. At the completion of drill I want to speak to them in the presence of my company. I also ask you to be present at the drill that evening and Mrs Coxon also and join my wife and myself for supper afterwards.

Till then I am both gratefully and sincerely, yours ever,

Frank Beck

As one might imagine Frank Beck offered up a fine tribute of thanks to those who had helped to start the Sandringham Company. Lieutenant Coxon was presented with a book of signatures of all the Sandringham Company as a gesture of thanks on 15 June 1906 for his help establishing the company. Beautifully bound in regal red leather with tasteful gold tooling on the inner turns of the cover, it was inscribed:

To Lieutenant Coxon

3rd Volunteer Battalion, Norfolk Regiment

We the men of the Sandringham Volunteer Detachment wish to testify by our signatures our gratitude for the help you have given us.

To your initiation the formation of the Company is due and it is by the efforts of your generous enthusiasm that this company mustering over 100 has been made ready for camp at Aldershot within three months of starting. We hope you will be spared many years to command your own company and to promote the Volunteer Cause that you have so much at heart.

[See Appendix 1]

The officers and men of the company faithfully attended their drill instruction and training nights, were issued their uniforms, rapidly became smart and efficient soldiers and attended their first Volunteer Infantry Brigade annual camp at Aldershot just one month after they were formally created. King Edward paraded the Norfolk volunteer units he had fostered – the King's Own Royal Regiment Norfolk Imperial Yeomanry (under the command of Colonel H.A. Barclay MVO) and the entire 3rd Volunteer Battalion, The Norfolk Regiment (under the command of Colonel G.F. Cresswell MVO), including the new Sandringham Company, together at a review on Sandringham Park on 1 December 1906.

The king was accompanied by King Haakon of Norway, the queen, the Queen of Norway and the Princess of Wales. The military units on parade arrived at Hillington Station where they formed up and marched the three miles to Sandringham behind their respective bands, their dress uniforms resplendent, their badges, buttons and accoutrements glistening in the winter sunshine. Tenants and employees of the estate were allotted positions and crowds of people from all walks of life came by train and

The newly-formed Sandringham Company getting ready to entrain at Wolferton Station for their first Volunteer Infantry Brigade Summer Camp, at Aldershot in 1906.

Centre left to right: Colonel H.A. Barclay, Commanding Officer KORR Norfolk Yeomanry, HM King Edward VII and King Haakon of Norway reviewing the Norfolk volunteer forces on parade at Sandringham Park on 1 December 1906.

a host of vehicles from carriages to bicycles from miles around. It was an occasion the likes of which had not been seen before at the Sandringham Estate.

The Sandringham Company also provided numerous guards of honour for visiting monarchs, always a remarkably impressive sight in their scarlet tunics with yellow facings, polished buttons and home service helmets. There would always be a fine turnout from all companies of the 3rd Volunteer Battalion for these. The local companies paraded in the station yard at Wolferton and the Sandringham Company under Captain Beck would parade in front of Sandringham House.

King Edward VII had been a keen supporter of the Haldane reforms so when the old Volunteers were discontinued and the Territorial Force was created in 1908 His Majesty asked Captain Beck again to form a company from men on the estate and the surrounding villages. Many of the original volunteers gladly transferred over and with new recruits he soon had over 100 men enlisted into E Company (Sandringham) of the 5th Battalion, The Norfolk Regiment (TF). They were unique for they were the only company in the Territorial Force, indeed the entire British Army, to be raised from the staff of a royal estate. This royal connection meant they were often simply referred to as 'The King's Company'.

Under the new Territorial Force scheme the company required a subaltern and Captain Beck and Lieutenant Knight were joined by Second Lieutenant John Valentine

O. H. M. S.

A Guard of Honour will be mounted by the Batallion at Wolferton on 4th Nov. 1907.

If you are able to attend, draw your arms and parade at the Corn Hall on Monday next, 28th October, in plain clothes, at 8.0 o'clock. Pm

E. M. BELOE, *Captain,*
3rd V.B.N.R.

The specially printed card sent to members of 3rd Volunteer Battalion, to muster a Guard of Honour at Wolferton for the arrival of King and Queen of Spain on Monday 4 November 1907.

King Alfonso of Spain and King Edward VII inspecting the 3rd Volunteer Battalion Guard of Honour at Wolferton Station 4 November 1907.

Band of the Sandringham Company c1911 pictured by the lake with the West Front of Sandringham House in the background.

Betts in September 1908. Betts had been born on the royal estate farm at Babingley that was run by his father Edward. John was educated at Gresham's School in Holt where he was also a member of the Officers' Training Corps. Fit and keen to progress, John would become a company commander in the Royal Fusiliers during the war with whom he served in France and would retire as a major.

The Sandringham Company continued to hold their drill nights at West Newton and staged their local manoeuvres and camps at the nearby estate village of Wolferton. When interviewed by *Great Eastern Railway Magazine* in 1911, Wolferton Station Master Harry Saward stated:

> *I am proud also to be a Sergeant in the Sandringham Company of the 5th Battalion, The Norfolk Regiment and have thoroughly enjoyed attendance at five camps in lieu of holiday-making elsewhere. Moreover, I am sure, that in addition to making one more efficient to serve King and Country should the need arise, the annual training does much good in other directions, not least of which is the establishment and maintenance of that degree of physical fitness which is so essential to the proper performance of everyday duty.*

King Edward VII encouraged the growth of the Sandringham Company until his death in 1910 and his son, King George V and the late king's widow, Queen Alexandra, maintained a keen interest in the progress of their Sandringham Company, especially after they were mobilized for war service.

Men of E Company, 5th Battalion, The Norfolk Regiment TF (Sandringham) at Wolferton Camp, 19 June 1912.

Back Row Left to Right: G. Batterbee, R. Ringer, E. Watts, B. Borley, G.R. Dove, H. Harlow, A. Ford, W. Finch, E. Emmerson, G.H. Batterbee, V. Wells, G. Wells, A. Watts, E. Hudson, C. Hunter, R. Bridges.

Second Row: W.H. Yaxley, G. Daniels, Hunt, F. Melton, J. Dye, B. Reynolds, A. Batterbee, J. Nurse, J. Batterbee, W. Goodman, W. Bridges, G. Deaves, W. Jakeman, A. Bridges, A. Emmerson, P. Smith, P. Loose, A. Waters, F. Wells, H. Lindford, S. Goodship, W. Humphrey, W. Grimes, W. Ringer, H. Elworth, C. Beckett, H. Garney.

Third Row: G. Melton, W. Grapes, S.A. Lines, G. R. Primrose, F.P. Sharpe, F.W. Bland (Head Keeper), T.H. Cook (Head Gardener), E.W. Crosbie, Lieut. J.V. Betts, Capt. F.R. Beck, Lieut. Col. J.B. Petre, Rev. A.R.H. Grant (Rector of Sandringham), Capt. A. Knight, H.L. Saward (Station Master), R. Crome,. G. Riches, H. Bugg, R. Barrell.

Fourth Row: F. Crow, W. Standaloft, W. Cross, B. Grimes, F. Patrick, A. Daniels, P. Daw, A. Grimes, G. Playford, W. Mindham, T. Houchen, A. Nurse, H. Wasy, D. Godfrey, C. Grimes, P. Hammond, H. Dawes, E. Bunting, H. Todd, E. Bland.

Fifth Row: J. Woods, J. Crome, E. Steele, J. Hanslip, L. Curson, R. Mussett, O. Carter, W. Hipkin, H. Willmott, A.W. Nurse, J. Hudson, F. Woodhouse, G. Needs, J. W. Godfrey, E. Cox, F. Woodward, R. Overman.

Sixth Row: F.R. Kerrison, E. Melton, H. Merrikin, D. Howell. C. Howell, F. Turley, S. Carter, A. Bridges, S. Smith, C. Basham.

Some of the Sandringham Company during manoeuvres on Wolferton Marshes, 1912.

Frank Beck was 53 in 1914 and did not attend the Territorial Force Battalion's summer camp that year. His family would recall how, after greeting his company from summer camp in July 1914, he took off his jacket and slumped into a chair where he confessed to his wife Mary, 'I don't think I'm much of a soldier.' However, when war was declared, although too old to be obliged to fight with his company, Captain Frank Beck insisted on accompanying his men when they were called up. Despite the king kindly offering him the chance to stay on at Sandringham, Frank was determined he was going to go with his men. It was well recalled by Frank's family that he made his reasons very clear, saying: 'I formed them. How could I leave them now?' to others on the estate who tried to persuade him to stay, he was resolute: 'Oh no, I must go, what would the boys think if I backed out now?'

Captain Frank Beck MVO, Sandringham Company Commander.

On the morning of mobilization, 5 August 1914, Frank gathered the Sandringham Company on the lawn of his house, surrounded by their families, and gave a speech where he promised the wives and the mothers, 'I will do my best to look after them.' Amid cheers they marched off to serve their king and country. Frank left his younger brother Arthur to look after things on the estate in his absence and his older brother Edward sent his sons Alec (Albert Edward Alexander Beck) and Evelyn (Arthur Evelyn Beck) to join the Sandringham Company as subalterns. To avoid confusion between the various members of the Beck family in the battalion, colour-coded nicknames were given to each of them: Frank was 'black' and his two nephews Alec and Evelyn were known as 'white' and 'pink' respectively.

During the ensuing months Frank would often pop back to Sandringham to ensure everything was running as it should on the royal estate. On his last visit before leaving to proceed abroad his friend Sir Dighton Probyn presented him with a beautiful gold hunter pocket watch which had originally been presented to Probyn by Queen Alexandra. It had originally been inscribed with Probyn's initials and crest on the outer case but now there was a new inscription inside the back cover:

> *This watch was given to me some years ago by Queen Alexandra and I now give it as I know Her Majesty would be glad I should do to my old friend Her Majesty's Servant Captain Frank Beck on leaving England in command of the Sandringham Company of the Norfolk Regt to fight for his King and Country in the Great War now raging abroad, May 1915. Dighton Probyn, Genl*

Frank carried the watch with great pride when he and his company proceeded abroad, a treasured touchstone and reminder of his beloved Sandringham.

Chapter 4

Mobilization and Training

'Leaving all that here can win us;
Hence the faith and fire within us
Men who march away.'

Thomas Hardy

By August 1914 it was not a question of if there was going to be war with Germany, but when. Immediately after summer camp at Holkham the permanent staff of the Norfolk and Suffolk Territorial Infantry Brigade set up an office in the Royal Hotel at Great Yarmouth. The adjutants of the various companies made arrangements to place themselves in close contact with their respective headquarters. Captain Ward of the 5th Norfolks went as far as booking rooms in a Dereham Hotel specifically because of its close proximity to the battalion HQ and the Post Office that was then open all night for telephone and telegraph messages.

The order was given to the Territorial Force to mobilise at 7.30pm on 4 August 1914 and it was announced that war had been declared with Germany at 11pm the same night. The adjutant telegraphed the word 'Mobilize' to each of the detachment commanders and they, in turn, carried out the detailed mobilization orders that had first been issued back in 1913. Territorial Force regulations had stipulated that adjutants should ensure mobilization notices, checked twice a year against the nominal roll, and that all addresses were up to date and correct (a report to the effect was required to be sent to headquarters on 1 January and 1 July each year). Identity discs stamped with the name of the battalion and tied up in bundles of ten were also to be kept at battalion headquarters, ready to be completed on production of company rolls corrected after medical inspection on the day of mobilization. Soldiers' pay books were kept filed in the same order as the company rolls. No entry was to be made in the books, but a slip of paper was pasted on the outside and folded over inside. On the outside of the slip was the man's name and number and on the inside the necessary particulars ready to copy into the book.

The rest of the orders covered every aspect of mobilization, from exactly how it should be carried out and who was responsible for which duties, to the issuing of appropriate items from stores, ammunition, food and transport. For the latter two, contracts with suppliers were already established. In the case of the 5th Norfolks, stores were supplied by Messrs. Baker & Sons of Fakenham and upon instruction would be delivered to their headquarters on the first day of mobilization. Further supplies, such as preserved meats, biscuits and groceries were to be obtained from Dereham merchants Henry S. Kingston & Son, Mid Norfolk Supply Stores, corn from Robert Gray & Son and wood from Norman Smith. A list of horses and carts earmarked for purchase by the battalion was attached and arrangements had been made with J.W. Crow to examine all vehicles in Dereham market place once they had been brought in by the collecting parties and to carry out minor repairs if necessary.

Once assembled each company was to hand in their bayonets for sharpening at intervals of four hours to Hobbies Ltd, engineers, at their workshop at the railway station. To aid in this process the Quartermaster was allotted one officer, Serjeant Instructor Leverington, the Quartermaster Serjeant, Storeman (Army No.71 Private Seabrook, D Company), the Pioneer Serjeant, all pioneers and one man per company were placed at his disposal. Similar preparations were already in place for all Norfolk Territorial Force battalions and mobilization was achieved without a hitch.

During the evening and through the night of 4/5 August the men of the Territorial Force made ready to present themselves at their headquarters on the morning of 5 August 1914. As they formed up in the market places to leave their home towns civic dignitaries and local clerics often gave a short address before the townsfolk waved off the brave boys from their local detachments. The 4th Norfolks were embodied at the Chapelfield Drill Hall, where sentries were posted all day with fixed bayonets to ensure

Officers and men of the 4th Battalion rest as Serjeants check their muster roll books after marching up to their temporary billet at the City of Norwich School on Newmarket Road, 5 August 1914.

no-one except those connected with military matters entered the building. As the day progressed companies from outlying areas arrived in the city by train and marched up to the Drill Hall to report, drawing large cheering crowds along the way. At East Harling the local detachments of E Company were cheered along by a large gathering of local residents as they marched to Harling Road station under Colour Serjeant H. Pattinson en route for their headquarters in Norwich. The constituent platoons of D Company, 4th Norfolks from Harleston and Pulham mustered at their local company HQ at Diss, along with the town boys under the command of Lieutenant Coxon. They marched out of town led by the band down St Nicholas Street, through the Market Place, Mere Street and Victoria Road to the station presenting a 'smart and soldierly appearance, and every man looked fit and well'. They were followed by a large crowd who cheered the men in khaki on their way.

At the station, while the brakes were being loaded with kit, those in line chatted with relatives and friends, there were hearty handshakes and fervent God speeds were heard. As the train steamed out of Diss rousing cheers were given by the crowd who waved them off. Once they arrived at Chapelfield Drill Hall, Norwich the men were placed in ranks, medical inspections were carried out and new recruits wishing to join now our country was at war were enlisted. The billet for the 4th Norfolks was to be the City of Norwich School on Newmarket Road. All that remained was to safely lodge the battalion's colours. The military authorities at Britannia Barracks refused to accept custody of Territorial colours, so they were lodged at the home of the battalion commanding officer Lieutenant Colonel John Robert Harvey.

The companies of the 5th Norfolks were ordered to muster at the battalion headquarters in East Dereham. At Aylsham the local Territorials paraded in the Market Place and adjourned to the Town Hall where Captain Purdy addressed his men, urging upon them the importance of making themselves fit in every way, and not to grumble if they should be called upon to endure hardships. He asked them to take as their motto 'For God and the King'. The men replied with cheers. Captain Purdy then formed them up in the Market Place where the vicar, Canon Hoare, offered up a prayer and the men marched in high spirits to the GER Station headed by the band. As they were leaving, a number of local men offered to join up, among them ex-Aylsham Volunteer John Lee Goulder. A true upstanding countryman, aged 32, he was a member of Aylsham Rural District Council and Board of Guardians and Captain of the Blickling and Aylsham Cricket Club, who left behind his farming business in the hands of a friend and joined the ranks as a private soldier.

The Yarmouth men of B Company took with them some thirty recruits in civilian clothes. At Cromer the men of F Company, under the command of Captain Havard Noel Bridgewater, marched from the parish hall to the GER station to entrain for Dereham. The *Norfolk Chronicle* reported: '*All of them were in the best of spirits and were singing with great heartiness their company song "Roll the Chariot Along".*'

At Downham the members of Downham Detachment, B Company, 5th Norfolks mustered at 9am with Lieutenant H.G. Smith in command. Accompanied by Serjeant Major Ford, they marched to the station to the cheers of locals at 9.50am. Others

Despite the inclement weather the lads of Downham Detachment B Company, 5th Battalion drew a huge crowd to the Market Place, Downham Market for their send off on the morning of 5 August 1914.

followed on the 2.30pm train, including one man who had joined on the previous Monday in order to go with the local company. Before the last batch left, they formed up on the Market Hill and a short service was held, led by the senior curate the Rev E.T. Leslie, the crowd watching was several hundred strong and a circle was made by the soldiers, including five troopers of the Yeomanry. The curate led prayers for the army and the navy, gave a few manly and patriotic words to the soldiers and, led by the Hilgay Excelsior Band, the crowd gave an enthusiastic rendering of 'God Save the King' followed by cheers for the king and the soldiers, especially the boys from Downham. The soldiers then marched to the station and were cheered by crowds of local people along the way. It was estimated by the *Lynn News* that a crowd of some 2,000 saw the Downham boys off at the station and its vicinity.

At King's Lynn, despite the pelting rain, the men of the Lynn Companies of the 5th Norfolks were given a rousing send-off. The men fell in at the armoury on London Road and marched in batches to the St James's Hall. Here they were fully equipped and each man was given a Soldier's Pay Book – for use on active service – and ammunition was brought up from the magazine under special guard. When all the men had assembled the Rev A.H. Hayes, Rector of All Saints addressed them after they had been drawn up to attention by Captain Arthur Pattrick. After the special address and prayers, the dismiss was given and he shook hands with members of the company one by one, wishing all God-speed. At the station the crowds thronged the

The Hunstanton and District Detachment ready to leave from Hunstanton Station, 5 August 1914 bound for King's Lynn Station where they would join the lads of the 'Lynns' for the next leg of their journey to Battalion Headquarters.

Lynn Company Commander, Captain Arthur Pattrick (foreground), fellow officers, local A Company lads and Royal Naval Reservists receiving a rousing send off from in the Market Place, King's Lynn, 5 August 1914.

departing soldiers. The Lynn boys met up with the Downham and district platoons and Hunstanton men of the battalion leaving together on the 12.30pm train for East Dereham. As the train moved out to the accompaniment of cheering crowds and waving hands, a young man of the 5th Norfolks waved a union flag out of the window and the train blew its whistle several times, even when it had passed out of sight. Throughout the morning of 5 August, the companies of the 5th Norfolks poured into battalion headquarters at Dereham from Cromer, Yarmouth, Lynn, Swaffham, Downham, Sandringham and Fakenham.

Because of the numbers involved, as the men arrived they were sent to muster in the Market Place and as they did so a Union flag was hoisted over two businesses there and the troops broke into loud cheers and sang 'Rule Britannia'. Each man in the battalion had to pass through the Assembly Rooms and was examined to ensure fitness and freedom from infestations and contagious diseases, a task shared by doctors Belding, Duigan and Howlett. The drill hall could not accommodate all 800 men of the battalion so the maltings belonging to Messrs. F.D.G. Smith were requisitioned for the men and the officers were accommodated on the top floor of Hobbies Ltd warehouse. The place of assembly for the battalion was the Corn Hall with the Masonic Hall in Norwich Street used for stores and Assembly Rooms retained for military purposes. By nightfall of 5 August 800 men of the 5th Norfolks were accommodated in the town.

Men of A Company, 5th Battalion, with greatcoats rolled and kit bags packed, ready to leave from King's Lynn Station 5 August 1914.

Cheering crowds say a fond farewell to their local lads on King's Lynn station as they depart for their headquarters at East Dereham, 5 August 1914.

The companies of the 5th Battalion mustering in the Market Place at their headquarters town of East Dereham, 5 August 1914.

Training

The first alarm experienced by the Territorial Battalions was raised at 1.30am on 7 August 1914 when divisional headquarters sent a message to the 4th Norfolks' headquarters at Chapelfield by telephone to serve out 150 rounds of ammunition per man and prepare to leave at short notice by special train for Cromer as the Germans were expected to land there. The ammunition was issued without delay and by the time the men had unwrapped the packages and filled their bandoliers the battalion was left standing knee-deep in paper. At 6.30am the order was cancelled; the whole incident had been a false alarm originated by a nervous young staff officer.

On the morning of 9 August 1914 reveille was sounded for the 4th Norfolks at 2.30am and after a breakfast at 3am the battalion marched down to Thorpe Station where they left by special train for Ingatestone. After rising at a similar ungodly hour the 5th Norfolks caught their train to Billericay, Essex where they occupied their first war stations along with the rest of the Norfolk and Suffolk Infantry Brigade.

On 10 August, owing to the fact that the men only had the underclothes they stood in and the County Association having made no contingency, Lieutenant Colonel Harvey sent out an appeal to Norwich and Norfolk through the *Eastern Daily Press* and, thanks to many kind donations from members of the public, the men had spare shirts and underclothes. Neither battalion was particularly fortunate in finding good accommodation. On 11 August the 4th Norfolks left Ingatestone for Cold Norton from where they marched to their new billets at Purleigh. These billets were very poor, many of them had recently been fowl houses and barns. Their problems were compounded on 13 August when the regular drill instructors of the battalions were removed to act as drill instructors for the ever-growing Kitchener's Army.

Rumblings of discontent about soldiers' footwear began around this time too. Men had joined the battalions wearing their own boots which were starting to show signs of wear and tear; there were no replacements to issue to the men and complaints were soon lodged about worn and leaky boots. On 17 August the 4th and 5th Norfolks left Purleigh with the brigade and marched on a scorching hot day via Maldon to Great Totham where the 4th Norfolks found their new billets and the 5th Norfolks marched to Colchester. Lance Corporal Tom Williamson of F Company recalled, 'We really hadn't trained sufficiently enough to cope with our heavy packs fully laden to march 20 miles and some of the lads didn't make it.'

Once they arrived at Colchester the men of the Norfolk and Suffolk Infantry Brigade were expecting to be housed in the barracks. However, a message handed to the officers during the march informed them that no barracks would be available and alternative billets would have to be at the Eastern Counties Asylum for Idiots and Imbeciles on Mile End Road, some two miles north of Colchester. You can no doubt imagine some of the comments made by the men of the brigade and, to add insult to injury, the reason for the sudden change soon became apparent when they saw long columns of Kitchener volunteers still in their civilian clothes pouring out of the North Station on their way to the barracks that should have been for the Territorials.

Some of the Yarmouth lads serving in the 5th Battalion published in the Yarmouth Mercury.

Accommodation in the Asylum buildings soon became overcrowded, some men even ended up sleeping in the chapel above and beneath the pews like bunk beds and the officers were placed in what had been the wards for paying patients. Others ended up in empty houses or tents. Private Hubert Attoe of 'F' Company, 5th Norfolks wrote home to Briston:

Dear Mother,

Sorry I have not written before but you know I don't like a lot of writing. I am glad to tell you I am getting on fine. All F Company went for a 4 mile march this morning (Sunday) that is all we have to do today we have the rest of the day to ourselves. Jack and myself thought of going into the town this afternoon and having our tea at the soldier's home we can get a good tea for six and then we shall not have to tramp back to barracks as it is 3 miles into the town. We have all just been given a new shirt 2 pr socks / undervest 1 Karki [sic] *handkerchief and we are going to have a woollen headgear later on, they are being given by private people for F company only. We have shifted from the asylum in to tents we had a rare wet night last night but we never got wet. We went to the Hipper last night it was tumbling down when we came out there.*

We have got 9 in our tent myself Jack, Louis, Dick, G. Bell, E. Eke, A. Gibson a chap from Hasbro and Thompson from Holt who is on Melton Works...Perhaps you could make me a little bag to keep my brushes separate from my shirts, socks and other things about the size of a net bag and you can send me a few short cakes, also a dessert spoon. The cakes will be nice for supper as we don't get any here send them as soon as you can but you will think I am a lot of trouble but I'm not costing you a sight now. We got 7/- this week but have got some more to come for the time we put in at Dereham. We have not drawed the five pound yet or heard anything about it. We have got a Kaki [sic] *coat but hope to have our other things about Wednesday.*

Hoping you are all in the best of health and don't forget to send the shortcake not because we don't get enough grub as we have plenty of it.

I think this all now write soon
and I remain be
your loving son
Hubes

Officers of the 1/5th Battalion, The Norfolk Regiment T.F. Colchester, October 1914: Back Row, standing Lieut. W.L. Blake, Lieut R.J.F. Pearce, Lieut. H.W. St George, Lieut. Randall Cubitt, Lieut Alec Beck, Lieut. Evelyn Beck, Lieut. N.B. de M. Greenstreet, 2/Lieut. E. Gay, Lieut. A.H. Mason, 2/Lieut. Eustace Cubitt, 2/Lieut G.W. Birkbeck, 2/Lieut. Victor Cubitt, Lieut. E.R. Woodwark, Lieut. H.A. Durrant, Lieut. Cedric Coxon, Lieut. William Wenn, 2/Lieut. S. Coles.

Middle Row: Capt. Cross, Capt. Frank Beck, Major H. Ellis Rowell, Capt. Arthur Ward (Adjutant), Colonel A.W. Thomas, Major H.R. Morgan, Captain W.J. Barton, Captain Thomas Woods Purdy, Capt. Arthur Pattrick.

Front Row: 2/Lieut. L.F.W. Willson, 2/Lieut. Randall Burroughes, 2/Lieut. Julien Randolph, 2/Lieut W.F. Norris, 2/Lieut. Reginald Cubitt, 2/Lieut. H.G. Smith.

Army Form, E. 624.

AGREEMENT to be made by an officer or man of the Territorial Force to subject himself to liability to serve in any place outside the United Kingdom in the event of National Emergency.

I (No.) 2/29 (Rank) Pte

(Name) E Emmerson of the

(Unit) F Co. 5th Batt. Norfolk Regt. do hereby agree,

subject to the conditions stated overleaf, to accept liability, in the event of national emergency, to serve in any place outside the United Kingdom, in accordance with the provisions of Section XIII. (2) (a) of the Territorial and Reserve Forces Act, 1907.

Ernest Emmerson
Signature of Officer or Man.

[illegible]
Signature of Commanding Officer.

Station Colchester

Date 20. 10. 14

The form signed by Territorial Force soldiers volunteering to serve abroad on active service. This example was signed by Dersingham soldier and Sandringham Company stalwart Private Ernest Emmerson.

The Imperial Service badge presented to all Territorial Force soldiers who signed the overseas commitment.

Seventeen-year-old Private Burton Stearman 1/5th Battalion of Cromer proudly wearing his Imperial Service badge.

The War Office knew that Territorial soldiers were under no obligation to fight overseas but it soon became painfully apparent the war could not be won by the BEF alone, so a general appeal was put out to the Territorial battalions for volunteers for overseas service. The first call of this nature was presented to the men of the Norfolk Territorial battalions on 21 August 1914. The response was very positive, with all Norfolk Territorial battalions sending in returns of 90 per cent or more volunteering 'to do their bit' overseas. Indeed *The Times* reported on 2 September 1914 that the 100 men of the Sandringham Company had volunteered as a body for active service. A white metal pin-backed badge bearing the legend 'Imperial Service' surmounted by a crown was issued to all members of the Territorial Force who volunteered for overseas service before 30 September 1914. It was worn with great pride above the right pocket on their tunics. By the later months of 1914 both Territorial battalions had a reserve battalion, the 2/4th and 2/5th battalions;

later further reserve battalions were raised numbered 3/4th and 3/5th and thus the original battalions were designated 1/4th and 1/5th and were known as such for the rest of the war.

Great interest was always shown in the 1/5th Norfolks and care was taken to note it amongst the staff corps because of the king's personal interest in his Sandringham Company under the command of his agent, Captain Frank Beck. After he had conducted his inspection of the brigade in late August, General Sir Ian Hamilton, at the time of the inspection a senior officer in Central Command with responsibility for anti-invasion forces, but who would ultimately go on to be in overall command of the allied forces in Gallipoli, wrote to King George V's private secretary Lord Stamfordham at Buckingham Palace:

My dear Stamfordham

Even in these dreadfully anxious and momentous times I think it is possible that the King might like to hear what a fine appearance the Sandringham Company of the 5th Norfolks put in yesterday when I inspected them at Colchester. They stood 100 on parade and the officer commanding the company said he expected to be 120 strong in three days' time. Every single individual of all ranks has volunteered for service overseas, and a finer, smarter, keener looking lot of young soldiers it would be difficult to find.

Believe me

Yours sincerely

IAN HAMILTON

On 14 October 1914 the Norfolk and Suffolk Brigade marched to Elmstead, near Colchester to take up a new line of defence on the Clacton Road, because authorities were still fearful the Germans might attempt to make a landing on the Essex coast. The 4th Battalion marched out to Elmstead Market in order to dig trenches at Keeler's Tye near Arlesford and on 29 October two companies of the 1/4th Norfolks marched to Clacton-on-Sea under Captain Rudd and occupied billets there so they could dig trenches on the sea front. These duties were shared in rotation with the 1/5th Norfolks and other battalions in the brigade until they left Colchester early in 1915.

The problem that lingered was the accommodation provided for the men as winter rolled in, especially those staying in canvas tents. Captain Purdy had cause to write to the Adjutant on 1 November 1914:

Sir,

I think it necessary to represent to you the condition of the tents in which my company and E, F and H are sleeping. Very few are watertight, the walls in most cases are much torn and owing to the hardness of the ground till recently and the numerous changes of position very few pegs are of any use so that the walls cannot be kept down and the tents are extremely wet at night.

The ground is too wet and in the morning the men's blankets and clothes are very damp and owing to the wet weather of the last few days there has been little opportunity of drying them. If the men have to stay under canvas much longer there will I fear be a considerable amount of sickness among them.

I have more than once asked the late transport officer for another water cart without result, one cart not being nearly sufficient for 4 companies and I suggest that two carts to always be stationed on the field and each filled four times a day. It is impossible for the men to keep themselves properly clean under the present conditions.

As the month progressed there were hopes the brigade would be deployed to France but it would only be the 1/4th Suffolks who were to leave. They landed at Le Havre on 9 November, their place in the brigade being filled by the 1/8th Battalion, The Hampshire Regiment (Isle of Wight Rifles) (1/8th Hants) in April 1915.

On 10 November 1914 the Norfolk and Suffolk Infantry Brigade, under the command of Brigadier Reginald Bayard DSO were inspected by King George V on the Braiswick Golf Links near Colchester. His Majesty had been driven up by motor car with Major General Inglefield, the commander of the East Anglian Division, and General Sir Ian Hamilton. The brigade was formed up in line of quarter columns and marched past the king in column of route.

Captain Beck greeting the king after His Majesty had inspected the Norfolk and Suffolk Infantry Brigade on the Braiswick Golf Links near Colchester, 10 November 1914.

Lieutenant Colonel Horace George Proctor-Beauchamp, appointed commanding officer 1/5th Battalion, November 1914.

On 12 November the Norfolk County Association had begun to send in supplies of clothing and boots to the battalion and by 14 November 500 suits had been received. During this time at Colchester, the battalions had been training in company work and musketry courses on the Middlewick Range. On 14 November Lieutenant Colonel Thomas was transferred to the Territorial Reserve and replaced by Brevet Colonel Sir Horace George Proctor-Beauchamp of Langley Hall as commanding officer of the 1/5th Norfolks. An experienced cavalry officer, Beauchamp had served with distinction in the Sudanese Campaign and in South Africa and was twice Mentioned in Despatches. He had retired from the 20th Hussars in 1906 thus he had not been part of the development of the Territorial Force new military operations guidance and had only ever known a cavalry command in peace and war. Not a young man, he assumed command of the 1/5th Norfolks in his fifty-eighth year. The gap in his military knowledge was apparent to the men when he gave them a start by issuing an occasional cavalry order, but he was popular with his men. One of them recorded his memories of Beauchamp:

> *Two or three times a week parades were held and each night the commandant was at his post dominating the proceedings by a combination of geniality and strictness which mark the leader apart from the led...No one could have been more inspiring, yet no one would have kept us more alive to the seriousness of what we were attempting.*

The battalions undertook more route marches, training for war with bayonet and on the ranges, on sentry duty and keeping an ever-vigilant eye out for spies. Shortages and the conditions the soldiers were staying in were still a matter of concern and men were often reduced to sharing a loaf of bread and tin of bully beef between eight. The cooks tried hard and filled many a wanting stomach with a good supply of hot soups. Mr Alfred Whitehouse, Head Teacher of the St Nicholas Boys Elementary School in King's Lynn, the father of Private Bertram W. Whitehouse, wrote to Captain Arthur Pattrick on 1 December 1914:

> *Dear Sir*
>
> *My son with several others from Lynn is at Boxted near Colchester and they appear to be having rather an uncomfortable time chiefly owing to poor and insufficient*

food. As his mother and I are rather anxious about his health from letters received (he has been on the sick list for several days) I feel sure you will enquire into the matter for me.

Captain Pattrick and other company commanders presented their concerns to the Adjutant and there was some improvement in the situation. Accommodation and living conditions were still far from ideal. The chapel at the asylum became so overcrowded that if men did not have a pew they slept in commandeered empty houses on floorboards on a straw bed with a waterproof sheet and a few extra blankets from home, if they had brought them, or had them sent down by post. The buildings were cold and damp, a situation made worse after a gale in late November tore a number of tiles off the roofs of the houses. Broken windows remained unrepaired, water came in when it rained and the mud along the driftway and paths on the Boxted Road became so deep the men could not arrive on parade with clean or dry boots. The Norfolk Territorial battalions made the best of it and along with the majority of the brigade, spent their first Christmas of the war at the Eastern Counties Asylum. There was very little home leave granted, but every battalion had a good Christmas Day meal and plenty of beer, although the teetotallers grumbled because they were the ones who had to do their turn on guard duty afterwards.

The first draft of men from the reserve battalions at Peterborough joined the 1/4th and 1/5th Norfolks at Colchester in January 1915. The first batch of lads for the 1/4th Norfolks consisted of twenty-five boys all under 19 years of age, six of whom were rejected by the regimental doctor as physically unfit. The number of sick also increased

Officers and NCOs of B Company, 1/4th Battalion, Colchester 1914.

owing to the wet weather and insanitary billets occupied by some of the men who could not be accommodated at the asylum. In the 1/4th Norfolks alone some days there were 200 men on the sick list, many of them suffering with influenza.

In January 1915 all Territorial Battalions had to be reorganised to comply with the new British Army 'four companies to a battalion' system. The new set-up for the 1/5th Norfolks was published in the Battalion Standing Orders of 9 January 1915:

Old Companies	**New Company**	
D and G	A	Officer Commanding: Major Barton Second in Command: Captain Mason Supernumerary: Captain Willson Platoon Commanders: Lieutenant Norris, Lieutenant Birkbeck, Second Lieutenant E. Cubitt Attached: Second Lieutenant Culme Seymour (Machine Gun Officer) Company Serjeant Major: Colour Serjeant Wells Company Quartermaster Serjeant: Colour Serjeant Smith
A and B	B	Officer Commanding: Captain Pattrick Second in Command: Captain Knight MVO Platoon Commanders: Lieutenant Woodwark, Lieutenant Coles, Second Lieutenant V. Cubitt Second Lieutenant M. Proctor-Beauchamp Company Serjeant Major: Colour Serjeant Hipkin Company Quartermaster Serjeant: Colour Serjeant Parker
E and F	C	Officer Commanding: Captain F. Beck MVO Second in Command: Captain E. Randall Cubitt Platoon Commanders: Lieutenant T. Oliphant. Lieutenant Pearce, Lieutenant Alec Beck, Lieutenant Evelyn Beck Company Serjeant Major: Colour Serjeant Spalding Acting Company Quartermaster Serjeant: Colour Serjeant Simpson
C and H	D	Officer Commanding: Captain T.W. Purdy Second in Command: Captain Coxon Platoon Commanders: Lieutenant Gay, Lieutenant Pearce, Second Lieutenant Randolph, Second Lieutenant Burroughs,

Second Lieutenant Archie Beck
Company Serjeant Major: Colour Serjeant Edwards
Acting Company Quartermaster Serjeant: E.W. Simpson

With so many men fiercely proud of the local associations and identity of the companies, every attempt was made to make the transition as smooth as possible to keep up morale and, although merged, the companies were still led by familiar officers and NCOs and the platoons retained as much local identity as possible. Some researchers correctly point out that the Sandringham Company ceased to exist from this time, but they seem also to latch on to the erroneous notion that the officers and men of the company were dispersed, however, the rank structure and platoons of the Sandringham Company actually changed little within the new structure of C Company. Just like the other companies of the 5th Norfolks, the 'Sandringhams' did not forget who they were and there were several occasions, because of the king's interest in their progress, when the men of the Sandringham Company were requested to parade as a separate company during inspections by the most senior officers so the visiting general could report back to the king on their progress. Even months after the action of 12 August 1915, those who were still serving with the 1/5th Norfolks were paraded separately as the Sandringham Company for inspection by the Prince of Wales before he inspected the rest of the battalion in Egypt in April 1916.

In the aftermath of the first Zeppelin raid on Great Britain on 19 January 1915 orders were issued for all lights to be extinguished or screened from 5pm to 7.30am – not an easy request in some of the buildings where the men were billeted, so many experienced long hours in darkness. On 23 February 1915 news was received that the forts in the Dardanelles had been bombarded by the British and French fleets but no-one in either battalion dreamed that in just a few months they would be serving in that same theatre of war.

On 1 April 1915 the Norfolk Territorial battalions were inspected on the Colchester golf links by General Codrington who was accompanied by Major General Inglefield and Brigadier Bayard; it was to be their last formal parade in the town. On 8 April 1915 the 1/4th and 1/5th Norfolks left Colchester for Sudbury. Billeted in the town for the night, the following day they marched to Bury St Edmunds via Long Melford. Bury was reached at 4pm and the Norfolk battalions were billeted in the north end of the town. Many of the men were accommodated with local families; all were in better accommodation and enjoyed the benefits of the open fields around the area for training and manoeuvres.

On 15 April 1915 orders were given to the 1/4th Norfolks to send two companies to watch the road to Newmarket and the Stowmarket railway lines. The men of the Norfolk Territorial battalions also had a very near miss when Bury St Edmunds was bombed during a Zeppelin raid on 30 April. Private Hubert Attoe, now in the amalgamated C Company, 1/5th Norfolks, wrote home from his billet at 17, Prospect Row:

Lieut H.M. Taylor (seated centre) and the Machine Gun Section, 1/4th Battalion, Bury St Edmunds, 1915.

> *...Well the bomb had not much effect on me they dropped some about 100yrds from my billet and set some stables on fire. My mate heard an explosion but I never heard anything he work* [sic] *me up at 1 o'clock there was a couple of big fires then. The one in the main thoroughfare had got a proper hold and it done a good bit of damage. I think they dropped about 40 bombs altogether they meant doing this place in properly, but luckily no one was killed or injured only a collie dog.*

In his next letter Hubert commented:

> *...the poor old landlady's* [sic] *were afraid to go to bed for two or three nights afterwards. Well the bombs helped to liven this place up a bit. They dropped a few at Southend early the other morning the devils seem to be everywhere and then the sinking of the* Lusitania *I reckon the people at Briston think the world is coming to an end.*

While in Bury the men took part in divisional and brigade training, chiefly on the Wordwell, Elveden, Thetford Road but they were also kept busy responding to continued reports of spies being harboured and active in the area, and a number of shops were 'hallmarked and blanked' as holding suspected enemy collaborators. Matters came to a head on 14 May when Theodore Jacobus, landlord of The Griffin pub on the corner of Cornhill and Brentgovel Street, was claimed by rumour to have been spotted standing on the roof of his pub signalling to the Zeppelins with a light. Incensed townspeople and some of the locally-billeted Royal Engineers assailed the

The Buttermarket, Bury St Edmunds after being bombed during a Zeppelin air raid on 30 April 1915. Soldiers from the Norfolk Territorial Battalions were billeted just a few doors away.

pub, hurling bricks through the windows and threatening to lynch the landlord if they could catch him. Troops from the brigade were drafted in to help restore order with the police and guard the premises from looting.

On 17 April the 1/4th Battalion was asked to hold itself in readiness to proceed overseas; this came to nothing and the 1/5th Norfolks were still left wondering if they would ever get an overseas posting. Private Hubert Attoe summed up how a lot of the men were feeling at the time in another letter home:

> *We have not heard anything about getting any more leave it was said we were going to St Albans in Hertfordshire to-day Wed but we are still here. I daresay we shall go strait* [sic] *from here to France the old Colonel said we should be facing the music in three weeks time, but you know Dad we have been going so many times. I shall be damned glad when we do go as I have got sick of messing about from one place to another.*

On 18 May 1915 orders were received that the Norfolk and Suffolk Brigade would move to Watford at midnight the next day. This was achieved using two special trains and the battalions had arrived at Watford by about 5pm on 20 May and were billeted in the town. The troops greatly endeared themselves to the people of Watford, for the previous unit in the billets was one of the 'London class corps' who had made

Officers and NCOs, C Company 1/4th Battalion, Watford, May 1915.

themselves unpopular by complaining about the lack of baths, or if baths existed, the owners of the houses used them for coal or storage. They had also refused to 'crowd' and would not put more than two men in a double bed. An officer of the 1/8th Hants recorded:

> *The 163rd Brigade had none of the fastidiousness of the Londoners, and were therefore, extremely popular and pampered. Such petting by the people was much to the chagrin of some officers who felt this gave the men no experience of hardships inseparable from a campaign.*

Brigadier Bayard had left the brigade on sick leave so on 21 May all commanding officers were summoned to the brigade office to meet the new commander – Brigadier Capel Molyneux Brunker DSO. From 21 May the 1/4th and 1/5th Norfolks became part of the 54th Infantry Division with the 1/5th Suffolks and 1/8th Hants, known henceforward as 163 Infantry Brigade. While at Watford brigade training was principally carried out, together with some battalion training, in Moor and Cassiobury Parks. On 16 June 163 Brigade left Watford for Gadsbridge near Hemel Hempstead, where they bivouacked with the 54th Division and took part in divisional manoeuvres under General Inglefield in Gadsbridge Park, then marched back to Watford.

Brigadier Capel Molyneux Brunker was 56 (two years younger than Colonel Proctor-Beauchamp of the 1/5th Norfolks). He had served with distinction in Egypt and the South African War during which he commanded the 2nd Battalion Lancashire Fusiliers. He was Mentioned in Despatches twice and was awarded the Distinguished Service Order (*London Gazette*, 27 September 1901) 'In recognition of services during

Men of 1/4th Battalion parading in full marching order, ready to march off for more training, Watford, June 1915.

Men of 1/4th Battalion on one of the regular route marches out of Watford, June 1915.

Soldiers of 1/5th Battalion sitting on their large packs that were filled with their blankets (every comfort helps) at a halt during a route march, Watford, June 1915.

Lieut. William Morgan clearly needs to have his hat adjusted, much to the amusement of all as 1/4th Norfolk make a roadside halt during brigade manoeuvres, Watford, June 1915.

the operations in South Africa.' He had not retired from military service in the years between, however his methods and leadership saw him described thus in the covering letter for the 1/8th Hants War Diary:

> *The brigadier was also a man of considerable age and service and was said to have been invalided from France in 1914. His ideas were early Victorian – on one occasion he informed the officers of the Brigade that no officer should ever smoke a pipe, not even in the seclusion of his own quarters. As a leader he inspired no confidence whatever. About a fortnight before going on active service, a Company Commander had occasion to tell his company before dismissing them that he was dissatisfied with their work and unless they showed more keenness they would have extra parades. The parade ground was the street in which they were billeted and the officer's lecture was listened to by the inhabitants, who sent a deputation to the Brigadier. The Brigadier listened to the deputation, and without waiting for explanation or investigation, reprimanded the Company Commander in their presence.*

Colonel Proctor-Beauchamp was also to suffer censure from Brunker. A complaint about Beauchamp's management of the battalion was sent by the Adjutant, Captain

Officers of 1/5th Battalion, The Norfolk Regiment, Watford 1915.

Back Row, Left to Right: Lieut. T. Oliphant, Capt. E.R. Woodwark, 2/Lieut. R. Adams, 2/Lieut. A. Beck, 2/Lieut. Alec. E. Beck, Capt. R.G. Ladell (Medical Officer), Lieut. E.H. Cubitt, Capt. E. Gay, Capt. G.W. Birkbeck, Capt. Evelyn Beck, Capt. Culme Seymour, Lieut Victor M. Cubitt, Lieut. R. Burroughs.

Middle Row, Left to Right: Lieut. M.R. Parker, Capt. A.C. Coxon, Capt. A.D. Pattrick, Major W. . Barton, Lieut. Col. H.G. Proctor-Beauchamp, Capt. A.E. Ward (Adjutant), Major T.W. Purdy, Capt. A. Knight, Capt. A.H. Mason.

Front Row, Left to Right: 2/Lieut. A.R. Pelly, 2/Lieut. M.G.B. Proctor-Beauchamp, 2/Lieut W.G.S. Fawkes, 2/Lieut. M.F. Oliphant.

'Ginger' Ward, to Brunker. Ward suggested he was not alone in his opinion and that 'a number of the officers had lost confidence'. But Ward was known in the battalion to have a problem with his attitude and at best his relationship with his fellow officers was 'difficult', the core of the problem being that Ward was a Regular Army officer and resented being attached to a Territorial unit. Again, Brunker did not investigate properly and soon Colonel Beauchamp was only allowed to stay in post subject to his adjutant taking on additional administrative responsibilities. Tragically, Brunker's leadership on the battlefield was to have fatal consequences.

Further concern over the standard of equipment and training of the brigade is recorded in the 1/8th Hants war diary:

> *Purely from the military side, the training was worse than useless. What little training ground there was around Watford, was almost useless on account of the congestion of troops and often a Company Commander, in despair, resorted to a route march as a means of finding something to occupy his men. In wet weather nothing would be done, as there were no halls to take the place of barrack rooms. The weapons and methods of warfare introduced by the war were untaught...The rifles were the ancient long barrel Lee Enfield, and the equipment was a very shoddy leather affair that more or less dissolved in wet weather. The only ball ammunition fired before active service was a short rapid course lasting one day. No trouble whatever being taken to profit by the exercise. As the whole Brigade succeeded in firing their course on an eight-target range in two days, it will be readily understood how useless the whole proceeding was. In every battalion a number of men unavoidably missed this opportunity to fire ball ammunition, and their first experience was against the enemy.*

Some of the Yarmouth Lads of 1/5th Battalion, The Norfolk Regiment wearing their newly issued foreign service uniforms and helmets, Watford, 1915.

Briston soldier Private Hubert Attoe, C Company 1/5th Battalion, (seated) and some of his pals in their new foreign service kit, Watford, July 1915.

Corporal Arnold Groom (standing far right) with his pals in their new foreign service uniforms, Watford, 1915. There were plenty of jokes about who or what each soldier looked like in their Wolseley pattern sun helmets.

Chapter 5

To Foreign Shores

'But other shells are waiting
Across the Aegean Sea,
Shrapnel and High Explosive,
Shells and hells for me.'

Patrick Shaw Stewart

Just as the men were beginning to wonder if they would ever see service abroad, warm climate khaki drill uniforms and Wolseley pith helmets were issued to all ranks. It came suddenly and as quite a surprise and the new look soon became the butt of endless jokes. The men were still wondering where they were going to be sent, could it be Mesopotamia? Others were convinced it would be Egypt. Some feared they were being relegated to garrison duties out in India, but despite all their trials and tribulations their optimism as they prepared to depart remained high.

On the eve of their departure for active service the king sent a telegram to Captain Frank Beck:

> *My best wishes to you and to the Sandringham Company on the eve of your departure for the Front. I have known you all for years and am confident that the same spirit*

Officers and men of 1/5th Battalion trying the new kit out on a march, Watford July 1915.

of loyalty and patriotism, in which you answered the Call to Arms, will inspire your deeds in the face of the enemy. May God bless and protect you.

George R.I.

Captain Beck had clearly kept himself abreast of his duties at Sandringham and had even taken headed notepaper with him for official correspondence. His reply to the king was very much in his typical loyal and upbeat style. Sent to the king's assistant private secretary Sir Frederick Ponsonby, on 28 July 1915, it was written on Sandringham Estate Office notepaper, the pre-printed address had a single line through it and was simply replaced with 'Watford':

Dear Sir

At last we are really off to the Front. The King's gracious message to the Division and His Majesty's more than kind telegram to the Sandringham men makes us all so proud and grateful. May we only prove ourselves men.

Your faithful servant,

Frank Beck

The men of the Norfolk Territorial battalions had greatly endeared themselves to the townspeople of Watford and, despite their train departing for Liverpool at the early hour of 4am on 29 July 1915, they were given a lovely send off and many a tear was shed when they left the town. The men would look back on these happy times throughout the dark

HMT Aquitania, *one of the biggest troop transport ships in the world, which safely transported the men of the 54th Division the 3,000 miles to Gallipoli.*

times of war. They carried on writing to those they had stayed with and many of those evacuated home wounded or sick returned to visit to the friends they had made there.

The majority of the 54th Division, some 7,000 men, made that same journey and boarded the HMT *Aquitania* at Liverpool Docks. At hardly two years old *Aquitania,* sister ship of *Mauretania* and *Lusitania,* was the newest of the three grand express liners of the Cunard line, and one of the largest passenger-carrying vessels in the world at the time. It is no wonder she left quite an impression on the men, most of whom had only ever seen the likes of the herring fishing trawlers, paddle steamers or maybe a battleship in the distance off the Norfolk coast. All men and equipment were loaded aboard, lifebelts were issued and were expected to be worn by all personnel at all times. *Aquitania* lay in dock overnight and into the following morning, then in the afternoon they cast off and moved into the river. They finally set off at 11pm on the moonlit night of 30 July 1915 and the men watched the twinkling lights of England slowly fade into the distance as they left the Mersey and made headway into the Irish Sea. Most of men aboard still had no idea where they were going.

Officers proceeding with the Norfolk Territorial Force Battalions overseas, 29 July 1915:

1/4th Battalion

Commanding Officer: Captain E.W. Montgomerie

(Montgomerie was the Adjutant and took command because Lieutenant Colonel Harvey was ill. Harvey rejoined his battalion on 15 August.)

Captains
Burrell, Charles William Wilborne
Page, Sydney Durrant
Hughes, Burroughes Maurice
Jewson, William Henry
Fisher, George Kenneth Thompson
Boswell, Bernard

Lieutenants
Flatt, Thomas Norman
Corke, Vincent Charles Clement
Morgan, William Vanstone
Hampton, George Kenneth

Second Lieutenants
Caton, Richard Bewley
Elliott, Charles Arthur Bertram
Bradshaw, Harold James

Culley, George Charles Henry
Steel, Stanley Joseph
Burrell, Robert Eden
de Poix, Ralph Claud Busick Marie Tyril
White, Spencer John Meadows
Thurgar, Ralph William
Collison, Edgar Henry
Wood, Guy Havat
Spackman, Charles Basil Slater
Jewson, John Howlett

Lieutenant Quartermaster: Moore, Richard William

Medical Officer: Hosken, James Gerald Fayrer

1/5th Battalion

Commanding Officer: Colonel Sir Horace George Proctor-Beauchamp, Bart CB

Majors
Barton, Walter John
Purdy, Thomas Woods

Captains
Ward, Arthur Edward Martyr (Adjutant)
Beck, Frank Reginald MVO
Pattrick, Arthur Devereux
Knight, Anthony MVO
Cubitt, Edward Randall
Coxon, Arthur Cedric Meers
Mason, Arthur Humphrey
Woodwark, Ernest Reginald

Lieutenants
Oliphant, Trevor
Beck, Arthur Evelyn
Birkbeck, Gervase William
Gay, Edmund
Cubitt, Victor Murray
Cubitt, Eustace Henry
Culme-Seymour, Arthur Granville

Second Lieutenants
Burroughes, Randall
Proctor-Beauchamp, Montagu Barclay Granville

Beck, Albert Edward Alexander
Pelly, Arthur Roland
Oliphant, Marcus Francis
Adams, Robert
Fawkes, William George Stewart
James, William Charles
Buxton, Murray Barclay

Lieutenant Quartermaster: Parker, Samuel

Medical Officer: Captain Robert MacDonald Ladell

Serjeant Jack Dye C Company, 1/4th Battalion.

Attleborough man, Serjeant Jack Dye of C Company, 1/4th Norfolks recorded the departure and journey in a letter home:

HMT Aquitania

Somewhere in Mediterranean Sea

4th August 1915

It was on Wednesday night 28/7/15 that we were paraded at 12.30 to leave Watford; never shall we forget it. It was a magnificent send off and without boasting I may honestly say the 1/4th Norfolks had once more kept up their reputation and made themselves much liked by the people generally.

It was a sight to see them carrying the men's kit-bags for them all the way to the station and when we arrived there and the public were not admitted the sight came to a climax; some were singing, some were crying and hanging round the chaps necks and the officers and us NCOs had all we could do to get them apart; they had up to now marched hand-in-hand or arm-in-arm and any other way that others have till suddenly they find they are not allowed to go any further; it was a sudden stop but it had to be done and we soon find ourselves alongside the train; there was no platform and nearly dark but we soon are all on board when the first thing for us to unload ourselves for our equipment is now up to full war strength and that's heavy. The men are put eight in each compartment and quite enough; what with the man, his equipment, his kit-bag and rifle; 6 of us Sergeants had the good fortune of playing the 'old soldier' and had a 1st Class compartment.

Precisely at 2.35am on 29/7/15 we steamed out of Watford to an unknown destination, rumours of course were many and being dark and tired we saw and troubled little as to where we were and not till we reached Rugby at 4.45 did we attempt to take our bearings. We stayed here some little time, some us managed to get a cup of hot coffee and breath of fresh air and a little exercise. Passing through several coal fields, tunnels etc. we arrived at Liverpool at precisely 10am. And here we soon detrained and were marched straight away to Alexandria Dock; and a hot, slow march it was with all our gear. It was a wonderful sight as we turned into the dock and saw the mighty Aquitania *there looking already packed with troops upon her decks waving and beckoning us on; this we soon were for not 3 minutes did we wait but straight away along the gangway in single file we went into the side of the ship, all lit with electric light; a ship's officer at once showing us our bunks and as soon as we had taken off our equipment we had to clear off up on deck and glad we were to get there and rest.*

The rest part of the day and Friday we were interested in watching the loading of guns, wagons and cases of food and about 7,000 tons of coal which in itself is a marvel. About 12.30 to 1.00 we were all on the decks that could get there and see the tugs make fast to tow us out into the mouth of the River Mersey. Before this could be done two dredgers were at work deepening the channel and finally it was a marvel the way the great ropes 2' to 3' thick were handled. Three tugs were made fast and her own self helped as well as she began to move. You may guess this was great excitement and as soon as we were clear of the Harbour and the tugs let go and soon her own engines were throbbing away and we soon got into mid-channel. There we remained till night, a skirmisher or smaller ship kept coming out to us and brought various oddments and some of the crew who had been left on shore. It so happened I was Battn. Orderly Sergt and one duty is to go round with Officer to see all lights out and so being about the decks late we saw her start on her trip.

It was all dark as the windows are all painted black and for the life of us we couldn't see which way we went out of Liverpool; I might say we saw no end of shipping while lying there and we saw the large two funnelled steamer go past us before dark on Friday night which we hear the Germans claim to have sunk thinking it was our vessel. We got up at 5.45am on Saturday morning (They never start in open sea on a Friday being considered by sailors an unlucky day) and we were out of sight of land all around and it was a peculiar sensation, but I felt quite alright. We have a torpedo boat destroyer on each side and one ahead of us to protect us from submarines; it was of course an exciting time whilst we were in the danger zone and it was a very queer time while we were going through the Bay of Biscay. Oh! My word we all felt it, some more and some less, mine didn't last long; the old ship rolled from side to side. I can tell you it was a funny experience to see and feel such a mighty great vessel leaning over so much. One machine gun toppled over into the sea and the cargo toppled about and boxes of potatoes broke, I can tell you it was a fair old spree.

On Saturday 31/7/15, the clock was been put back 40 mins. It was really on Sunday August 1st that the gun went overboard and we had a kind of service on one of the decks and two whales and two sharks were seen. On the Monday Bank Holiday I woke up at 2am as my head banged against the side of the bunk owing to the ship rolling so much and had to keep shifting into bed to keep from rolling on to the floor. We suggest a party of us spend Bank Holiday down at the seaside somewhere. At 2.30pm there is a great shout, the siren blows and we find there is land in sight, it is Tangiers on the coast of Africa we also see the Morocco coast, the wonderful Rock of Gibraltar – to describe these is beyond me. It is truly a marvellous sight to see the mighty rocks reaching up to the clouds it seems and many look like pumice stone. In places the coast was plainly visible to naked eye but of course our glasses helped us to enjoy the scenery much better and with the band playing you may guess it was fine fun to sit on the top deck and look around.

On 23/7/15 we enter the Mediterranean Sea and are soon out of sight of land again, the time is put forward new half an hour in the morning and 10 mins more in the afternoon, it was about mid-day when we lost sight of land. It was very interesting watching other ships, many of them foreigners, who all saluted our Flag which flies on the mast at the stern and some waved and shouted as we to them. It is now getting unbearably hot, sweat runs (not drops) off us, we go about almost naked now, many having no shirts on and the men who do physical exercises do it without them and take a towel to wipe down with. Most of us have very bad arms now from vaccination. The sea is now absolutely like a pond.

Well-known King's Lynn Town football player Private Frank Rogers, 1/5th Norfolks, also wrote home about his experiences on the voyage:

I suppose you already know that we are now sailing to an unknown destination. As far as I can make out it is not to Egypt that we are going, but to the base which is now nearer the seat of operations. I think most of the men have felt more or less the parting from England; indeed, when we left Liverpool that was the last we saw of our country, as we steamed away at night, and by next morning had got away down past Land's End. We were escorted by several destroyers, but after the first day we were going too quick for them, and they turned back. You know we are going on one of the fastest ships, doing about 22 knots per hour on an average, and simply fly through the water more like a train than anything else. The last trip the ship did proved to be very nearly her doom; the destroyers left her as on this trip, and about a quarter

Norfolk Territorials aboard HMT Aquitania.

of an hour afterwards a German submarine attacked her. However, her speed saved her, as the torpedo missed by about 30 yards. Naturally we were on the look-out all day for submarines, but unfortunately did not see any. There's one thing about the matter – we should have been an excellent prize had we been sunk.

There was very little sea-sickness amongst us, perhaps because we had such fine weather. We only had one rough day when we passed the Bay of Biscay; that day, of course, there were plenty of sick, some of them very bad. For my own part I took some special medicine I got at Watford, and but for a beastly headache I was little the worse. We were on the look-out each day for any special sights. Of course it was a great thing to see Gibraltar. We had been travelling some 800 miles or so before we saw any land whatever, and it was the south coast of Spain which broke the monotony. Being my first voyage over the water, I feel rather proud of the way in which I've got over the new experience. There's only one thing amiss, and perhaps is peculiar to a troopship, i.e., the meals. We dine in the saloon, but the noise is something awful and the manners a little worse, if possible. I thought I had got used somewhat to such things but it seems there is still some more to learn.

We are getting in the warm now, and it is the usual thing to get about in shirts, trousers and shoes. I don't think it would hurt to go about naked, especially below decks. It is here that you are warned about stopping, as it is liable to bring on sickness. However, each night I get an eight hours guard down against the meat stores. How we stick it I don't exactly know. A guard is seldom of more than two hours duration and four off, but we (there are two of us) get eight straight off the reel. We can't help going to sleep; the monotony of the job, the time it is done, and the smell is enough to shut anybody's eyes for a week. It's all in a life-time, though. Still, we go on – water, water, water, occasionally we see a ship, maybe a merchant or a hospital ship; only once have we seen a war vessel, that was when we went through the Straits of Gibraltar. We encountered an English patrol boat and an Italian torpedo boat destroyer, but that's the total. The land is visible here and there; the mountains, of course, giving a lovely contrast on the horizon, and we see some lovely sunsets.

Once at sea their destination of Gallipoli was revealed to all ranks of 54th Division and most of the men scratched their heads and wondered where on earth Gallipoli was. For most country lads, world travel was beyond their means and beyond the comprehension of many in the days when some folks were still happy to spend their entire lives in the village where they grew up. A trip to the nearest town or city would require planning and usually a special reason. Notions of the world and its geography learnt at school mostly covered knowledge of the British Empire and at Sunday School the Holy Land from the Bible, the Gallipoli peninsula or Turkey didn't feature in either.

Why Gallipoli?

Germany had sought to foster a relationship with Turkey since the late nineteenth century and Turkey had welcomed a military mission headed by General Otto Liman von Sanders to re-organise the army of the Ottoman Empire in 1913. Even though there was already a German influence in Turkey it was not a forgone conclusion that there would be a guaranteed allegiance on the outbreak of war in 1914, but they decided to ally with the Central Powers, closed the Dardanelles Straits and laid sea mines. With those actions Turkey closed a vital supply route to Russia. Britain and France declared war on Turkey and its Ottoman Empire on 5 November 1914 and Secretary of State for War Lord Kitchener and First Sea Lord Winston Churchill began to formulate offensive operations against Turkey with the aim of forcing them out of the war. Churchill was of the opinion a successful attack on the Gallipoli peninsula by fleet action and naval bombardment alone would give the Allies control of the Dardanelles and enable them to dictate terms at Constantinople. A combined British and French naval bombardment of the Turkish defences along the Dardanelles Straits commenced on 19 February 1915 and culminated on 18 March 1915 when British and French battleships attempted to force a passage through the Dardanelles. Success, if any, was limited, but the reconnaissance had been valuable.

Churchill and Kitchener then formulated a plan for a joint naval and land forces assault on the peninsula. A Mediterranean Expeditionary Force (MEF) of 63,100 British and ANZAC soldiers was assembled over the following weeks to which was added a French division of a further 18,000 men. Kitchener appointed General Sir Ian Hamilton to overall command of the MEF on 12 March 1915.

Hamilton was a brave and audacious officer who had come to Kitchener's notice during the South African War when Kitchener had entrusted the then Colonel Ian Hamilton with the command of a drive against De La Rey's commandos. Hamilton drew on the mobile columns under his command to create four 'super columns' of veteran troops led by reliable, experienced officers. In an attempt to break out of the ever-closing area they were being driven into, the Boers delivered a mounted charge in close order, firing from the saddle against what they believed to be one of the lightly held British positions at Rooiwal on 11 April 1902. Hamilton's troops were not as thin as the Boers expected and with rifle and artillery fire they managed to smash the charge, killed the Boer commander, scattered the commandos and with due diligence Hamilton sent his mounted troops in pursuit of the enemy, during which they took fifty prisoners and recaptured the British artillery that had been lost at an earlier engagement. Kitchener had not forgotten how this victory had helped him to gain the upper hand he needed as he entered the discussions of terms to end the South Africa War and invested the same faith in Hamilton in 1915 to deliver similar in the Dardanelles.

General Sir Ian 'Johnny' Hamilton, Commander of the Mediterranean Expeditionary Force.

Hamilton was keen to get on with the planning immediately after his appointment, but he soon found he had to press Kitchener to get any further guidance out of him or useful intelligence from the War Office. Hamilton would later comment that had he been a German general he would have been supplied with meticulously detailed plans that would have been compiled months or even years before just in case a need for them arose. What he received from the War Office amounted to little more than a tourist guide to the area with a totally inadequate map, a 1912 handbook on the Turkish Army, and one sheet of general instructions from Kitchener. However, Hamilton did have a three-hour meeting with Kitchener on 12 March 1915 to discuss the scope of the operations and, with his team of staff, a plan for the assault upon the Gallipoli peninsula was developed.

On 25 April 1915 a successful landing was made by British, French and ANZAC troops on six beaches along the peninsula. The Australian and New Zealand forces landed at what soon became known as ANZAC Cove and the British and French at Cape Helles. The campaign, however, rapidly stagnated into trench warfare akin to that on the Western Front. General Hamilton requested reinforcements to reinvigorate the offensive; he was given IX Corps which comprised the 10th (Irish) Division, 11th (Northern) Division and 13th (Western) Division of Kitchener's New Army, the 53rd (Welsh) and 54th (East Anglian) divisions and the 2nd Mounted Division.

Hamilton wanted an experienced field commander for his new division and requested either Lieutenant General Sir Julian Byng or Lieutenant General Sir Henry Rawlinson, but Kitchener would not withdraw either them from the Western Front. Indeed, all the most experienced generals were already deployed there and the pool of available senior officers was not extensive, so by process of elimination and primarily because of his seniority on the Army List, Lieutenant General Sir Frederick Stopford was appointed by Kitchener to command IX Corps. Amiable and the possessor of great charm, Stopford had held mostly staff appointments throughout his campaign service when he performed such roles as aide-de-camp to Sir John Adye, Chief of Staff for the Egyptian Expeditionary Force and ADC to Major General Arthur Fremantle, commander of the Suakin Expedition in 1885. He had been military secretary to General Sir Redvers Buller and Secretary to the GOC Natal during the South African war and back in the UK he became Director of Military Training at Aldershot. In the years immediately before the war his health had not been good, he had retired and had been given the predominantly ceremonial position of Lieutenant of the Tower of London. Critically, he had never held a senior command of troops in combat.

Hamilton formulated a bold new plan with ANZAC commander Lieutenant General William Birdwood, an experienced senior officer who had served many years in the Indian Army. Fresh troops would land at Suvla Bay to the north of ANZAC Cove on 6 August. Co-ordinated attacks would then take place whereby ANZAC troops would force their way north while the newly-landed troops at Suvla would push on to take the hills at Kiretch Tepe and Teke Tepe. At the end of the second day it was intended that Suvla would be secured and the British and ANZAC forces would join up in a joint break-out and head for Maidos. The key to the success of the whole operation was the speed with which it needed to be enacted.

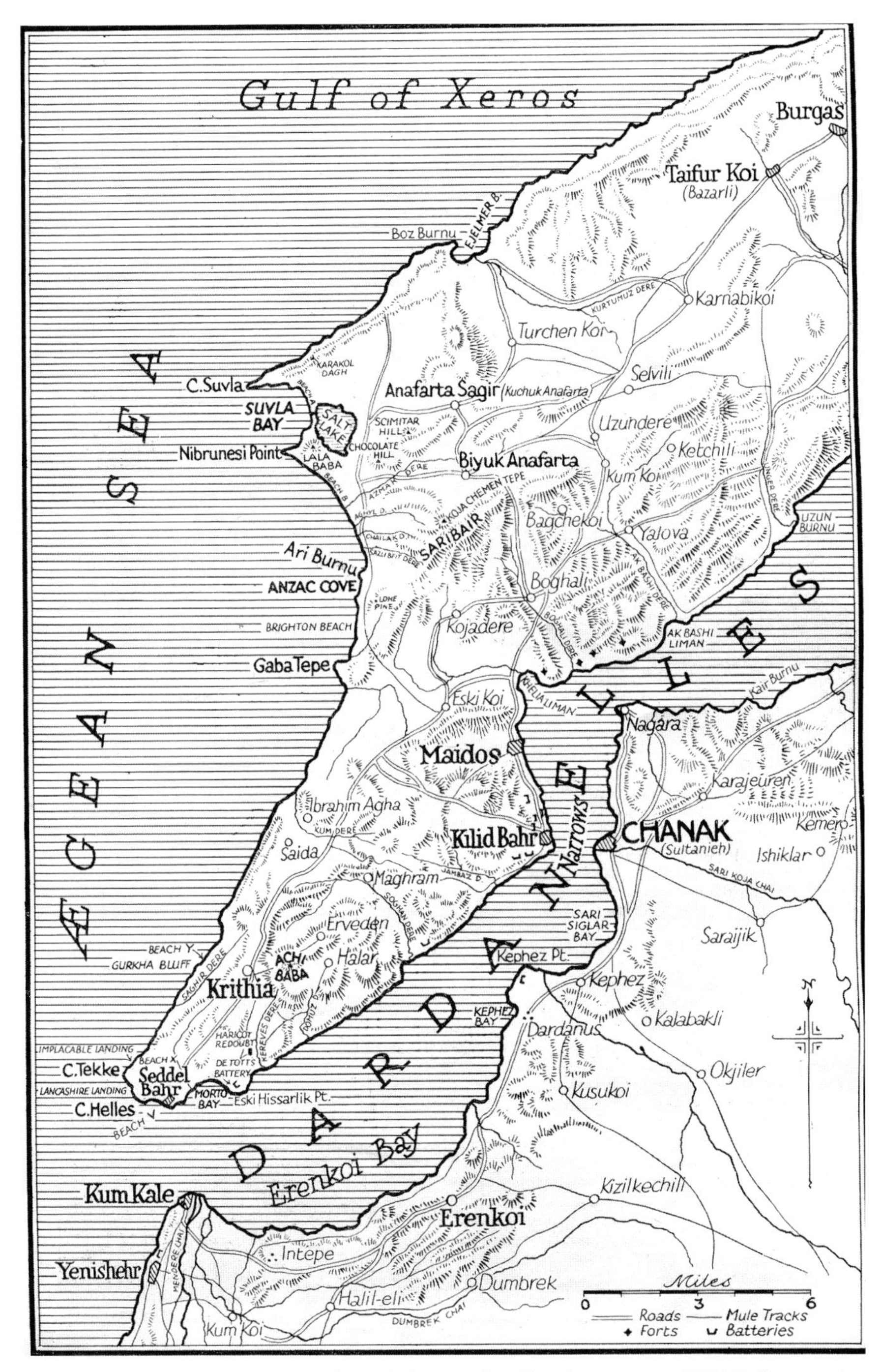

Map showing the Gallipoli Peninsula and the Dardanelles Strait, note ANZAC Cove and Suvla Bay.

Aboard the *Aquitania*

While still at sea all ranks of 54th Division were handed a written address from the GOC dated 3 August 1915 in which he wished to impress upon everyone that now the period of training was over they should not forget what they had learned:

> *...by observing at all times:*
>
> *(a) A resolute determination to press forward the attack and close with the enemy with the bayonet.*
>
> *(b) An equally resolute determination to hold on at all costs in the Defence.*
>
> *These are matters of extreme importance, concerning which it is well to remember that retirements are usually much more costly than advances and that boldness and vigour in the attack are essential to success...*

A second, shorter letter from Serjeant Dye, 1/4th Norfolks on 5 August 1915 related:

> *We are soon to finish our journey now I expect as all our kit-bags are to be packed ready by 6pm. We saw much coastline again, including the island of Sardinia's convict settlement...It has been terribly hot again today; almost baked we are. We had a grand concert on deck tonight after tea, the band played and to hear the thousands of our throats singing was a treat. We expect to land at the island of Lemnos on Friday and I understand there are a lot of Turkish prisoners on there.*

He continues, probably on 8 August:

> *Today we start preparations for landing, our kitbags, we are informed, we may not see again, if ever, from orders read out this morning it looks as if we shan't be long before we are in the fighting line. All seems in high spirits as yet. We don the khaki drill today for the first time.*

Every evening of the journey the brass band of the 1/8th Hants played for two hours concluding with the regimental marches of the battalions on board. Decades later Company Serjeant Major Walter Hipkin DCM would recall that the last tune they played for the men while on the ship was '*There's a Silver Lining*' and said that he would '*always remember it if I live to become a hundred'*.

The *Aquitania* pulled into Mudros harbour in Lemnos Island at 8am on 6 August 1915. The men then remained on board their ship for the next two days, but it gave them time to soak up the view. Captain Fair and Captain Wolton described the scene in their *History of 1/5th Battalion, The Suffolk Regiment*:

> *Mudros Harbour was full of craft of all kinds and there was always something interesting in the medley of shipping. French transports filled with Colonial troops,*

54th EAST ANGLIAN DIVISION.

The arduous period of training being over the General Officer Commanding, in thanking all Units for the care that has been bestowed on the work of ~~prepation~~ preparation desires to impress upon all ranks that full advantage of this work can only be obtained by observing at all times:——

(a). A resolute determination to press forward in the attack and close with the enemy with the bayonet.

(b). An equally resolute determination to hold on at all costs in the Defence.

These are matters of extreme importance, concerning which it is well to remember that retirements are usually much more costly than advances, and that boldness and vigour in the attack are essential to success. Indeed so valuable is the latter consideration, that at times it has compensated for incomplete training.

There are instances in the present war where partially trained troops have achieved marked success by their gallant and energetic bearing in attack.

This Division has now had the advantage of a prolonged period of training. It is imbued with the same spirit of Devotion to Duty which has characterised other units already sent to the front from East Anglia.

These facts render it capable of holding its own, and more than holding its own, with any other Division with which it may become associated. But if the Division is to do so, it is necessary that the considerations enumerated above under headings (a) and (b) be constantly borne in mind, and that all units vie with each other in upholding in the East Anglian Division, the reputation which other Territorial Divisions with earlier opportunities have earned for gallant conduct and efficient work in the field. These are matters which concern more particularly the Regimental Officers.

With the fine spirit which animates all ranks, the General Officer Commanding feels well assured that the action of the troops when called upon to take part in forthcoming operations will be such as to justify to the full the message of confidence which His Majesty the King was pleased to send to the Division on the eve of its departure from England.

E. C. Da COSTA, Lieut-Colonel,
General Staff,
54th (East Anglian) Division.

At Sea.
August 3rd, 1915.

The printed instructions emphasizing the need for 'a resolute determination to press forward in the attack' *distributed to every man of 54th Division on 3 August 1915 while still at sea.*

our own transports arriving or departing, hospital ships and all kinds of war craft made a continuous spectacle of vivid interest.

Yarmouth man Scout Wilfred Ellett of A Company 1/5th Norfolks wrote home of what he saw:

In the distance we can see a Greek town with a Mosque in the midst of it. Small Greek boats come alongside selling chocolate, Turkish delight, cigarettes, nuts etc. They have to be hoisted in tins up the huge side of our ship.

Major Tom Purdy of the 1/5th Norfolks takes up the story in his diary:

At 6pm (9 August) we had orders to parade in marching order at 9pm, picks and shovels to be taken. Now when we embarked at Liverpool, not a single 'Brass Hat' had gone forward to superintend the embarkation and the embarkation officer there was an old man, much-harried, whose idea was to get things on board and his job over as quickly as possible. He had the picks and shovels, tools and signalling apparatus which happened to come off the train first at Liverpool and had them pitched into the bottom of the hold first, and the heavy stuff such as field cookers, machine gun wagons and limbers put on the top.

But now we wanted our equipment and the ship's Captain said it was impossible to get them out without clearing the hold. The Brigade Staff looked grave but were helpless. The Divisional Staff dressed for dinner. Luckily, Major Woodwark, whose signalling apparatus was with the picks and shovels, being a man of business, got hold of one of the ship's officers and talked him round to having a hatchway opened and a special effort made to get the tools and apparatus, and luckily it was successful.

At 9pm we paraded on A Deck. I made my men take their equipment off and go to sleep. At 2.30am we embarked on the SS Osmaih. *About that time, orders came that we were not to move that night, so the other regiments might have gone back to their bunks and had a quiet night, but the Divisional Staff had gone to bed. So, ourselves, the 4th Norfolks and about 150 Hants (1700 or so, in all) were crammed on the SS* Osmaih *with accommodation for about 500. The men had to lie down just where they could, few could wash and latrine accommodation was woefully insufficient.*

Coffee and bread was served out about 6am. D Company, under the efficient guidance of Sergt. Smith, showed their aptitude on service conditions by commandeering 9 out of 20 cans of coffee and about half the bread. The rest of the battalion got the coffee, and the 4th Norfolks, whose Officers were all asleep, were very sick to find, when they arrived, that all the coffee had gone. However, we had more than we wanted, and some more was made, so they did all right.

The Officers breakfasted on the Aquitania *and men and Officers had lunch there. Captain Gay, as Company Mess President somehow managed to get our three boxes of stores on board, a very good move, and about 2.30pm on 9 August we steamed out of Mudros Bay and along the east coast of Lemnos. We soon came in sight of Imbros on our left and Tenedos on the Asiatic coast on our right and we could see the shells bursting on Achi Baba in front of us. But really it was hard to realise that desperate fighting was going on within 4 or 5 miles of us. The sun was going down behind Samothrace which rose sheer out of the sea behind Imbros, a vast cone-shaped mass of purple, all soft and shadowy in the evening light, while the level rays of the sun fell eastwards clear and bright on the round hill of Tenedos and the red coast of Asia behind. To the North the guns thundered, but the puffs of smoke on the hills looked so fat and lazy as they slowly floated up into the sky, it seemed impossible that they should be to those beneath them the black pall of driven shattering death.*

We passed through the minefield and anchored in Imbros harbour, crowded with liners, tramps, monitors, submarines, cruisers and battleships of every description… As the darkness grew, the hospital ships with their line of green lights from bow to stern and the bright Red Cross amidships made the whole picture like a place of fairyland, or to compare great things with small, a scene on a modern stage. In the evening D Company Officer's Mess opened a stores box and made an excellent dinner of sardines and tongue, cake and marmalade and a small loaf of Greek bread (this latter item obtained from the Greek Steward of the Osmaih *at the exorbitant sum of one shilling). From the same source a whisky and soda was also to be had in exchange for 1s 3d.*

After a good night we all got up about 6 and I had a bath and a shave in comfort and then breakfast. No more bread was to be had, and as we did not like to be the only ones to have a good meal, we gave one of our boxes of food to the rest of the officers.

British troops aboard one of the transports from Mudros Harbour to the landing beaches along Suvla Bay on the Gallipoli Peninsula.

> *About 2pm we steamed out of the harbour in the direction of Suvla Bay. We all carried on us two day's supplies of nasty little oval biscuits and bully beef and two emergency rations. As we came near land we could see several other transports close in to shore and three or four cruisers and a monitor at the south end of the bay firing inland.*

The thunder of the naval guns prompted Sandringham soldier Private John Dye to remark to Captain Beck, *'I don't think we are going to be made very welcome here, Sir,'* to which his captain laughingly replied: *'I don't think we are...'*

Major Purdy continues:

> *We came to anchor at 4pm half a mile from the shore and for some time watched shells bursting inland. Anafarta was being treated to 14 inch projectiles and large columns of smoke and debris rose up from time to time among its houses. In due course a lighter came alongside and A and D Companies and part of C got on board and we were quickly taken to the landing stage and at 5.30pm* [10 August] *I set foot on Turkey. One of the Divisional Staff told us to get on quickly, follow the others, and we should find the Brigade Major and get orders, but we must look out for land mines as two or three had been found and caused some casualties, so we moved along the edge of the shore over ground whose vegetation very much reminded me of Blakeney Point, and after two or three halts found the Brigade Major who directed us to bivouacs. Each man was issued with two pints of water which they were told had to last for three days and it was suggested that they keep a small pebble in their mouths to stimulate saliva.*

Troops of IX Corps, including 54th Division, on the beach after landing at Suvla Bay, Gallipoli, August 1915.

We piled arms, took equipment off and were trying to find out about water and make some preparation for food, when our Brigade Staff Captain Bridgewater came up and said he wanted two senior officers to make a reconnaissance with him. The Staff had told him there was not a Turk within miles so we need not bother about equipment or revolvers. So off we went, Captain Tony Knight and myself from the Norfolks, Captains Oliver and Fisher from the Suffolks (three of us Old Haileyburians). Our job was to find the right of the 10th Division who were pushing along the ridge of hills running North East along the coast.

The party came across some Dublin Fusiliers entrenching across the base of the Northern Horn of Suvla Bay who showed them a track which they said would take them to the Lancashires. Through the ragged old Turkish lines, passing the fetid bodies of dead Turkish soldiers, they found a company of Lancashire Fusiliers lying along the bed of a dry watercourse which they had roughly entrenched. A subaltern informed the reconnaissance party the firing line was about quarter of a mile in front of their position. He also warned them of snipers who lay in trees. The party told the sub they were going to bring their men up to prolong their line on the right to the Salt Lake. Then borrowing a serjeant to guide them back, they returned under cover of darkness.

Major Purdy recorded:

At 8.45 I got back to the company, warned them to be ready, piled the packs, detailed Ralph Wade and another as baggage guard and bolted some biscuits and cheese not having fed since lunch. At 9pm sharp we stood to. After a long wait the Suffolks moved off, and we followed with the Hants beside us in column of route. It was the slowest and most wearisome march imaginable. We halted every 10 minutes and eventually got to our position soon after 1am on the 11th. We lay down in two ranks with bayonets fixed and a couple of listening posts about 50 yards in front of each company. Where we lay the air was fragrant with a delicious spicy smell of some balsamy plant which grew in profusion, but every now and then a gust of wind brought the loathly sickly smell of some unburied body near our front.

On the 11th at about 5am we ate some bully beef and a biscuit or two, and soon afterwards got orders to advance in line of platoons in double file. The going was rough over rocky ground with dried up watercourses running from the high ground on our left to the Salt Lake. We (D Company) halted under a low ridge of scrub-covered rock and walked forward with Fox my observer to see what was happening and found the two leading Companies on the right were going to dig in from the ridge towards the Salt Lake. I then walked back, not paying any attention to the ships' guns booming from the bay or the Turkish guns replying. I had just got through a fence when a whine overhead coming from the foothills East of Chocolate Hill, to my great surprise exploded over my head and spattered the tree I was under with shrapnel. I hustled the company across the field and got them into a deep ditch under a fence running parallel with our position as the Turks opened up. We stayed there about an hour with shrapnel coming over every few minutes. A and B Companies suffered about 5 minor casualties. One shell burst over Captains Knight and Birkbeck and knocked them down without hurting them but Birkbeck had his glasses smashed.

Then C Company relieved A and B as we moved to the right and relieved the 10th London who were in a ditch to the right rear. D Company then relieved C Company and luckily by that time the shelling had almost stopped and we did not have any losses. We were much bothered by a dead horse in the field to windward and 'Black' Beck [Captain Frank Beck] *got a party together and burnt it – it was a rather nice looking bay, and I suppose had been killed by a ship's shell.*

During the morning QMS Smith and the fatigue party we left behind on the Osmaih *came up. Smith says they are issuing rum at the Base and brought some – good water would have been more welcome. About 1pm we knocked off under Colonel's orders as it was getting very hot. Got some water from a hole in a field, which the doctor said was good, and ate some lunch – bully and biscuit. The water hole was about 8ft deep and about 2ft of brown water collected in 3 hours. The only other well was one nearer the beach, about one and a half miles off but the water there was excellent and worth sending for. We then lay down under the ridge getting what shelter we could from the sun and rested.*

About 3pm some rather heavy rifle and machine gun fire was going on in the valley in front of us and we stood to for a bit. For the rest of the afternoon we were undisturbed except by snipers' bullets which came singing over our ridge and 'phitting' into the ground behind us. In the afternoon the ships banged away at Hill 971 on our right and on the foothills beyond Chocolate Hill towards Anafarta Kuchuk. We could see a column of Turks with transport on a ridge east of Chocolate Hill who seemed to be getting it pretty hot, a good many shells too were raising huge columns of dust in Anafarta.

In the course of the day I saw 2 hares and two or three small hawks – hobbies I should think – and Sgt John Goulder told me he heard some partridges. I also saw a dead snake about 3 feet long in a ditch. About 6pm we had some food again, and soon afterwards put out a listening post, and about 8pm I lay down on a bed of dried sage bushes and had a good night's rest.

Lieutenant Colonel Harvey of the 1/4th Norfolks recorded a description of the country as seen from the sea:

On the left Sulva Point with Nebruniessi Point to the right, form a small bay known as Suvla Bay some mile and a half across...Inside and immediately in front was a large flat sandy plain covered with scrub, while the dry salt lake showed dazzlingly white in the hot morning sun. Immediately beyond was Chocolate Hill and behind this again lay the village of Anafarta some four miles from the shore. As a background, the Anafarta ridge ran from the village practically parallel with the sea where it gradually sloped down to the coast. Beyond the plain a number of stunted oaks, gradually becoming more dense further inland, formed excellent cover to the enemy's snipers.

The men of the 1/4th Norfolks remained on the beach to unload stores after the landing on 10 August, moving up to support trenches of the brigade shortly before 12 August. It was thought an attack was impending, but no clear orders had arrived. Due to a disparity of numbers within the different companies they were reorganised to try and balance the numbers of men in each. This was not a popular decision; many of the men had grown up together, enlisted together, trained together and had grown to know and rely on each other. Now at the moment when they thought they would need each other most some of them were being separated.

Lieutenant Colonel Harvey recorded his understanding of the situation in retrospect:

> *On 12 August 1915 Sir Ian Hamilton decided to make another attempt to take the Anafarta Ridge and directed the 54th Division to make a night march that night and attack at dawn on 13 August the twin heights of Kavak Tepe and Tekke Tepe, the chief summits of the Anafarta Hills. General Stopford, the Corps General, agreed but considered it necessary to clear first the cultivated area of Kuchuk Anafarta Ova, in order that the night march might be unobstructed...orders were also given to clear the Turkish snipers out of the valley in the immediate front then join up with the 53rd Division.*

Chapter 6

Anafarta and The Gallipoli Campaign

'Good-morning; good morning!' the General said
When we met him last week on the way to the line.
Now the soldiers he smiled at are most of them dead,
And we're cursing his staff for incompetent swine

Siegfried Sassoon

Just two days after landing in the sweltering heat of the Gallipoli peninsula the men of the 1/5th Norfolks were to be plunged into front-line action on 12 August along with the rest of 163 Brigade, with the 1/4th Norfolks in reserve. On that day the losses were heavy and the battalion fought on bravely deep into the enemy lines. Out of this action arose one of the most persistent myths of the First World War. The supposed 'disappearance' of the 1/5th Norfolks, including the Sandringham Company, at Anafarta Ova during the advance on Kavak Tepe-Tekke, Gallipoli peninsula, has been the subject of books and numerous articles in magazines and periodicals, both academic and, frankly, sensationalist.

The truth of what happened is not hard to find. The cost in life was heavy but neither the Sandringhams nor any part of the battalion were entirely wiped out, nor did they disappear never to be heard of again. A number of survivors wrote home shortly afterwards and their letters were published in local newspapers and parish magazines; others wrote diaries or later memoirs and, by careful compilation of these accounts of the action in the words of those who were there, a clearer picture can be established.

Major Thomas Woods Purdy, C Company Commander, 1/5th Battalion.

One of the most detailed accounts was written by long-serving Territorial Force officer Major Tom Purdy of Aylsham, a well-respected company commander who did much to collate a true account of the action. He drew upon his personal experiences and the recollections of other survivors he encountered and managed to contact over the days, weeks and months directly after the battle. How the day of Thursday, 12 August 1915 began is recorded in Major Purdy's diary:

> *Reveille about 5.00am. Night not so cold as last. Got an empty jam jar and Fox* [Purdy's batman] *boiled some water in it in which we dissolved an Oxo tablet, soaked biscuits in the result and had an excellent breakfast. Early on the 12th Colonel da Costa and some of the Divisional Staff came round and said he wanted us to get in touch with the 53rd Division on our right front and reconnoitre the path that led through our front. Sent out two reconnoitring patrols under* [Lieutenant] *Burroughes to find out the left of the 53rd Division and 3 men to push up the path as far as they could go. Fox brings word that the Stretcher Bearers have some condemned water they are washing in. Make tracks for them at once, and find an old biscuit tin holding about 2 pints of water in which some 20 men have washed. Have a very welcome shave and wash.*
>
> *The water in our hole being temporarily interdicted by the MO, arrange to send a party to the well near shore about 1½ mile back. As this well is under continuous shrapnel fire, only one man at a time can approach it, so we send 8 men per company under an NCO with all the company water bottles that want refilling and they have to halt about 200 yards from the well and send out one man at a time with bottles – a long job.*

It transpired later that, fatefully, a number of men from the battalion had gone into action with little or no water in their bottles and were incapacitated by dehydration.

> *The patrols come back – Burroughes reports the left of the 53rd were about 800 yards in front of us, half right. The patrol along the path got about 1200 yards on the other front and were fired at by 8 or 10 Turks. They said the path opens out and becomes a fair sized track running in the direction of two Lombardy poplars one can see about a mile in front. Reported to de Costa accordingly. Later on sent out another patrol under* [Serjeant] *John Goulder to the 53rd. They report being fired at on their return, and finding one of the Cheshires dead, whom they want to bury, so sent out a burying party and six men as escort. They managed to get the man buried but were under fire most of the time. From their report it was evident there were a good many Turks in front. Sent a report to Battalion Headquarters.*
>
> *Have lunch at 1pm of hot Oxo and biscuit. Sent another party to the well near the beach for water.*
>
> *At 2pm Acting Sgt.-Major Wells came up and told us that we had to be ready to move* [at] *4pm. About 3.15, having heard nothing more, I strolled back to Battalion Headquarters and found the C.O. and Adjutant giving orders to the other company officers. He said the Brigade was to move at 4pm and clear snipers out of the valley to our front, join up with the 53rd Division on our right, and the 10th on our left, and dig ourselves in for the night, and that we should probably attack the Turkish position early next morning; that we were to move in attack formation A Company on the right, D next, B on the left, C in reserve* [the overall attack consisted of] *5th Suffolk,*

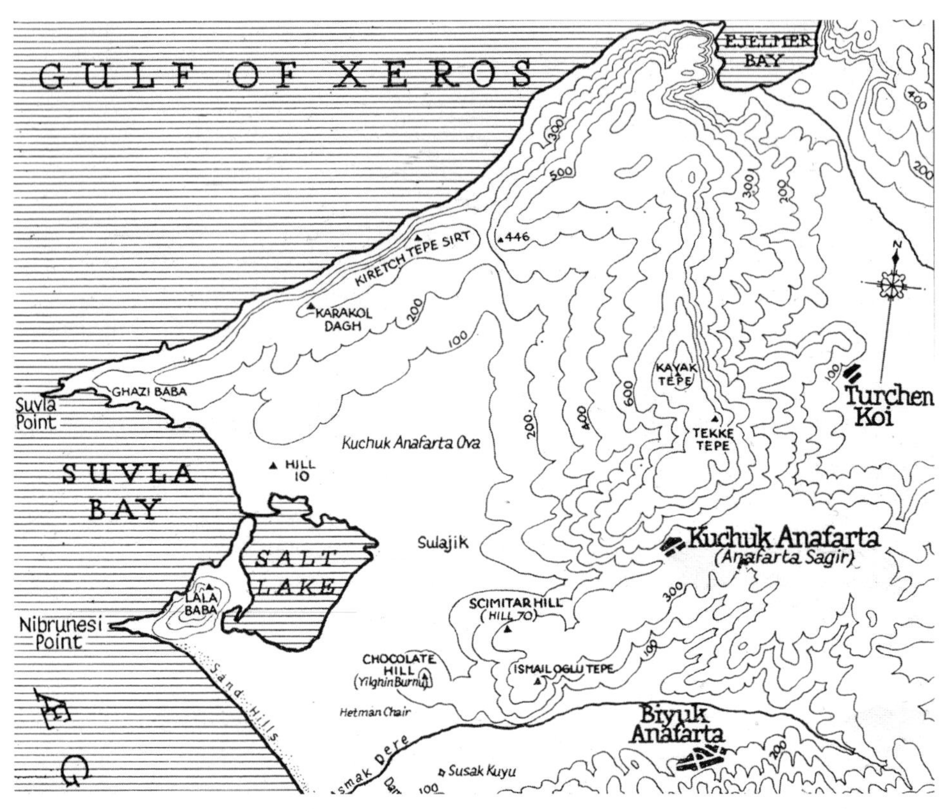

Map showing Suvla Bay and the area of the attack of 163 Brigade across Kuchuk Anafarta Ova.

> *8th Hants, and 5th Norfolk in front, with 4th Norfolk in support. We were on the right of the line, the Hants next* [to] *us and the Suffolks on the left. The left was to direct. Talked things over with other Company Officers, and we decided, the country being very close, to advance with 3 platoons of each company in snake formation, the leading section of each of these 3 platoons extended to 5 paces, and to be about 100 yards in front of the rest of the Platoon, the 4th Platoon to follow in support.*

Apparently, no indication was given at the time of where brigade headquarters, dressing stations, reserve ammunition were situated. Objections were also raised by some officers about attacking in daylight over unfamiliar ground with little cover, but these concerns appear to have been ignored. The officers, except the colonel, dressed as soldiers and carried rifles in the hope they would make less of a target for the Turkish snipers. As Purdy was returning to his company the adjutant, Captain Ward, called him back and told him to take a pile of maps:

> *...as much, rather more than one man could carry – and distribute them among the Officers and NCOs. I said I could not possibly do so in time to move off by 4pm, but*

he said I must, and that they had only just received them from the Division. There were about 8 different maps of different parts of the peninsula, about 12 copies of each, 2 or 3 inch I should think, and they were mixed up anyhow. I eventually got them distributed amongst the Officers and NCOs, served out picks and shovels to all the company except the leading sections of the first 3 platoons, detailed Sgt. Goulder to take command of the first line [of] *the extended section, Coxon the 2nd line, the 3 platoons in snake and the Sgt Major Wells and I joined No.4 Platoon in support and moved into position. Thanks to the maps, we were 15 minutes late, the other Company Commanders with more wisdom having chucked their maps into a gorse bush.*

Second Lieutenant William George Stewart Fawkes, aged 32, was, like Major Purdy, a solicitor on civvy street but had only volunteered and obtained his commission in April 1915. On the day, Fawkes was a subaltern in B Company, he recorded:

On the 12th August 1915 the 163rd Brigade lay entrenched some 2 or 2½ miles south of the northern extremity of Suvla Bay with their left resting on the ridge of hills which descend to the sea at Suvla Point. At 3.15 on that afternoon Col. Sir Horace Beauchamp rode up to the battalion and called the officers together. He said 'We move at 4 o'clock, set about it.' And he added 'I am sorry my orders are so vague but I give them to you as I received them from the Brigadier.'

A statement confirmed in the 1/8th Hants War Diary, the brigade advance was to be directed:

...immediately towards the hills marked on the map under the names of Kavak, Tepe and Tekke Tepe. The advance was to be pushed at all costs, but it was not expected that there would be any opposition, but snipers would cause a certain amount of trouble. When asked what the objective was to be, the CO said that Brigade were unable to tell him. He was also uncertain as to whether there were to be any troops on the flanks of the Brigade. The CO also said that he had protested strongly to the Brigadier [Brunker] *at the vagueness of the orders, but without success...None of the Officers knew the nature of the operation nor the position of the enemy trenches. There was however a general impression that the object of the move was to be a 'sniper drive' for the country was infested with snipers and they had been annoying us continually for 2 days.*

Shortly after Beauchamp's address, Captain Ward gave Second Lieutenant Fawkes maps for his B Company. The B Company officers also found there were too many to examine or compare with the country around and consequently, as Fawkes remarked, they '*found themselves obliged to select those most likely to be useful and leave the rest behind*'.

As 54th Division did not have its field artillery support at Gallipoli, the guns of the Royal Navy vessels lying off the coast opened up a preparatory bombardment at 4pm. There was also an 18pdr battery and mountain guns, but the latter two had no

Turkish officers taking observations from the high ground overlooking Anafarta, 1915.

definite targets and they were not even sure of the position of the British front line. In their *History of 1/5th Battalion, The Suffolk Regiment* Captain Fair and Captain Wolton make the point that *'the naval guns supported the attack with High Explosive. This sounded comforting even if it was unable to do much harm. High Explosive is useful for pounding trenches and other known positions, but its effect is very local, and for open warfare with an enemy in unknown positions it is of little use.'* Indeed some were to comment that all the bombardment served to do was draw attention to the fact an attack was coming.

There has been confusion over the years in other articles and histories about the times for the attack; to be clear the bombardment by naval guns started at 4pm and the attack commenced at 4.45pm. Lieutenant Colonel H.M. Lawrence DSO OBE who was the adjutant of the 1/5th Suffolks at the time of the attack on 12 August wrote up his comments for the manuscript that had been sent to him for the *Official History of the War, Military Operations, Gallipoli* in which he stated:

> *It was not until after 4.00pm that 1/5th Suffolks knew anything of even a contemplated advance and then only because the Brigade Major 163rd Bde. arrived at Battn. H.Q. and wanted to know Why the!! What the!! etc. etc. hadn't the Battn moved off? This was easily explained to him, as nothing was known of a move anywhere. It was then ascertained the orders had been sent to one of the other Battns on a memo form to be noted etc and passed on and return by last named. The 1/5th Suffolks was the unfortunate Battn to be the last named and had never received the orders. The Battn*

A Turkish artillery battery in Gallipoli, 1915.

staff were trying to get some rations up from the beach, in lieu of a large consignment of boxes containing maps and some rum. The latter did help but the former were very little use as they were found when opened to be for the Helles front. The only information obtained was that the advance was purely a sniper's drive and would be about 1,400 yards. No objective could be pointed out and so the advance began...

The brigade began their advance at 4.45pm. Serjeant Walter Tuddenham, 1/5th Norfolks, of Hilgay recalled: '*The boys lined ready for the attack just as they would on a field day.*' The brigade advanced in the direction of Anafarta village. Colonel Proctor-Beauchamp and Captain Randall Cubitt led the attack. Both men were smoking and the colonel carried his mackintosh over his arm, he waved his cane above his head as a number of survivors recalled in their letters home '*...as if on a British parade ground*' and spurred his men on with cries of *'On, Norfolks! On!'* Private John Dye noted Captain Beck was *'walking with his stick, just the same as he did at Sandringham, putting it down at the same time as he did his left foot'*.

Serjeant Tuddenham continued: '*We got about a quarter of a mile and the shells and shrapnel burst all over us. We kept going for about a quarter of a mile when we came under rifle fire. The hills were alive with rifles and machine guns, it was a perfect hell,*' but the 1/5th Norfolks pushed on, the officers and men showing daring and coolness under increasingly intense fire. Private Cliff Harrison recalled Lance Corporal Tubby shouted *'Come on Yarmouth'* and other the NCOs were heard urging the men on with shouts of *'Come on the Lynns, Good old Downham'* and *'Onward Sandringhams'*.

A recent photograph of Anafarta Ova viewed from near the 163 Brigade start line for the attack of 12 August 1915.

Captain Edward Randall Cubitt led the advance of the 1/5th Norfolks across Anafarta Ova with Colonel Horace Proctor-Beauchamp on 12 August 1915, neither of them survived the action.

As the battalion moved forward they received orders to move half right. For some reason none of the other attacking battalions received this order and as the brigade advanced, a dangerous gap developed between the Norfolks and the rest of the attacking line. Major Purdy, seeing the danger, halted his company (D Company), as did Captain Knight (A Company), to allow the companies on the left of the line to come round and catch up. Captain Beck (C Company) had begun in support but continued their advance through Purdy's supporting platoon. Purdy continues:

> *Then Brigadier Brunker came up and asked why I had halted. I told him. He ordered me to fix bayonets and extend the whole company. Till then we had been in artillery formation, with the leading section in each platoon extended. I did so, and of course a couple of guns from our*

right, somewhere east of Chocolate Hill, opened on us with shrapnel. Soon after that, the platoons in front moved, and word was passed to double. All the time we were being enfiladed with shrapnel from the right. They had our range beautifully and the fire was very accurate, but I think they must have been firing at extreme range, as there were not many casualties. My observer (Fox) was hit next me, but the ball never penetrated. We went on in 50 yard rushes through a lot of small fields, 3 or 4 acres each, with high fences and deep ditches round them and numbers of low, thick oaks with wide spreading, thick leafy branches.

After going about a mile like this we came under rifle fire, we then got to a farm and went through it. There were only a few men visible in front, and one could not see more than 100 yards in any direction. The fire began to get very hot and we were all very much done. By this time I had not more than 20 of my original platoon with me, but picked up some of C Company and I think some of B. We shoved on but did our rushes at a slow quick time instead of at the double. We had not a double left in us.

After we had gone about half a mile past the farm, we came to a deep ditch running between two fields, about 400 yards from the foot of the hills in front, and about 600 yards from the hills on our left. A heavy fire was enfilading us from the left and there was also heavy fire from the front and bullets came singing along from behind us as well. No-one was coming up in support, but under a fence about 150 yards off on our left front there were more men firing hard. I judged it best to halt in the ditch and get our wind before reinforcing, as the fire was too heavy for any more walking. Just as I was getting the men ready for the rush, the Adjutant [Captain Ward] *came along from the right and said we were wanted in front at once to rush the enemy's trenches with the bayonet. So we got out of the ditch together and started off as fast as we could, but before I had got 5 yards I was knocked over* [wounded].

Captain Cedric Coxon took command; leading the men on, he vaulted a stone wall followed by the bugler, Drummer Donald Swann. Captain Coxon was then wounded, shot in the throat narrowly missing the carotid artery. Coxon was a fit man, an accomplished pre-war athlete who had some medical training. Applying pressure to the pressure point near the wound to avoid bleeding to death, he attempted to make his way back to our lines but, weakened through loss of blood, as the Turks closed in, he was taken prisoner. He later made a full recovery from his wound. Subsequently Swann was also wounded and they became two of only fourteen men of 1/5th Norfolks taken prisoner during the Gallipoli campaign.

Private John Bridges, of King's Lynn was also in the attack:

I was in B Company ...our officers were Capt. Pattrick, Capt. Woodwark (he was with the Signallers), Lieut. Cubitt, 2nd Lieut Fawkes and 2nd Lieut. Beauchamp. We began the advance at 4 o'clock in the afternoon of August 12 with fixed bayonets, going in platoons and then after about a quarter of a mile, in sectional rushes in long lines. I was right in the middle. We went for two miles – it may be more, for it is difficult to judge in a country like that and with such conditions – with heavy firing going on. There was the firing from our own ships behind us, right over our heads, with firing

Captain Arthur Deveraux Pattrick, A Company Commander. Last seen being taken prisoner on 12 August 1915. Nothing further was heard of him.

Second Lieutenant Montagu Proctor-Beauchamp, nephew of Colonel Proctor-Beauchamp, said he joined 1/5th Norfolk to 'keep an eye on his uncle.' Killed in action, 12 August 1915.

> *from guns in front of us, with snipers in the trees and with rifle fire from the enemy here and there. It was simply hell. For a long time I saw no officers except Second Lieut. Fawkes. I lay alongside him several times in the course of the advance. The enemy had a big gun on Anafarta Hill and were firing at us with shrapnel, and there were trenches deep down near the forest and village – so deep down that I could not see them. They must have been entrenched up to their necks.*

Second Lieutenant Fawkes continues his own account of the day:

> *As the advance continued progress became more and more difficult owing to the nature of the ground. The country was very broken and dotted with stunted oak trees which grew at first sparsely but more and more thickly as the advance proceeded. The ground between the trees was in many places covered with thorn scrub which clung to the men's legs and many were hit trying to make their way through it. There was also here and there a patch of ground which showed indications of having been roughly enclosed and cultivated. Platoon commanders and section leaders found it increasingly difficult to keep in touch with those on their left and right of the line as the advance became more and more broken. Moreover, the Turks set fire to the scrub and in this way some sections were held up altogether.*

As the men of the 1/5th Norfolks pushed on they moved further away from any form of support the rest of the brigade might have been able to give. The battalion, now well in advance of the rest of the brigade, had left its rear totally exposed and the Turks began to surround them trying to cut off their line of retreat. Fawkes continues:

During the whole advance men fell rapidly under the steady fire maintained by the enemy. After proceeding about 1400 yards I came up with Lieut Trevor Oliphant who with a party of about 10 men was taking cover in a kind of sunken road 100 or 150 yards in front of the Turkish trenches which lay at the foot of the hills. I myself had about 15 men of my platoon with me. There were no other troops visible either on our right or left and I therefore told Oliphant that I thought we ought to remain where we were for support. He agreed and was then hit in the arm and asked me to take over his men as he could not go on. At that moment I looked round and saw Colonel Beauchamp alone about 200 yards in the rear. He shouted and waved us to go on. I told Oliphant that that settled the matter and called on the men to follow me. Stretching from the road where we lay up to the Turkish trenches was a clear field of fire, but in order to get into it from the road it was necessary to pass through a gap about 10 feet wide. Unfortunately, the gap was covered by a machine gun and as the party bunched in order to get through, they were practically all brought down. Four or five including myself got into our stride but we were picked off one by one as we approached the enemy trench. I believe that I myself was the only one to actually reach the trench. Just as I reached it I was hit twice, once below the right breast the bullet passing out at the side and again behind the right hip. I fell against the parapet of the trench.

Fawkes lay by that parapet in a concussed state for about ten hours, coming round dazed, he made some movement which attracted the attention of the Turks within who took him prisoner and took him to a dressing station and eventually captivity for the rest of the war.

Major Purdy had been floored by his wound:

I lay there some minutes with bullets zipping all round and then, on trying to get up, got another knock on the other side. My left arm was good for nothing, so I crawled back to the ditch where I found a skulker who put my field dressing on and tried to retain my watch.

There was very heavy rifle and machine gun fire all this time especially on our right front, and a good few bullets were hustling

Serjeant Tom Robinson, 1/5th Battalion (Cromer) killed in action, 12 August 1915 age 24.

Private Geoffrey Griston, 1/5th Battalion (North Walsham) killed in action, 12 August 1915 age 18.

Private Cecil Bullimore, 1/5th Battalion (Westwick) killed in action, 12 August 1915 age 21.

> *about. The Turks seemed to be counter attacking from the hills on the left, but no reinforcements came up and what few men there had been on our original left, began to retire.*

Purdy limped back:

> *When I got to the next fence I heard my name called out, and in the ditch I found some 8 or 10 men, some of No.4 Platoon (the second line) among them, and poor Derby the platoon Commander, looking ghastly and in great pain with a bullet through his stomach, and next him, Corporal Green of B Company, with a bullet through the lower part of his throat. He said he was in no pain but had no sensation in his body at all. He too, looked very bad. I gave them both some brandy...I went along the fence towards our original left and there I found Lawrence, the Adjutant of the Suffolks with about a platoon of men. He made me lie down, took my equipment off, took my flask and said he would look after my glasses and revolver, and with an entrenching tool handle as a splint, bound my arm up. Marsh of the Hants came up apparently off his head. It seems he had set fire to some crops on the right and our men had to retire as a result. Then* [Captain] *Tony Knight came up and asked for reinforcements. He said Birkbeck was holding out in front on the right but was very hard pressed. Lawrence could not spare any men and said he thought he would have to retire as soon as it was dark. They decided that Knight should go back to Brigade Headquarters and tell them how things were, and ask for reinforcements, so he took off his equipment and went back.*

Then some officer came up behind me. I heard him tell Lawrence that he was 4th Norfolk, that he had 20 men with him, that he had left the rest of the company who were lining the fence behind us. It was now getting dusk and Lawrence said he would soon retire and that I had better get back to the field dressing station, so with the help of Lockwood, who had been slightly hit in the head, I walked back.

After a long walk and dressing of his wounds Major Purdy was evacuated on a stretcher to the hospital ship *Salta*.

The Brigade attack had been observed by a number of officers and men from commanding viewpoints with the supporting gun batteries of the division and in the surrounding area. It was clear heavy enemy machine gun and artillery fire had slowed the advance of both the 1/8th Hants and 1/5th Suffolks, but the Norfolks had found themselves less strongly opposed and pressed on. However, as they probed further the casualties mounted; the physical heat of battle and lack of water took its toll on the men, dehydrated and exhausted many could not fight on.

Lance Corporal Herbert Beales, 1/5th Norfolks, of Leziate, was just taking cover in one of the many ditches when he saw Captain Trevor Oliphant get hit and fall. Beales climbed out of his ditch and in full view of the enemy and under heavy fire ran and crawled the 200 yards to reach Oliphant and dragged him to cover. On his way back he heard a cry for help and found a soldier of the 1/8th Hants lying wounded in a gorse bush. Beales ran to the rear of his own position, collected some stretcher bearers and had the man taken to safety, he then returned to his own position and rallied his men ready for an expected Turkish counter-attack.

Despite the desperate casualties Colonel Proctor-Beauchamp, with 250 officers and men, continued to advance through the scrubby terrain towards Turkish positions. Private Bridges continues:

...the Turkish trenches were a kind of horse-shoe shape. The village and forest buildings, including a farm and wood some of whose trees had been burned away – occupied the centre of the horse-shoe. It was when we were getting up there that I saw some of the officers, Col. Beauchamp, Captains Pattrick and Woodwark and Capt. and Adjutant Ward. The Colonel was leading his men on, and I heard him shout: 'Come on, boys, give 'em the point.' I didn't get as far as these. I was a little distance away from the village and in the smoke I saw the four officers, with men, just in the place of which I was practically on the outskirts. The last words I heard the colonel say were: 'Now, boys, we've got the village. Let's hold it.'

As they cleared the cottages Beauchamp was heard saying '*Hound them out, boys!*'

Private Bridges continues:

Directly afterwards we got the order to retreat. Those who did get out and managed to retreat were lucky. Poor chaps lay about wounded all over the ground. Some had been hit by shrapnel and some had got caught by bullets. The first man I saw laid out

Corporal Arnold Groom, 1/5th Battalion, (Fakenham) Killed in action 12 August 1915 age 30.

Corporal Robert John Crowe, 1/5th Battalion (Sandringham) wounded in action 12 August 1915.

Sandringham Company Serjeant George Needs. Killed in action, 12 August 1915 age 28.

was Sergt. Jakeman, of the Sandringham Company. I was one of those who wasn't wounded. With some more I got into a gulley that runs between one field and another, and we had to hold that position till night.

[Serjeant William Jakeman was evacuated wounded and made a recovery but was left in great pain. Two years later he had to have another operation to remove a piece of shrapnel from his thigh.]

The problem was that the scrub was on fire, whether as a result of shelling, a result of the terrible mistake of Marsh of the 1/8th Hants, or a deliberate tactic of the Turks to cut the battalion off is impossible to prove. What is certain is that many of the men who followed Colonel Proctor-Beauchamp this far were not seen alive again.

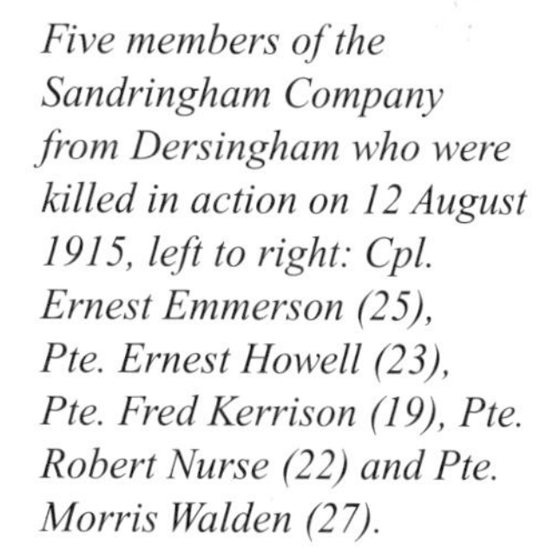

Five members of the Sandringham Company from Dersingham who were killed in action on 12 August 1915, left to right: Cpl. Ernest Emmerson (25), Pte. Ernest Howell (23), Pte. Fred Kerrison (19), Pte. Robert Nurse (22) and Pte. Morris Walden (27).

Serjeant Theo Randall of Cromer was one of those who made it to the forward area and lived to tell his story:

> *I rushed my platoon on as fast as possible to get out of the area that was being shelled but we kept losing men fast. Once I lay panting for breath in a ditch with about eight men, a shell got us properly and five of the party were wounded. I felt the bullets hitting the ground all round me but none touched. We got up again and off, just out of the artillery zone, thank goodness, and we lay down for a breather behind a fence. As we lay there, small parties kept coming up and I got those near me into something like a line and off we went once more, over very deeply ploughed land now, and horrible going.*

Serjeant Theo Randall 1/5th Battalion (Cromer) was one of the few survivors of the furthest forward advance across Anafarta Ova on 12 August 1915.

Very few of the fellows could do more than stagger along and here the enemy opened fire with rifles and machine guns. The noise was frightful and it seemed a miracle how anyone could get along at all without being hit. Luckily, there was plenty of cover till I had about a dozen men with me and then made a rush as far as I could run or until I came to another ditch or hedge. Still, onward we went and now we came to the remains of a village built of stones, which was held pretty strongly. Into it we went and here I fired my first shot and saw the first of the enemy. They scurried away as soon as we got anywhere near them, though they laid out many a good man as we advanced...

As the men of the 1/5th Norfolks pushed on, they had moved further and further away from any form of support the rest of the brigade might have been able to give. The battalion, now well in advance of the rest of the brigade, had left its rear exposed and the Turks began to surround them trying to cut off their line of retreat.

Private Gordon Browne, 1/5th Norfolks gave an interview recounting his experiences to the *Yarmouth Mercury* when he was back home recovering from his gunshot wound:

We advanced 300 yards at a time, and the bullets began singing overhead. Sniping had been going on for some time, and I was one of a party of ten who had to take the water bottles and fill them at a well. The snipers were at us, but we got out all right, though another party was not so fortunate. We went forward in open order till we reached a gully, when we made a rush across to our first line of trenches occupied by other troops who were glad enough to see us. We passed beyond the trench into a field and lined a fence on the other side of it. Several fellows were hit here, and firing was continuous.

From this fence we charged several blockhouses under shrapnel fire, and then came to a half-finished trench which the Turks had just evacuated. That was the first we saw of them. Snipers continued to pot at us from trees which we had left behind us. We occupied this trench, but came under an enfilading gun fire, and lost a lot of men there. At nightfall the order was given to retire, but this order was not passed down on the left, and about 50 of us remained there. After wandering about we fell in with some Cheshires and Norfolks mixed up, and we caught ten snipers that night. They were painted green and cleverly hidden, and some had a fortnight's supply of food and water. They used a forked stick in which to rest their rifles when aiming.

Great Yarmouth soldier, Private Maystone, 1/4th Norfolks, one of a number of Priory School old boys out with Norfolk Territorial Battalions adds:

We continued to advance in the daylight with the 5th Norfolks, but we were cut up cruel. Shrapnel continually burst over us and bullets were thick to the right and front of our positions, but our battleships kept up the shelling of the Turk's positions and pieces of soil flew in all directions, some as big as a tramcar. It was a tough job while it lasted and one we won't forget. There is one thing about the work that none of us like, that is the methods adopted by the Turkish snipers. They get up trees and fire down upon us. You cannot see them, for they are painted green like their rifles which are even disguised with branches, twigs and leaves bound around them. We have even found Turkish girls at this work who have pocketsful of the discs which we wear around our necks but which they rifle the dead and wounded of after an engagement or this horrible sniping.

No wonder when the bodies of the fallen of 1/5th Norfolks were eventually discovered years later in 1919 only two had identity discs to enable identification.

Private Gordon Browne 1/5th Norfolks continues:

Early next morning we came across our own men again, and then we resumed the advance till we came across the first line of Turkish trenches. After a fairly stiff engagement with the bayonet, we got them out of it. They shouted 'Allah' when we bayoneted them. The first man I met when I jumped in was a huge fellow who was big enough to eat me, but he slipped, and I got him through the stomach. He carried my rifle over with him, and I had to put my foot on him to pull it out, and he screamed 'Allah'. They ran out of the trench, and we bayoneted more in the back than we did face to face because they did not stay long.

We then continued our advance towards Anafarta, which seemed little more than a farmstead and outbuildings. My water bottle had been shot through, and I had lost all my water. Just as we were going into the village I was shot by a sniper in the thigh. I managed to crawl back about a mile when I was picked up by the stretcher-bearers and carried the remaining four miles to the beach. We were under shell fire all the time. Every time a shell was heard coming, the stretcher-bearers went down and I fell off the stretcher and had to struggle back. This happened a dozen times. It was not very funny then, but I can laugh when I think of it now. The charge of our fellows went on towards some fortified houses. A party of eight men rushed into a house but did not come out. I heard afterwards we were partly surrounded and had to fall back.

Drummer Frederick Wells, aged 17, was another one of those who pushed furthest forward. He wrote home in a letter: *'I think myself lucky as there were 41 of us surrounded and only five of us came out again. I was one of the lucky five, but I had five bullets enter my haversack, which was on my back.'*

Serjeant Theo Randall continues:

At last we could stick it no longer, no reinforcements reached us and the enemy were in force about 20 yards in front of us. So back we had to crawl about 200 yards until we came to some of our fellows holding a long lane. Here we stuck for about half an hour under fairly decent cover and then we got news that a party of our fellows were holding a line 100 yards in front, so we collected about 50 men and rushed forward to give them a hand. We found one of our Lieutenants [Evelyn Beck] *holding a short line of hedge and trying to get in touch with other small parties on either side of him. We were uncertain as to whether we had any of our own men in front of us and as it was now dark, we were in a somewhat peculiar position. After a short consultation the officers decided to retire to our line 100 yards in the rear. This we managed all right and held on there for five days till we were relieved.*

The remainder of the battalion was also stopped by Lieutenant Evelyn Beck who had seen the danger as Turks began to encircle the colonel and his men. The brigade gradually fell back to a natural line in front of some wells. After dark a weak counter-attack was repulsed by machine guns which had finally been brought into action after problems moving and deploying them in the earlier advance. However, digging in and sandbagging were difficult due to the loss of shovels and picks during the action and the lack of sandbags with the men. All through 13 August the brigade held the line without any food or reinforcements, but did find some water in the nearby wells. Some of the lads pinned down in the trenches a little further forward were not so lucky, the journey to collect the water could still be perilous and not always richly rewarded as Private Fred Frostick of D Company, 1/5th Norfolks recalled:

I had a little water in my bottle which I poured into my mess tin, put my tea ration in the water to brew in the sun, a change from plain water. I heard of a water well not far from us in a vine-yard, taking my mess tin and my puttee to lower the tin into the water. Not much water there, it was mud and water. A sniper spotted me, I heard bullets passing near my head, I quickly left for cover, went back to where I had left my rifle and kit. I put my dirty handkerchief over the part of the mess tin to suck the water from the mud.

The 1/8th Hants War Diary recorded:

At about 5 o'clock on the morning of the 14th the Essex Brigade appeared advancing from the rear and upon sighting the 163 Brigade immediately opened fire with machine guns. A young signaller of the Norfolks saved the situation by standing up and signalling to the Essex, who immediately ceased fire.

Captain Evelyn Beck, 1/5th Battalion. Awarded the Military Cross for his bravery and initiative that saved many lives during the attack on Anafarta Ova.

Private Harry Palmer, 1/4th Norfolks, had advanced in support and was one of the stranded soldiers in the trench with Fred Frostick. Both men recalled the actions of the brave signaller who almost certainly saved their lives, Harry tells the story:

I was one of a party of about 20 cut off that night and mistaking us for Turks, a party of Essex fired into our rear, causing slight casualties. The bugler sounded ceasefire but it was ignored because it was said the Turks might copy our bugle calls. Signaller Copeman then stood up and signalled 'Cease fire we are Norfolks'. The Essex moved off and we were eventually joined by another party with our Brigade padre Rev. Pierrepont Edwards, complete with monocle.

Evelyn Beck wrote home on 25 August 1915 with his account of his experiences of the battle:

We were suddenly told we had to make an advance that afternoon (12 August) at 4 o'clock; this we did and came under a very heavy shell fire as soon as we left our position. Anyway, we kept on with the attack, and very sorry to say it was not a success, the Battalion was very badly cut up indeed, I think there were more Turks than we supposed. We had to advance across a piece of country very much like what our farm looked like... The fields had very high rough hedges and deep ditches round them. This caused our men to get into small parties, and the Turks, knowing the country, cut us up awfully. Out of the whole battalion we have left 384 men and 4 Officers, Major Barton, Birkbeck and one Cubitt and myself. As to where all the others are gone, no one knows, but I cannot believe all, and I think they must have been taken prisoners. The last I saw of Alec and Uncle Frank, they were just one field behind me and at least Alec was going strong, Uncle Frank was more on my right.

Now all I can tell you is about myself, we went on until the Turkish fire and machine guns held us up when we opened fire upon them until dark. I found myself with about 40 men of the Norfolks and four other regiments. At about 9 o'clock the Turks worked round on my left flank and killed some more, then the beggars set the corn and grass on fire in the fields in front and drove us out. I then took up another position further back, then they worked round on my left and enfiladed me, so had to leave that and retire again until I came into the line the remnant of our Brigade had taken up arrived there at 3 o'clock Friday morning...We held on to that line until relieved Sunday night by the Essex who took our place.

Lieutenant Murray Buxton in his diary concurs with Beck and adds '*...the only officers left with the battalion after the action of 12 August were Major Barton in command; Lieutenants Birkbeck, Beck, Cubitt; 2nd Lieutenants Buxton and James and Lieut and Quartermaster Ford*'.

The gallantry awards for the action of 12 August 1915 were announced in the *London Gazette* early in 1916. Alec and Evelyn Beck were both recognised for their gallantry with Military Crosses, Alec's award of course was a posthumous one. Lance Corporal Herbert Beales, 1/5th Norfolks, and Private Tommy Copeman, 1/4th Norfolks, received Distinguished Conduct Medals for their conspicuous acts of gallantry. The Reverend Pierrepont Edwards, chaplain to the 1/5th Suffolks, who had also led a volunteer stretcher party into the forward area and recovered a number of injured men, was also awarded the Military Cross. They were all rightly and highly praised by their comrades and in their local newspapers for their deeds and there were many others whose brave and selfless deeds sadly went unrecognised. However, one man judged by many survivors to deserve the highest award for his deeds on the

The modest hero Private Herbert Saul, 1/5th Battalion.

day never received a gallantry medal. A cutting from the *Yarmouth Mercury* dated 16 October 1915 tells his story:

The Heroic Devotion of Herbert Saul
Rescuing Wounded Under Fire

Not many weeks before the outbreak of war there was a mock parliamentary debate at the YMCA rooms in Great Yarmouth on the ever-burning subject of National Service. The stoutest and most skilful debater against it and militarism generally was Herbert Saul. His were ways of peace and his gentleness of character led him to think everything of helping other young fellows and nothing of noisy jingoism. There were those who thought slightingly of such a man – would name him unpatriotic, even a coward. But when war came he volunteered for military service learning the soldier's task with grit and spirit. He remained just the same, quiet, peaceable, deliberate 'Old Saul', liked by all, giving a helping hand here and there as was always his wont. For some slight defect he was almost rejected from the Imperial Service battalion, but he qualified as a stretcher bearer and there are many today who give thanks that he was with them...

It was during their awful ordeal that Herbert Saul proved himself a man. One of the non-commissioned officers who owes his life to him has said 'If Old Saul lives to come back to England shake him by the hand, for you will shake the hand of a real man. All the men simply idolise him for what he did during that trying time. I was hit by a piece of shell in the side and fell. Saul came up, dragged me behind a rock and looked at my wound and dressed it calmly. 'Not enough blood for you, eh Saul?' I said. Then he helped me down to safety.

Saul efficiently dressed shocking wounds with calmness and steadiness of nerve and an utter disregard of danger and fatigue. The doctor himself was wounded but Saul took charge with quiet capacity and as the men state, he seemed to be everywhere with his medicine chest binding up wounds and cheering the men. He worked ceaselessly in the firing line getting the casualties away and minimising the difficulties which necessarily arose because no dressing stations or base hospital had yet been organised.

They say too that he bore a charmed life. The men yelled to him often to come back – begged and prayed him not to go – when he went out into the bullet swept country to fetch in some poor chap who laid there helpless. 'It's all right,' he would say in that deep slow voice of his, 'they can't hit me – they haven't done so yet.' While there was a man to be reached, the heaviest fire did not stop him. He was unmoved by his great danger and happily always untouched. In this way he brought some of the poor boys into safety and the others felt all the better for having such a brave spirit with them.

His heroic devotion and presence of mind during a most trying and unnerving period received almost instant recognition, for amid the pleased shouts of his comrades he was promoted a sergeant on the field, a tribute to his ability and qualities of leadership as well to his courage. Those with him vehemently declare that he deserves the V.C. and we shall all rejoice with the first fifths if he should be recommended to the King for some distinction. All reports agree he has richly earned it.

Other 1/5th Norfolks soldiers praised Saul for his coolness in the height of battle. Private Gordon Browne was attended by Saul when he was wounded and recalled when he expressed concerns over the fighting Saul simply replied 'in his quiet, staid way *"It's pretty hot. It's looking a bit black."*'

Herbert Lepard Saul was born in Great Yarmouth in 1879, the third son of the late Mr Thomas John Saul JP, employed as a partner in the firm Thos. Saul and Son Ltd, timber merchants. Up until the outbreak of war he lived with his family at Waveney House, Euston Road, Great Yarmouth. Herbert was a teacher in the Park Baptist Church Sunday School and a keen supporter of Lichfield Football Club. Many of the soldiers in the 1/5th Norfolks were in their twenties, Herbert was in his mid-thirties, hence the nickname 'Old Saul'.

He was returned to England suffering from shell-shock in 1915. Judged recovered the following year, he took a commission as second lieutenant in the 7th Suffolks and in November 1916 was sent to serve in France. Returning briefly to get married in June 1917, he was back at the front by July. Herbert was killed in action less than a month before the end of the war on 24 October 1918. He lies buried in Vendegies Cross Roads British Cemetery, Bermerain, France.

Aftermath

Private Bob Overman, a pre-war member of the Sandringham Company, 1/5th Norfolks, wrote home to his parents Walter and Rachel Overman who lived in the Sandringham Royal Estate village of Flitcham to reassure them he was OK:

No doubt you hear a lot of rumours but it is no use meeting trouble half way as we have had it a bit rough out here, but it is fairly quiet again and I don't think the Turks will hold out much longer. They seem to think it will soon be over here anyway and we shall not be sorry if it is. We are living fairly well out here now, about as well as you can expect anyway, but if you choose to send a parcel out be sure to do it up safe and sew some sack round the tin or else it will all get lost and don't send anything that would go bad at all. A piece of chocolate and cake I should think would keep and it might be a bit dry but that would not matter as it would be a treat you may depend...You will see by the paper, we have suffered heavily with officers and we have got very few left but they all proved themselves men, every inch of them and there was nothing that they could not do for the men they would not do if they could.

In another letter Private Overman wrote of how he had been told his home village had reacted:

Lacky told me there was a bit of a do in Flitcham when the news came through how we had been cut up. He said people had been going to the Post Office every minute of the day. That was the very thing me and Percy Hammond and Teddy said when we was sitting in a trench a day or two after. We have talked more of home since we have been out here and likewise learned to respect our homes more than ever we had done before...

Meanwhile, on HM Hospital Ship *Salta* Major Purdy found fellow 1/5th Norfolks officer Trevor Oliphant in the next-door cot. Oliphant had been struck in the right arm with a bullet which had severed an artery and had been pulled to safety in a hail of fire by Lance Corporal Herbert Beales. Purdy also found Second Lieutenant Rollo Pelly who had suffered a sniper's bullet which had smashed his jaw, ribboned his tongue and knocked out most of his teeth, leaving a gaping wound on the right side of his face. There was also Captain Culme-Seymour who had commanded the battalion machine guns and a number of men from D Company of the 1/5th namely: Privates Colman, B. Bullock, Strong, E.J. Keeler and S.G. Bircham from 1 Platoon; Lance Corporal Pawley and Privates Busby, Spurling, Allison, W.H. Tooke and Smalley from 2 Platoon and Privates Dawson, Francis, Marjoram, Medlock and Megitt from 3 and 4 Platoons.

Talking to the survivors on the ship and while he was in hospital in Malta over the ensuing weeks, Purdy became increasingly horrified by the emerging casualty figures for his battalion and incensed by the apparent incompetence of the senior commanders of the action. Returned to Britain for hospital treatment, Major Purdy was disembarked at Devonport on Friday, 27 August 1915 and was removed to the Royal Free Hospital in London.

His diary continues:

On the Saturday learnt from Col. Woodwark the awful news about the battalion and for the next few days did nothing else but answer enquiries from relatives and friends of missing Officers...Since coming home, I have seen Knight who tells me that when the battalion were getting into position on the afternoon of the 12 August he kept A Company halted so as to give the rest of us a chance to get round, but the Colonel cursed him and made him move; that his leading platoons went off so quickly he could not keep in touch with them.

When he got to the trenches held by the 53rd Division he halted his reserve platoon considering that he had gone as far as he had been ordered to, but the 53rd said he was drawing shrapnel on them and begged him to go forward. He did go a little way, and then sent out a patrol to find out where the platoons in front were. He got hold of [Lieutenant] *Birkbeck's platoon and withdrew it. He then found* [Serjeant] *John Goulder who told him that the rest of the battalion was considerably to the left, so he* [Knight] *left a section to watch his right flank and withdrew the rest of the two platoons and then advanced half left till he came to some farm buildings where he bayoneted 5 or 6 Turks.*

He could not advance beyond this as there was a very heavy rifle and machine gun fire on them from the Turks 50 yards ahead, so he halted under a wall. Just the other side of the wall was a patch of nettles in which lay [Major] *John Barton, who after a bit came back over the wall to him. While he and Barton and Goulder were sitting there discussing what was to be done, Goulder was shot in the head by a sniper up a tree. Knight took up a rifle and shot the sniper. After this, the Turks began to work round his left, so he withdrew to a fence further back. Barton took command of about 20 of the men and Knight with the rest worked towards the left along the fence the left of which was held by Lawrence* [Adjutant of the 1/5th Suffolk Regiment] *as before related.*

After he left Lawrence he ran back about 2 miles till he found Brigade Headquarters and Swan who said he would send two Companies of the 4th Norfolks to reinforce. Knight then went back to tell Lawrence and on the way was shot in the foot by a sniper. He sent word on to Lawrence by a Stretcher-Bearer and got another Stretcher bearer to help him back to a field dressing station.

A wounded man told Knight that the reason our men went so fast was the Colonel kept urging them on in spite of Ward who tried to get him to wait for reinforcements.

Tragically, Captain Knight's personal efforts to call for reinforcements, were viewed by some as an act of cowardice. Back at Sandringham, Sir Dighton Probyn never spoke to Knight again.

As the weeks passed Major Purdy heard from more of his men, a letter headed 'Gallipoli, October 30th 1915' from Company Serjeant Major William Edwards is typical of the correspondence:

Dear Sir

Received your letter today of 3rd inst, thanks for kind wishes. The CQMS and myself have not stopped any Turkish metal yet though we have been extremely lucky. We often speak of you and wish you were with us again though we are now a sorry remnant of the old company. There are only 52 of us left and I believe a five mile march would knock us out. We heard you were wounded a few days after the battle. Most of the news of the fight we get from home, it is surprising how little we know of what is going on around us.

Rudd was killed by shrapnel on Aug. 13th. Cousins was not missing as he only left the Battalion last week with a wound in his wrist. Several of the wounded have rejoined, though Miller, Bullock, Eggett, Bowers and Busby of D Company, am sorry can hear little of the missing. Sgt Nurse and Kidle are still with the Company. Plant and Simmons are Acting Sergeants. Have not seen the 5th Suffolks since the first week landed but will speak to Major Lawrence about your glasses and flask when I see him. Lieut Balme of the Essex Regiment is in command of the Company now.

I went so far to the right on the day of the battle and missed you and got into a hot corner near that village but was rescued by the Cheshires at dusk. Had to go into hospital next day for 24 hours with sunstroke, rejoined about 140 of the Battalion who were in the firing line and as I was senior had to take charge of them until they sent an officer of the 4th Norfolks to help me. After five days the remainder of the Battalion joined us with the officers who were left. We have been in the trenches since. Sickness has been the trouble since. Hope to see you again when things are better...

Major Purdy continues in his compilation of accounts:

I have also seen [Lieutenant] *Trevor Oliphant who said he was in command of the two rear platoons of C Company, the Reserve Company. That when the line moved he wanted to wait till the three companies forming the front line should get about 200 yards, but Kennedy of the Divisional Staff ordered him to move off with the front Companies saying there were not any Turks within two miles. The result was that C Company got mixed up with the leading Companies and so we had no reserve at all...*

Significantly, Major Purdy begins his conclusion:

I have also seen General Inglefield's report to the King (which he annotates with his own comments). Inglefield there states that our orders were:

(1) To take the village of Anafarta Saga. No such orders ever reached us.

(2) That the left of the line met with more resistance and came under heavier fire than we did on the right, and we pushed on and lost touch with the others. This is a lie. If anything, the resistance to the front of the right was more than on the left.

(3) That our men were soft, and out of condition and so a large number could not keep up and the others went on unsupported. No doubt some did fall out, but how could anyone expect otherwise after a mile and a half double in very hot sun over broken and enclosed country?

The question is, were we expected, by ourselves, to take the village of Anafarta Ova a mile or so in front of the 53rd while the 53rd on our right and the 10th on our left stayed in trenches? A 53rd officer told me that they had no orders to advance and were told that we were coming up to relieve them. The 10th had no orders to advance either.

If we were meant to do a proper attack, why were we not told:-

(1) Our Objective

(2) The position of Brigade Headquarters

(3) The position of the Field Dressing Station

(4) The position of Reserve Ammunition

(5) The position the Machine Guns had to take up

and why were orders not given to the troops on either flank to advance with us?

Why too, were we ordered to fix bayonets and double a mile and a half before we got to the Turkish position? Our bayonets disclosed our advance at once to the enemy's gunners on the right and they were not slow to take advantage of it.

A double of 1½ miles ensured that we should be too exhausted to move with any dash when we did get at the enemy's position. Why was not the Reserve Battalion brought into action earlier; and why were the two other Brigades of the Division left kicking their heels at the base?

Under the orders we got, Knight was perfectly right in halting when he got to the 53rd, and our front line should have been halted on that alignment.

Major Purdy sums up his final feelings of why the action had the outcome it did in his closing paragraph:

I believe Brunker was sent home next day, but it seems to me that the Divisional Staff were the people mainly responsible for the whole ghastly muddle, and they only exhibited in the real thing the same criminal incompetency that has characterised their methods during our 12 months of training.

After Anafarta

The attack by 163 Brigade had been crushed, all three of the forward battalions had suffered terrible casualties and those who remained had to find their feet again. Lieutenant Colonel Harvey of the 1/4th Norfolks commented on the terrain and warfare confronting the troops:

The peninsula was a mass of diversified heights, difficult to traverse in time of peace and formidable obstacles in war when courageously held. Except in a few valleys there was little cultivation, though cypress or occasional olive groves, broke the monotony near one or other of the small and infrequent hamlets. Roads were even fewer and the scanty inhabitants of the peninsula preferred to make their journeys from place to place by boat. Water was scarce and none at all was found at most of the points selected for the land attacks. The disheartening nature of the Gallipoli operations, in the form in which they were undertaken, was that each successive height surmounted seemed only to reveal further ridges beyond.

Private Bill Ely, 1/5th Norfolks survived the action of 12 August and remained in the forward lines with the remnants of the battalion until they were relieved, he recorded in his diary:

Next to the nerve racking bullets and shells thirst was the worst torture we had to withstand. Food was nearly as scarce, iron rations the only food we were relying on for an indefinite period. Haven't had a wash for last four days. Most of us look like tramps. Living on biscuits, Oxo cubes and water.

On the evening of 15 August the 1/5th Norfolks were relieved and returned to base camp to rest and to begin to take stock of their losses. The three officers and 147 NCOs and men that had been left aboard the *Aquitania* at Lemnos joined the 1/5th Norfolks. One can but wonder what they thought upon arrival and saw the decimation suffered by their battalion. On 16 August the draft of two officers and 156 men left the *Aquitania* and arrived aboard the *Minnetonka*. On the afternoon of 18 August they were moved to a position near Hill 28 where they rested until nightfall, taking cover from troublesome snipers, and moved again to the north side of the hill under cover of darkness the following night.

On 20 August the battalion dug in; it was also Private Bill Ely's eighteenth birthday – he had lied about his age to join up. He recorded the day in his diary:

> *Up at 5.00am cold as a rat. Feeling very weak, having had very little grub and water. Had some cold tea out of the water bottle and some biscuits for breakfast. Laid about all morning, sleeping at intervals. Managed to eat bully and biscuits about midday, also a little water, which is more precious here than gold dust. Had a dip in the sea, which was grand, while the enemy had a few pot shots at us, but they were a little too far off to reach us.*

On 28 August they were relieved and the 1/4th and 1/5th Norfolks removed to the north side of Kapanji Sirt, marching five miles in single file across Salt Lake to the Lalababa rest camp by the coast. There was still no company transport, everything had to be carried and the soft and yielding ground they had to cross in full marching order made it heavy going. Once there, however, the men were able to stop and have a proper rest, bathe in the sea and have a change of clothes. It was also the first chance they had to re-organise the battalion.

On 29 August the men took part in a communion service led by the Rev Pierrepont Edwards. Lalababa was remembered as probably the best place the battalions had to stay while on the peninsula but it was still a dangerous place to be at times. While there, enemy aircraft dropped two bombs, one of which fell close to divisional headquarters, the other brought down a big shard of the cliff. The only casualties were the mules of the 1/5th Suffolks. The rest camp was also occasionally troubled by shell fire and three men were injured early on the morning of 30 August while drawing rations.

The 1/4th and 1/5th Norfolks were sent to ANZAC in early September 1915 and attached to 9 Corps, which consisted of Australian and New Zealand troops. The 1/5th Norfolks were attached to 162 Brigade which consisted of the 10th and 11th Londons, 4th Northamptons and 5th Bedfords. Arriving on 3 September, they were inspected the following day by the GOC, General Ian Hamilton. They held a line of trenches stretching along the brow of a ridge which rose above Aghyll Dere (or valley). The 5th Norfolks manned the trenches on Gloucester Hill where Regimental Serjeant Major Ford was wounded while the 1/5th Norfolks were occupying the firing line. On 9 September the trenches and dug-outs were inspected by Lieutenant General William Birdwood, the ANZAC Corps Commander.

The 1/5th Norfolks alternated its time in the front line here with the 1/10th London Regiment, each spell in the trenches consisting of about a week. After a week in the line the regiment went into rest on the other side of the ridge, only 200 yards from the trenches, and there they were employed in fatigues, carrying parties, digging trenches and improving the extant defences. It was possible here to take bathing parties down the Aghyll Dere to the beach, which was about two and a half miles away.

The Turkish trenches opposite the 1/5th Norfolks were on the high slopes of the ridge connecting Khoja Chemen Tepe and Chunuk Bair, both of which were about 1,000ft high. The Turks were able to get as much timber as they needed from the thickly-wooded eastern slopes of the peninsula, and with this they constructed several lines of barbed wire entanglements and were able to provide head cover to their trenches, and wood for strutting and dug-outs.

On the western side the ridge was covered with scrub about 3ft or 4ft high and there were a considerable number of olive trees in the valleys about 20ft or 30ft high. Australian troops were on our right, their line stretching from the southern branch of the Aghyll Dere to ANZAC.

Lieutenant Colonel Harvey, 1/4th Norfolks, recorded the conditions the Norfolk battalions were living in:

The stench was awful owing to the number of unburied dead lying in between our trenches and the Turks. The order was to occupy the fire trenches for 6 successive days and then six days in reserve, but as the reserve bivouac was only about 200 yards behind the fire trenches there were usually as many casualties from stray bullets as in the firing line. The fire trenches occupied by 4th and 5th Battalions were as little as 15 to 30 yards from the Turkish trenches and it was certain death to show a head over the parapet in daylight. There was continual musketry fire and bombing all day and night.

The greater part of the trenches were built over corpses and there were many legs and arms protruding along the parapet line...Up to now the Turks made no concerted effort to drive us out and after the failure of the previous British attacks, day succeeded day with desultory artillery duel morning and evening, the afternoons presumably spent by the Turks in a siesta. Little was accomplished by the artillery fire, beyond the annoyance caused by shells falling amongst the stores and dug-outs at the bases. It was astonishing to see high explosive shells bursting in what appeared to be crowded areas and to learn afterwards from the men there that comparatively few casualties had resulted. Certainly, at times a shell would cause considerable damage, especially if it fell on rock or hard ground; one of these killed and wounded upwards of 100 mules and another, which I saw, killed 9 men and wounded 7, but these are exceptions.

The efforts of the Norfolk Branch of the British Red Cross Society, regimental and other comforts associations, were particularly appreciated as they sent out large consignments of cigarettes, tobacco, chocolate, fly nets and other luxuries. Perhaps the most timely of all was a consignment of 2,000-3,000 sandbags, made by various ladies in Norfolk, which arrived early in September at a time when sandbags in the front line were very scarce. This consignment was put to excellent use and added not a little to the safety in the trenches and the comfort of the men in the dug-outs. Private Bill Ely recorded how they made the most of their rations in his diary entry for 7 September 1915:

> *Had a little flour issued so we set to make something nice. We ground some meal biscuits to powder by putting some into a ration bag and laying it on a rock, then hitting it with an entrenching tool handle. We mixed this with the flour and water and made it into a paste, rolled it out on a tin lid, spread apricot jam over it, rolled it up in a cloth and dropped into a dixey of boiling water. Had a jam roll for dinner as a result. It was heavy but very tasty. The boys made short work of it.*

The month of September saw nights get much colder and flies began to abound and became a constant curse. It was impossible to prepare any food without it becoming covered with a horde of filthy black flies and at all times of the day they were continually tormenting the troops and spreading disease. Dysentery began to take its toll among the battalions to the degree that by 19 September 1915, fifty-four men were recorded as sick in the 1/5th Norfolks war diary and the fighting strength of the 1/4th Norfolks was reduced to 11 officers and 287 other ranks.

On 22 September Lieutenant Colonel Harold John Kinsman (author of the military training manual *Tactical Notes* (1914)) of the 4th Inniskilling Fusiliers was taken on the strength of the 1/5th Norfolks to take command. Kinsman began to bring the battalion back to fighting order as best he could. He conducted daily inspections of the fire trenches and dug-outs accompanied by Major John Barton and bombing courses under Captain Evelyn Beck but it was very much an uphill struggle with so many men becoming sick.

October saw heavy rains, all ranks regularly got wet through, dug-outs became flooded and there was no means of drying out their clothes. Six badly needed fresh officers arrived from the 2/5th Norfolks on 7 October and some of those who had been wounded returned to the battalion, but as the month progressed men continued to succumb to sickness,

Grave of Aylsham soldier Private Ralph Wade 1/5th Battalion who died of enteric fever on 13 October 1915 after being evacuated to Alexandria Hospital in Egypt.

especially dysentery and were evacuated to hospitals in Egypt. In the days before modern drugs had been developed to treat it, if the sufferer was not removed from the environment that caused it and given sufficient and suitable fluids to rehydrate, dysentery could often prove fatal. Private Bob Overman, 1/5th Norfolks, was sent to the Citadel Hospital in Cairo suffering from dysentery, he described his treatment in a letter home to his parents:

> *I have been in here a month and two days and I was put on ordinary diet as they call it. It was eggs for breakfast and meat and pudding for dinner and then I went onto milk diet after 2 days of it ordinary and then I was kept on milk for 22 days and now I am on no diet as they call it, that is to say I get 6 eggs and 2½ pints of barley water and 4oz of chocolate. How long I will be on that I don't know.*

A number of them were also shipped home to England. Among them was George Robert Carr of 5 Bowling Green Walk, Great Yarmouth, who was revealed to be the youngest soldier in the battalion – he was just 14 years old. George had left school in September 1914 and went to work at Wenn's Ltd and was among a number of lads from the firm who volunteered to join the 2/5th Norfolks during their recruitment drive in the town in March 1915. He was then just two months past his fourteenth birthday but being a big-framed, tall lad he had no difficulty passing for 19. Naturally, his parents found out; his mother wanted his father to stop him, but the boy pleaded with him to let him go and his father was very much of the opinion 'if he is so set on going, let him go'. George had survived the action of 12 August but it was the dysentery outbreak that caught him and he was sent to hospital in England – and all before his fifteenth birthday.

George made a good recovery during his convalescence in Eastbourne and spent the latter part of the war in the Grenadier Guards. He was not alone as an under-age soldier in the battalion, because the Territorials had a minimum age of 17 for enlistment, whereas the New Armies were 19, it was inevitable that the Territorials contained quite a number of under-aged lads, especially in Norfolk where the country life produced many a tall, strapping young man who looked older than his years. Among them were Private Roland Reed of Northwold who was killed in the action of 12 August 1915 and Private George Harnwell who fought in the action,

Private George Harnwell 1/5th Battalion (Downham) wounded, 12 August 1915 taken prisoner of war, died 21 August age 16.

was wounded, taken prisoner and died a few days later. Both these lads were just 16 years old.

Meanwhile, back on the Gallipoli peninsula on 11 October 1915 the Norfolk Yeomanry, now working as infantry and retitled the 12th (Norfolk Yeomanry) Battalion, The Norfolk Regiment, had come over from England and were posted to assist the 1/4th Norfolks in the same trenches and receive some instruction in trench warfare while the Loyal Suffolk Hussars did the same with the 1/5th Norfolks.

The rations also improved and instead of bully beef and biscuits, beef, bread, cheese and all kinds of jam and marmalade were frequently sent up. On 16 October a demonstration attack was ordered along the line, consisting of firing one round, fixing bayonets and then cheering. The aim was to see if the Turks would show some indication of their military strength. The Turks were not taken in, only one machine gun opposite the 1/4th Norfolks returned fire.

In the closing nights of October patrols were conducted by the 1/5th Norfolks from the firing line on Gloucester Hill. On 28 October patrols encountered Turks on Sandy Knoll and a further patrol went out in front of Franklin's Post and located a Turkish listening post. The following night a patrol went out under Captain Edward Balme, who was attached to the 5th Norfolks from the 3rd Essex. The Turks had been in the habit of posting a listening post at night on a steep spur which led down from their line, but which could only be approached from our lines by climbing up, one at a time, a precipitous ridge which led to it. Balme took out a small patrol just before dusk to attack it. They succeeded in scaling the ridge without being spotted and were able to get into the enemy post before the men who were to man it that night arrived. The three-man Turkish patrol were successfully ambushed, killing two and the third rolled down the hillside. Captain Balme was able to bring his whole party back without a casualty.

On 1 November the 1/5th Norfolks left their line for reserve bivouacs in 62 Brigade's area. They were so reduced in numbers that the remaining members of the battalion had to be reorganised into just two companies. The 1/5th Norfolks returned to the Gloucester Hill lines again on 5 November and orders were received from Lieutenant General Birdwood complimenting Captain Balme and his men on their patrol work in late October. He was subsequently awarded the Military Cross for his personal bravery and leadership on the patrol. Captain Balme returned to his regiment after Gallipoli but sadly died of wounds at Ypres in April 1918 age 33.

The heavy rains and the cramped conditions continued; there was no adequate protection with only one waterproof sheet per man for cover and sickness took more men. The 1/5th Norfolks were formally withdrawn from the trenches on 30 November. For about a week before this there had been a great blizzard and the peninsula was covered with snow; the cold was intense. Later this turned to great storms of rain, and soon all the valleys which had been used as the chief means of communication for ration parties were changed into flowing torrents and the men were up to their waists in water in some of the trenches. Frostbite and trench foot became rife and some of the men lost toes or feet.

Lieutenant Colonel Harvey of the 1/4th Norfolks had become very ill with dysentery. Gradually becoming weaker every day, he was living on condensed milk and arrowroot and experienced great difficulty in walking. Captain Hosken, the battalion medical officer, insisted he be removed to hospital and on 4 December 1915 he left his battalion on a stretcher and was taken aboard the hospital ship *Glenarty Castle* which sailed for Alexandria the following day. Captain William Jewson then stood in as commanding officer, but he had only 10 officers and 170 men fit for duty. The 1/5th Norfolks were in a similar state; they were so few they had to be reorganised into two companies. The gradual evacuation of the Gallipoli peninsula by the British commenced soon afterwards.

Private Lewis Burton 1/5th Battalion of Cromer. Died of the dysentery he had contracted in Gallipoli at Floriana Hospital, Malta on 24 November 1915. He was 19.

When the 1/5th Norfolks left the peninsula on the night of 4 December and embarked at Mudros, Captain Eustace Cubitt and Lieutenant Murray Buxton were the only two officers of the original battalion, who had left England aboard the *Aquitania,* who were still with them. Gervase Birkbeck, the only other remaining officer of the original 1/5th Norfolks embarkation, had been detailed for duty as embarkation officer and remained with Private Harrod carrying out those duties on the peninsula until the final evacuation, and then rejoined the battalion. The 1/4th Norfolks, then in the Reserve Gully, ANZAC, went to Mudros on 7 and 8 December and with 11 officers and 237 other ranks and the last remnants of the 1/5th Norfolks, embarked on HMT *Victorian* along with the rest of the shattered 163 Brigade and steamed away from Mudros bound for Alexandria, Egypt on 15 December.

Chapter 7

Egypt 1916

'We catch the breeze and sail away,
Along the dawning of the day'

Henry Abbey

The officers and men of the 1/4th and 1/5th Norfolks disembarked HMT *Victorian* at Alexandria on 19 December, marched to Ramleh tram station and were conveyed by trams to the camp at Sidi Bishr. In complete contrast to the hellish cramped conditions, stench and deprivations of life in the trenches of Gallipoli, Sidi Bishr was a place of peace, calm and rolling countryside where the men were accommodated in neat rows of tents not far from the sea. The camp had been left in very good order and the men soon settled in; they would spend their first Christmas on foreign service there.

Private Bob Overman, 1/5th Norfolks, was at the Winter Palace Hotel, Luxor over Christmas 1915 (it had been closed to guests and used to accommodate convalescent soldiers) with a few of his pals from the battalion; most of them were recuperating from dysentery they had contracted while on the peninsula. Private Overman wrote home to his sister in January 1916:

> *I was pleased to hear you spent such an enjoyable Xmas. We had a fairly decent one considering we are out in a foreign country, but instead of being a nice sharp cold day it was hot as any summer day in England. In fact I could not think it was Xmas at all. The one thing was we never saw a piece of Xmas cake or a piece of mistletoe, but the mistletoe would not have mattered if we could have found the nice girls, but no such luck. I think we must have left them all in England.*

In other letters he often repeated how he was '*anxious to see the boys again*' and wanted to be back with his pals in the battalion rather than '*laying about all day long*'.

He concluded: '*...there is a strong rumour we are coming to England and then to France but I don't believe it as we hear so many rumours that we get fed up with it and we just let things go.*'

He was right about a move being in the air, but it would not be to France or Belgium.

On 31 January 1916 Second Lieutenant Tom Jennings and 46 other ranks from the 1/4th Norfolks and Lieutenant Leslie Shutes with 50 other ranks of the 1/5th Norfolks left Sidi Bishr as an advance party for Mena Camp, ten miles from the centre of Cairo. They were followed by the rest of the 54th Division on 2 February 1916. The site of the

Soldiers of the Norfolk Regiment Territorial Battalions 'on jankers' at Mena Camp at the foot of the pyramids, Egypt, February/March 1916.

camp was formerly used as an Australian Imperial Force (AIF) training base from late 1914 until they set off for the Gallipoli landings; it undoubtedly had one of the most picturesque views in the world, situated as it was at the foot of the Great Pyramid with the Sphinx only a short distance away. On 8 February General Maxwell GOC Egypt inspected 54th Division followed by a brigade route march. The divisional artillery rejoined a few days later and training, including night operations, commenced soon afterwards while the weather was still not oppressively hot.

The 1/4th and 1/5th Norfolks were also joined by several reinforcements of both officers and men throughout January and into April as the division was rebuilt. Some of these reinforcements had been members of the Norfolk Territorial battalions who had been evacuated wounded or sick from Gallipoli and were rejoining their old companies; some of the others were familiar faces from Norfolk who had joined up later. Lieutenant Colonel William Alfred Youden (late of the Highland Light Infantry) had taken over command of the 1/4th Norfolks in December 1915 and Lieutenant Colonel Christian 'Billy' de Falbe (late 1/1st Hertfordshire Yeomanry) was appointed commanding officer of the 1/5th Norfolks in January 1916.

It was also in January 1916 that General Hamilton's final despatch from Gallipoli was published and the 'disappearance' of the men of the 1/5th Norfolks who pushed on too far was picked up by the national newspapers. Particular press attention was paid to the King's Agent, Frank Beck and the men of the Sandringham Company and a number of men saw the newspapers out in Egypt and wrote to the press back home to try to redress the misleading reportage. Others who had known Frank Beck and the men of the 1/5th Norfolks who were still missing wrote home expressing their

Senior NCOs of 1/5th Battalion posing on camels during a trip over the hills from Mena Camp to the Sphynx, March 1916.

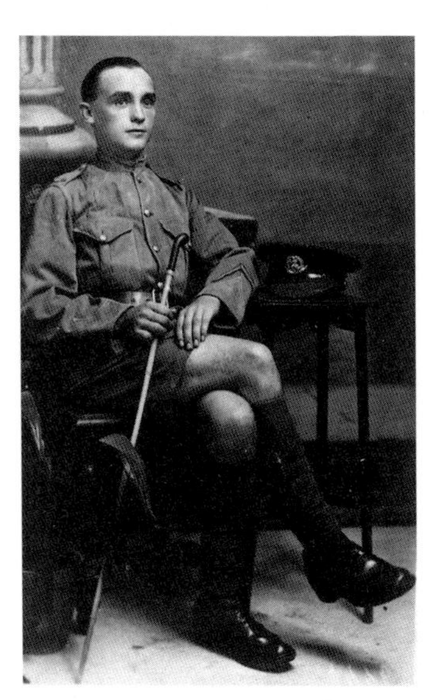

Private Frank Mayes 1/5th Battalion shows how smart the men could look on parades or walking out in Egypt.

sympathies, especially for the families they knew. Private Bob Overman wrote home stoically on 9 February 1916: *'I see by the papers that they cannot make anything out about Capt. Beck but I should think he is a prisoner of war, but I suppose his wife is in a way about him, but it is no use if the Turks will not let them know what prisoners they have got.'*

At Mena Camp, the men enjoyed their training, they felt good about seeing their old battalions rebuilt and they could get a pass and explore Cairo. Private Bob Overman had rejoined the 1/5th Norfolks in late February and wrote home on 25 March 1916:

> *We are having a good time out here now but the things are very dear out here as well, but we have a YMCA that we go to every night and have a nice cup of tea and cake or anything you like and it is very cheap. It is no use you sending anything out here at all because if you send cakes or anything they get so dry and sweets melt as it is nice and*

hot out here now and its only a waste of money. We get plenty of cigarettes and tobacco, in fact a lot more than I can smoke.

On the night of 30 March, the 1/4th and 1/5th Norfolks marched out of Mena to Cairo and entrained at Abu-el-ela Station to take up their defensive positions in No.1 (Southern) Section of the Suez Canal defences at Shallufa over the next two days. At the front line the battalions were split up into company, and sometimes platoon, posts. The men of the 1/5th Norfolks were initially divided between Salford and Oldham Posts near Shallufa. During the hours of daylight, the men would be engaged digging trenches, filling sandbags, reinforcing defences, constructing dug-outs and barbed wire entanglements. At night time the posts would be manned and patrols were sent out. On 25 April the Prince of Wales (who had been appointed staff captain to GOC Egypt) visited the camp of the 1/5th Norfolks with GOC 9 Corps and inspected the officers and men. Private Bob Overman 1/5th Norfolk wrote home:

We had the Prince of Wales to see us the other day and they had the rest of the Sandringham Company out by their-selves. He also shook hands with Captain [Evelyn] *Beck and his brother Lieut. Beck* [Archie] *then walked around our company and then all the other companies... We are getting a fairly good time now. We are doing guards and patrol on the desert and it is nice and warm I can tell you...*

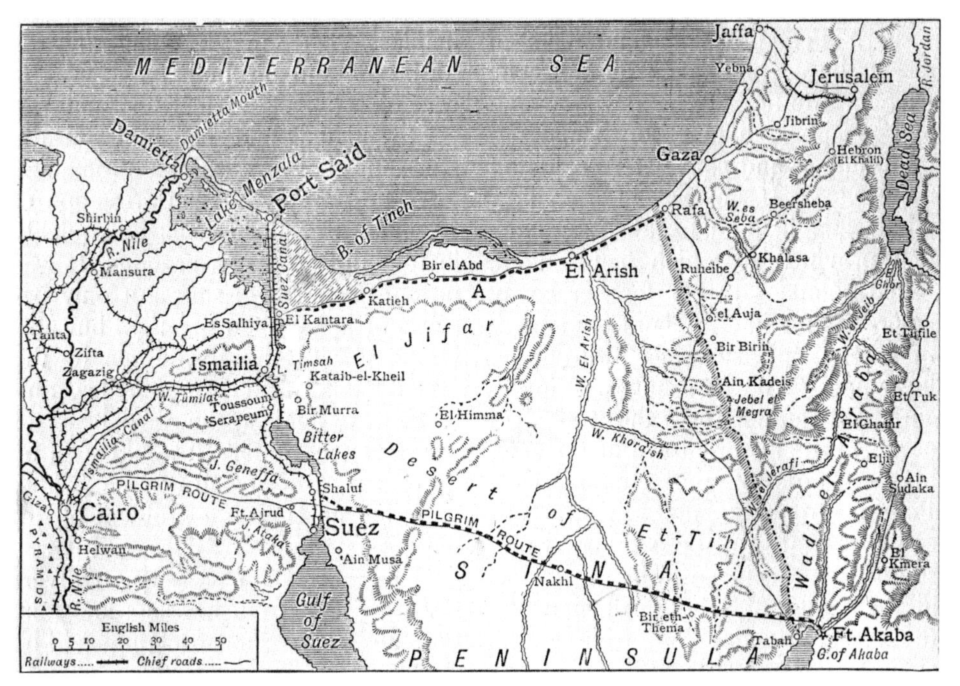

Egypt, the Suez Canal and Palestine. 1/4th and 1/5th Norfolks, along with the rest of 163 Brigade, 54th Division marched and fought along the coast to Gaza, Jaffa and beyond to Beirut.

HRH Edward, Prince of Wales who inspected the Sandringham Company and 1/5th Norfolks during his tour of the Suez Canal defences, April 1916.

Serjeant Frank Windsor 1/5th Battalion of Fakenham died of sickness at Suez on 17 May 1916 aged 20.

[Lieutenant Archibald 'Archie' Beck had been commissioned from the Norfolk Yeomanry into the 2/5th Norfolks in December 1914, and joined the 1/5th Norfolks in Egypt in February 1916.]

The Norfolk Territorial battalions, along with the rest of 54th Division, manned posts along the Suez Canal in the area of Serpeaum and El Ferdan north of Ismalia for the rest of the year. In June 1916 the Norfolk Territorial battalions moved to Serapeum East and, as ever in the Middle East, sickness took its toll on the men. On 4 June 1916 Lieutenant Colonel de Falbe went sick to hospital, was invalided home and Gervase Birkbeck took over command as temporary major.

On 13 June an enemy aeroplane dropped five bombs on the 1/4th Norfolks' camp on 13 June and passed over the 1/5th Norfolks' outposts between No.4 Post and Serapeaum; soldiers opened fire but the plane went on its way and fortunately there were no casualties. Groups of soldiers from both battalions were also given a break and some fresh air at the 'Sea-Side Rest Camp' at Sidi Bishr. On 24 July 1916 Lieutenant Colonel Bernard Salwey Grissell, a very able leader who had served many years in the 2nd Norfolks took over command of the 1/5th Norfolks (with Major Purdy now recovered and returned to the battalion taking over command as temporary lieutenant colonel during any period of absence) and it was under this leadership team the battalion really got into their stride and achieved a very high standard of efficiency.

The 1/4th and 1/5th Norfolks spent their Christmas in Egypt near Ismalia. Private Bob Overman wrote home:

We had an excellent dinner, 5 turkeys between 24 of us and they were good big birds and we had as much as ever we could eat and drink... I hope you had a good time and as you say,

I hope by next year we shall be able to have Xmas at home again if God think fit to spare us to come back again.

On the first day of the New Year orders were received directing all material from occupied posts to be salvaged between 7-9 January 1917. The Norfolk Territorial battalions then proceeded from Serapeum to Moascar by route march for divisional training on 10 January 1917.

The 54th Division spent a month in good hard training there and many an old soldier would remember this time for the route marches in full marching order, trekking along hard roads under the burning sun, especially how their feet ached after being softened by months in the desert sands and the combined agony and ecstasy of taking boots off on their return to camp. In those days blisters were lanced and hundreds were burst under the watchful eye of the medical officer or the sergeant of stretcher bearers as the men continued to march day after day to harden their feet again for the task ahead. When the men of the Norfolk Territorial Battalions struck camp at Moascar everyone was feeling fit and ready to get to grips with the enemy again.

Chapter 8

Palestine 1917-18

'No sooner were we over than hell was let loose.'

Private Bill Ely 1/5th Norfolks,
on the Second Battle of Gaza

Ottoman Turkish forces had invaded the Sinai Peninsula in an abortive attempt to raid the Suez Canal back in 1915. British forces evacuated from Gallipoli to Egypt had been brought back up to strength with reinforcements and an Egyptian Expeditionary Force was raised to retake Sinai and Palestine. The venture was given a real hope of being successful after the Arab Revolt of 1916 (famed through the exploits and writings of T.E. Lawrence 'Lawrence of Arabia') which had stimulated unrest throughout the Ottoman Arab territories.

On 1 February 1917, 163 Brigade left Moascar trekking to El Ferdan, Kantara, Gilban and Romani, where the battalions were able to have bathing parades and final preparations for the march across the Sinai Desert en route for the new campaign that was opening in Palestine.

Captain Murray Buxton, 1/5th Norfolks, noted in his diary:

Much of the march was along the 'wire road' which had been laid. It consisted of four strips of ordinary rabbit wire netting which was laid and pegged on the sand giving enough width for a battalion to march in column of fours. Marching was considerably easier on this than on the soft sand, into which often the men sank up to the ankles at every step.

As a short aside, it is interesting to think that some of this wire road may well have been made in the same county that so many of the battalions came from – in Norwich by Barnards Ltd Engineers who produced over 6,994 miles of wire netting under contract to the War Office during the Great War.

Buxton continues:

The general route was from Romani, by marches of about twelve miles a day, to El Arish. The brigade was led each day by the battalion which marched the best and in which the fewest men fell out. The 5th Norfolk Battalion led the brigade the whole way across, without a man falling out, until the day before the brigade reached El Arish, when a machine gunner got kicked off a refractory mule and injured his leg, so their place at the head was taken by the 1/5th Suffolk.

In their *History of 1/5th Battalion, The Suffolk Regiment* Captain Fair and Captain Wolton reminisce:

> *We proceeded by short daily marches over a splendid wire road to the East. The days' marches were very much alike, varying from five to nine miles under a cloudless sky. Walking on the wire netting was like walking on velvet, and as the bivouacs were invariably on sand, and the weather gloriously fine, conditions were very pleasant.*

1/4th Battalion Serjeant Major wearing his wool service dress jacket to keep off the chill early in the morning at a camp in the desert, 1917.

They were never far from the railway line that ran alongside the wire road with its regular train loads of supplies thundering by. There was also a pipeline that was destined to carry 1,500,000 gallons of the waters of Egypt 200 miles across the desert, which guaranteed soldiers would not go thirsty and gave truth to the ancient prophesy that Palestine would only be conquered when the Nile flowed through it.

As they march soldiers talk, they share stories when they halt and tell tales into the night where they bivouac. This is how rumours spread too and the rumour was that tanks, the new, great, secret weapon were being deployed to Palestine. They had heard they had been seen being landed at Alexandria, but no one had seen them for themselves and the officers denied they were being deployed until they were seen by the men of 163 Brigade who saw tanks in the field for the very first time at Gilban on 3 February 1917.

On 25 February 163 Brigade reached the coastal town of El Arish, their first real town in the desert. Much of the land around the village was cultivated and small melon plantations followed the course of the wadi and fig trees grew along its banks. There were large military camps spread out over the hills, plenty of canteens to supplement rations and even a sea to bathe and get clean in. After crossing the Sinai, it must have seemed like a heaven-sent oasis and a worthy journey's end. When they reached Gaza, the battalion had travelled 200 miles across mostly desert country from Moascar. The brigade then encamped and engaged in training.

On 7 March 1917 163 Brigade took over the left sub-sector defences at Wadi El Arish, the 1/4th Norfolks at Mount Murray and the 1/5th at Mount Dobell. Their duties mainly consisted of guarding the many wells that were scattered over the area and the divisional gas officer at the camp presented a lecture to the men on the new weapon of war. On 20 March the brigade set out for El Burj and via Rafa arrived at Khan Yunis on 25 March and rested for most of the day, then marched to In Seirat and

El Arish, their first real town encountered after crossing the Sinai, it must have seemed like a heaven-sent oasis and a worthy journey's end.

Anti-Gas Hood drill for the Norfolks in the desert.

bivouacked for the night of 25/26 March. On 26 March they headed to Mansura. The brigade lost its way in the darkness and as a result only had two or three hours rest before starting again at 4am for the first attack on Gaza.

At the time Murray Buxton was a temporary captain acting as brigade intelligence officer to Brigadier General Ward. He recorded:

It was most unfortunate that there was a very thick fog on the morning of the 26th, for no one had any idea of the country between In Seirat and Gaza. There were several 'wadis' to be crossed and the R.E. had only made one or two crossings which were very difficult to find, and were usually crowded with columns of troops crossing. For this reason we must have lost about three hours, and it was not until 8 o'clock that we crossed the Wadi Ghuzze at Shekh Nebhan.

The Brigade marched the eight miles to Sheikh Abbas in artillery formation, arriving there about 10 o'clock without firing a shot, and took up their position along the ridge. All day we remained there while 53 Division and 161 Brigade were attacking Gaza from the south and the New Zealand and Australian cavalry were attacking from the N.E. The Turks had much larger forces in Gaza than we had expected, and large reinforcements were marched from Beersheba and other places round, and so the attack was not so successful as we had hoped...In the afternoon we received orders to take up a position during the night west of Sheikh Abbas on Mansura Ridge. The Brigadier sent me down on my horse to find out the way, and I then came back and guided the columns to Mansura Ridge during the night.

General Sir Charles Dobell had assembled the core of his force 8km from Gaza near the coast and behind the Wadi Ghazi. He had used the thick fog effectively as a cover for his cavalry advance that successfully cut off the rear of Gaza east and south-east on the morning of the attack. Coupled with a deployment to prevent the supply of reinforcements to the town, there was every advantage in numbers of Allied troops and the element of surprise. Despite crossing difficult terrain, the infantry of 53rd Division made good ground and was greatly assisted by the encircling cavalry but, tragically, other infantry units were held up and the artillery bombardment did not commence until 9am. The element of surprise had been lost and the cavalry commander, Sir Philip Chetwode, was ordered by General Dobell, to withdraw his troops.

By 4pm on 27 March Turkish reinforcements were approaching from the east in readiness to attack the 53rd and 54th divisions. The attack came at dusk but was repulsed with machine gun and artillery fire from the whole British line. Corporal William Ward of All Saints' Street, King's Lynn described what he saw of this action in a letter:

...the artillery got going and we had to dig ourselves in. Fortunately, while we were digging no shells came over, so we got good cover. All this time on our left was very stiff fighting and with field glasses you could see the enemy in masses and the shells smashing them to pieces...we had dug ourselves into a splendid position with a lovely field of fire and just as the sun was setting Johnny Turk could be seen coming towards us...The attack lasted two days and the enemy brought up large reinforcements.

At 5.15pm the trenches occupied by the 1/4th Norfolks suffered the first casualties of the Norfolk Territorial battalions during the Palestine campaign. Their trenches were shelled killing Gallipoli veteran Lance Sergeant William Smith and Private Albert Kemp and wounding a further thirteen. At 8.15pm orders were received to withdraw via Sheikh Nebhan where parties from both the 1/4th and 1/5th Norfolks were detailed to remove eighty wounded soldiers to the 1/3rd East Anglian Field Ambulance back at In Seirat. The withdrawing troops passed the convoy coming up with rations, but they had to be sent back to Wadi Ghuzee, as there was no time for them to be issued. Consequently, the men got no rations or water that night.

The shortage of water carried by the men meant many of them were suffering from dehydration and any water supplies were being fired on by the enemy. Captain William Wenn and two of his men selflessly risked their lives to help fetch water; tragically all three were wounded and Captain Wenn died of his wounds three days later. The death

Captain William Wenn, wounded on 28 March while trying to obtain water for his parched troops. He died on 1 April 1917.

of this popular officer, particularly under these circumstances, was particularly felt by both the officers and men of the 1/5th Norfolks.

Buxton continues:

> *Directly it was light we saw a large force of Turks advancing on the ridge and they shelled us rather heavily. The 5th Norfolk were ordered to go forward and take up a line about 500 yards in front of the ridge. After a good deal of machine gun and rifle fire the Turkish attack was broken up and they never got much nearer than 400 to 500 yards. The 5th Norfolk consolidated their position and remained there all day.*

As 28 March progressed it soon became clear the danger of further counter-attacks from ever-growing numbers of enemy troops and lack of water supplies meant it was advisable to call off the attack. The 163 Brigade were given orders to cover the withdrawal of the 54th Division to the west bank of Wadi Ghuzee, while doing so maintaining communication with 158 Brigade, which was covering the 53rd Division. This operation was successfully achieved and the brigade began to arrive back at In Seirat from 5am on 28 March 1917 and were back at the comparatively quiet defences along the El Sire Ridge to El Adar and Sharta on the east side of Wadi Ghuzzi by 1 April.

Commander-in-Chief General Archibald Murray wrote to the War Office after the First Battle of Gaza suggesting Turkish losses were three times their actual figure and claimed the attack was far more successful than it was. His despatch was convincing enough to instil a feeling among his superiors that a second assault was all that was required to achieve a victory. A similar confidence was also felt by many men who did not get the chance to press home their attack in the advancing 53rd or covering 54th divisions in the first battle. As the divisions entered into more vigorous and extensive training, Captain Buxton reflected the mood by recording '*everyone expected that at the second attack we should gain Gaza with comparative ease*'. Corporal Ward was a little more cautious in his comments: '*I expect shortly we shall have another big attack, I daresay we shall manage to gain our objective, but I can assure you they* [the enemy] *are hot stuff.'*

The Norfolk Territorial battalions remained at In Seirat taking their turn in the defence and support trenches. Both battalions had a brief spell in rest camp and it was from there the 1/4th Norfolks proceeded to Sharta on 15 April.

Operations against Sheikh Abbas Ridge by 163 Brigade commenced at dawn on 16 April. The Turks only had a few outposts in this area and the capture and consolidation of the ridge was achieved without much difficulty by Hampshire and Suffolk battalions, preceded by two tanks, with the two Norfolk battalions in support.

Lieutenant Colonel Tom Purdy while attached to 1/4th Battalion, with some of his officers, Palestine 1917.

1/4th Battalion Officers Mess 'in the field' Palestine 1917.

1/4th Battalion Medical Officer and his dug-out, Palestine 1917.

The Turkish main line was along the Gaza-Beersheba Road. During the consolidation there had been heavy shell fire and A Company 1/5th Norfolks, under Captain Birkbeck, received the brunt of the enemy fire but, fortunately, suffered few casualties. One soldier was killed (King's Lynn soldier Albert Garnett Cobbold, 1/5th Norfolk) and two were wounded. The night of the 17/18 April and all day on 18 April was spent in this

Just behind the forward lines, Gaza, Palestine 1917.

Dug-outs and field operating theatre of the East Anglian Field Ambulance, Gaza, Palestine 1917.

position as the rest of the line also attained their first objectives.

Orders for the general attack on what was to become the Second Battle of Gaza on 19 April were issued so late on 18 April that they did not reach all the men until nearly midnight, resulting in most of the night being spent preparing for the attack and distributing rations and water. The 1/5th Norfolks' war diary for 19 April stated:

> *Artillery bombardment commenced on Turks at 0530, lasting two hours. 163rd Brigade ordered to attack 07.30. 5th Norfolks being on right of 163 Brigade frontage, 4th Norfolks on left with 8th Hampshires in support and 5th Suffolks as reserve. The trenches to be attacked were 2500 to 3000 yards from line held by 163 Brigade.*

Captain Gervase William Birkbeck, 1/5th Battalion (West Acre) died of wounds received at the Second Battle of Gaza, 19 April 1917.

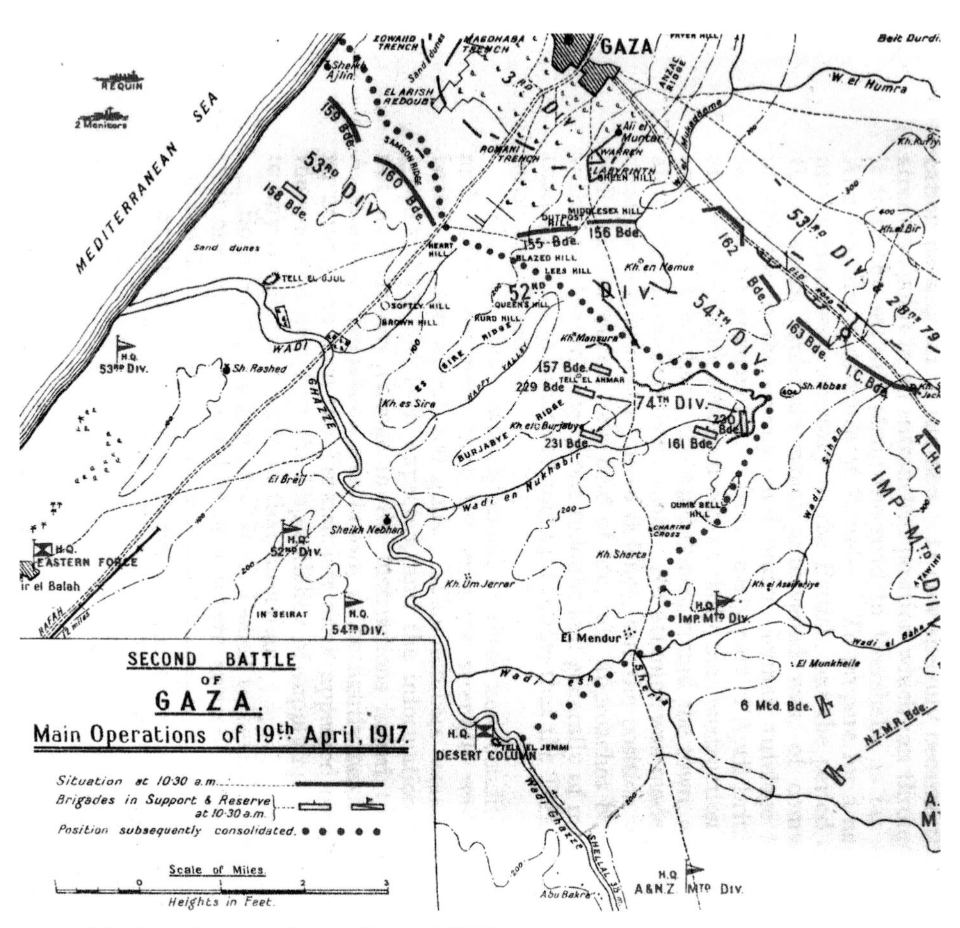

Map of the Second Battle of Gaza 19 April 1917.

Of the two Norfolk battalions' advance Captain Buxton recorded: '*it was a magnificent sight to see them going in extended order as if on a field day'*. His phraseology and the irony of it echoes the opening movements of the 1/5th Norfolks on 12 August 1915 and should not be lost on the reader, for this too was to prove a costly day for the brave men of the Norfolk Territorial battalions. In the interim the Turks had extended their formidable garrison defences south-east along the road to Beersheba, the Gaza fortifications had been reinforced and were far more formidable than before.

Each battalion covered a front of about 900yds. The right of the 1/5th Norfolks was directed on a Turkish redoubt which soon sprayed the men with heavy machine gun and rifle fire. The first low ridge was crossed by 8.30am and the second, about 500 yards further on was reached. The 1/8th Hants now advanced against the redoubt with one tank. On the opposite flank, to the left of the 1/4th Norfolks, the other tank advanced on another Turkish redoubt, but it had not taken long for the artillery to find them and the tank was hit by a shell and put out of action. The 1/5th Norfolks

Area of the advance of the 54th Division and Imperial Camel Corps at the Second Battle of Gaza 19 April 1917.

soon disappeared over the second ridge and communications between the battalions became strained.

The tank, known as 'The Nutty', with the 1/5th Norfolks and 1/8th Hants did sterling work inflicting heavy damage on the enemy, but followed a somewhat wayward path towards the redoubt whereupon achieving the knoll it was fired upon at point blank range by four field guns and set on fire. Despite suffering severe casualties taking the redoubt, the attacking troops from the 1/5th Norfolks under Lieutenant Arthur Blyth and the Camel Corps took it with a bayonet charge. The Turkish troops, some estimate at being some 600 in number, broke and fled to their second line defences with twenty taken prisoners of war.

The capture of what became known as 'Tank Redoubt' was undoubtedly the infantry's most significant gain of the battle, but this gain was to be short lived. The advance had been held up just below the Turkish line, and one could see our men lying out in lines, killed or wounded. The 1/5th Norfolks' B Company, under Lieutenant Blyth, had captured Tank Redoubt and had held it some time, till all ammunition was spent. No support came up, and those who did not get away, sixty in all, were captured in the Turkish counter-attack.

All this time enfilading fire from well-placed machine guns caused heavy casualties in both our Territorial battalions. The whole attacking force had suffered a similar hail of fire from artillery, machine gun and rifle fire which the British artillery, at a range of 6,000 yards, was unable to keep down.

Captain Buxton continues:

There were a lot of dead men and wounded all round us. Some of the latter we got behind our lines, in case the Turks tried a counter attack. We were about forty men

One of the wrecked hulks of the British tanks that lingered on the field after the battles for Gaza 1917.

Captain William Vanstone Morgan 1/4th Battalion (Norwich), killed in action 19 April 1917.

Lieutenant Eric Gardiner, 1/5th Battalion (King's Lynn), killed in action 19 April 1917.

and a Lewis gun, and no-one on our left or right for several hundred yards. The place we were holding was the top of a rounded hillock. The Turks kept us under pretty good machine gun fire all day. Indeed, by noon the attack had faltered at all points and any gains which had been made were too thinly occupied to be held for longer than minutes or hours.

Private Bill Ely, 1/5th Norfolks, vividly recorded his experiences in the battle in his diary:

Roused at 3.30am. Took over the front line, which consisted of several strong ridges of hills from the Suffolks. Laid low for about one and three quarter hours whilst our artillery let rip at top speed. Then, at approximately 6.30am we went over the top, or rather round the ridges and into the open.

No sooner were we over than hell was let loose. The ground we had to go over was devoid of any cover; nothing only short grass. The shells fell thick and fast all over the place. Before I'd gone 200 yards something bowled me right over. I thought I had clicked a good packet, but on examination I found a small piece of shell had only badly bruised the upper part of my right leg, so I got up and carried on.

About half a mile further on we came under a murderous fire from rifles, machine guns and heavier shell fire. Plenty of shrapnel dropping down like hail. The enemy gunners were simply sweeping the ground in every direction and men were falling thick and fast all round. Our chaps in front made a bayonet charge, capturing a large portion of trench, bombing and driving Turks out with cold steel. Casualties are terrible. Colonel wounded and rumoured a prisoner; adjutant killed and all officers except one bowled over. I stopped and helped bandage several of

Corporal Frederick Wells 1/4th Battalion, killed in action 19 April 1917.

Private William Albert 'Dolly' Bunn, 1/5th Battalion (Dersingham), killed in action while tending a wounded comrade 19 April 1917.

the wounded including Bob Etchells. Dolly Bunn and I lay behind the small ridge dressing Bob's wounds when Dolly rolled over suddenly dead with a bullet through his heart.

It was sudden death to go over to the redoubt which was 200 yards in front, so I decided to help Bob back to safety. I managed to drag him back at a time while shells were dropping all around us and eventually handed him over to two Australian stretcher bearers after giving him practically all the water I had left. Saw him safely out of danger, then returned across the thickly strewn battlefield to the boys under the ridge, who were nearly dead with heat. Suddenly the firing increased again, machine guns (the enemy must have had hundreds of 'em) spitting out viciously in all directions, excepting the rear. It was hell retiring to our old line across that ground, which was strewn with corpses and equipment, as the enemy guns opened up again and plastered us with high explosives and shrapnel until we reached safety.

Private Joseph Emms, of B Company 1/5th Norfolks, wrote home in May 1917 with his own first-hand account of the Second Battle of Gaza:

The 5th Norfolk Regiment was in the first line to advance and suffered rather heavy losses. No.5 and 6 platoons of B company were on the right of the line and 7 and 8 were forming support. About 5.00am we were told that we had to advance roughly 2000 yards and during the whole time we should be under rifle and big gun fire. We moved off at first in artillery formation but the fire got so hot for us to go in this order so we had to open out into extended order and at 5 paces interval. My friend Dent was on my left while a man named Eastic was on my right and it was not long before they were both hit so I began to think my time was coming, but luck was good for on that day I managed to get as far as any man in the line.

The Turks were holding a very strongly fortified redoubt which consisted of two lines of trenches one behind the other forming half a circle. Barbed wire entanglements had been erected in the front of these trenches and we were lying before these just wondering how to get past them when we suddenly heard a tremendous rattling noise coming from behind and, keeping my head as low as possible, I chanced a look behind and saw a tank coming at full speed not a hundred yards behind and firing all her guns which was a fine sight to see. The tank soon laid the barbed wire low and then we advanced behind her and I managed to get into the second trench and then a very lucky shot for the Turks hit one of the Tank's wheels and put her out of action, which made a great deal of difference to us in the trenches. The crew, rather than let the Turks have it, set fire to it and ran into the trench where I was in, there was an officer and 3 or 4 men and they all seemed to be wounded.

While I was in the trench my company officer Lieut Blyth came in and by the amount of blood on his shorts I saw that he was hit rather badly in the lower part of his body but he said nothing about it only smiled when I ask him if it was very bad and said 'Good Boys'.

Then a bad thing happened for us, the whole line retired and left 17 of us and two officers in the trench without us knowing it and this left us heavily outnumbered and almost at once there were lots of Turks swarming around us and I began to think it was all up with us, but we had two Lewis machine guns but had no ammunition for them, so we all emptied our pouches and used that but of course it soon all went as these guns fire nearly 400 rounds a minute and when it was all done we sat down on the dead Turks who were in the trench as there were so many that we couldn't help it and waited for the worst to happen, mainly to be rushed. We waited about two hours and then someone suddenly shouted 'They are in' and we saw about a dozen Turks jump in the next fire bay to ours and we only had our bayonets to fight them with. Someone managed to find a bomber's coat full of bombs and we kept them off for a short time with these and then our Officer shouted out that [we would] *either have to give in or run for it so we decided to make a dash for it and only one Officer and seven of us managed to get away. Lieut. Blyth got safely back and is now in hospital in Alexandria where he is doing well. All of us who came back recommended him for his coolness and bravery which he showed in many ways.*

Lieutenant Arthur Blyth recovered from his wounds and his gallantry at the Second Battle of Gaza was recognised with the award of a Military Cross.

At 2.23pm a counter-attack was launched, the 1/6th Essex on the left and 1/5th Suffolks on the right, with an artillery barrage firing on the enemy trenches. It soon became clear this attack would make no progress and the 1/6th Essex were withdrawn behind the Sheik Abbas ridge, while the remains of the Norfolk battalions and the 1/8th Hants dug in at the positions they occupied and held on there until daybreak on 20 April.

At around 4pm the 1/5th Suffolks was sent up in support and helped consolidate what ground our territorials had managed to hold. During the day a variety of stragglers found their way to Captain Murray Buxton's sector and reported that Captain Birkbeck had been badly wounded. The OC 1/5th Suffolks was given the whereabouts of Birkbeck and sent out patrols, but much to the frustration of Buxton 'these did no good at all'.

At about 7pm the brigadier came up the line and ordered the battalions to retire under cover of darkness to the start point. Buxton continues: '*We brought in a lot of wounded as we came back. The three attacking regiments of our Brigade had all had very heavy losses. Each was reduced to about 150 men.*'

In their *History of 1/5th Battalion, The Suffolk Regiment* Captain Fair and Captain Wolton recalled what was seen of the attack of the 1/4th and 1/5th Norfolks in broad daylight:

1/4th and 1/5th Norfolks, supported by 1/8th Hants, commenced the attack from the ridge. There was at most points more than a mile of almost level country with little cover to be crossed before the enemy trenches could be reached. A tank pushed on to Tank Redoubt and held it until occupied by the 1/8th Hants. It was however put out of action by enemy artillery fire and could not move from there. The tanks had not given as much assistance as was expected, but a very large amount of artillery fire had been concentrated on them...The Norfolks, on arriving about 800 yards from the enemy trenches, came under a very heavy and accurate belt of cross-fire from machine guns, which swept the ground entirely devoid of cover. They tried to press quickly on but could not pass through the belt, and suffered very heavy casualties, nearly seventy-five per cent of each battalion being seriously wounded or killed...

At dusk Brigadier Ward rode out to inspect the position. At intervals throughout the day small parties of wounded Norfolks came back through the line. The groans and calls of the wounded could be heard, but to send a party into that belt meant certain death and drew heavy searching fire on those that were there.

On 20 April 161 Brigade took over the line and the battle weary and decimated survivors of our Norfolk Territorial battalions retired to Wadi Nokhabir where they began to take stock of their losses:

1/4th Battalion

Killed
Major William Henry Jewson
Captain William Vanstone Morgan
Captain Sydney Durrant Page
Captain Ralph William Thurgar
Lieutenant Frederick John Cole
Second Lieutenant Josiah Levy
49 Other Ranks.

Wounded
11 officers and 312 Other Ranks

Missing
T/Second Lieutenant Reginald Cuthbert Chilvers
99 Other Ranks

1/5th Battalion

Killed
Lieutenant Colonel Bernard Salwey Grissell DSO
Captain Arthur Evelyn Beck MC
Captain Gervase William Birkbeck
Captain (Adjutant) Eustance Henry Cubitt
Lieutenant Eric John Gardiner
Lieutenant Richard Reeves Plaistowe
13 Other Ranks

Wounded
9 officers and 401 Other Ranks

Missing
4 officers and 299 Other Ranks

Both battalions suffered dreadful losses, 37 officers and 1,103 other ranks killed, wounded or missing. All told 265 officers and men from the 1/4th Norfolks and 228 officers and men from the 1/5th Norfolks died in the action or succumbed to their wounds between 19 and 30 April 1917. It was not just a loss in numbers, but in the 'life-blood' of the battalion, the characters, the friends and experienced men. For the 1/4th Norfolks it was the deaths of respected and well-liked battalion stalwarts like Major Jewson and Captain Page that hit hardest.

Major William Jewson, 1/4th Battalion (Norwich), killed in action 19 April 1917.

In the 1/5th Norfolks their commanding officer Lieutenant Colonel Grissell, the man who had really shaped the new battalion into a fighting unit, had died of his wounds. The ever-resourceful Captain Gervase Birkbeck (a man who had scored three centuries while playing county cricket for Norfolk before the war) had been reported as badly wounded but the patrol sent to his aid failed to locate him. His body was never found, or if it was it was not identified, and, like so many of his comrades who fell on 12 August 1915, he too has no known grave.

The villages of Norfolk felt the losses acutely, in Dersingham, for example, there were Nigel Duncan, George Riches, George Houchen and Leonard Fulcher who were all serving in the 1/5th Norfolks and all of them were wounded. Fred Cross was wounded and taken prisoner and William 'Dolly' Bunn was killed while tending a wounded comrade. Dersingham brothers Ernest, David and Jimmie Howell had charged together at Anafarta on 12 August 1915. They lost sight of Ernie, he didn't turn up after the action, and was among the many posted missing. The family were still holding out hope he would turn up in a hospital or as prisoner of war when Jimmie

Captain Sydney Page, 1/4th Battalion (Norwich), killed in action 19 April 1917.

Lieutenant Douglas Hervey, died of wounds received at the Second Battle of Gaza on 17 May 1917 age 21.

Second Lieutenant Terrence Capon Read, 1/5th Battalion, died 22 April 1917 from wounds received at the Second Battle of Gaza.

Private Jimmie Howell 1/5th Battalion (Dersingham), killed in action 19 April 1917.

and David were in action at the Second Battle of Gaza. Both were wounded but sadly Jimmie succumbed to his injuries before the end of the day.

There was also 28-year-old Captain Eustace Cubitt, the last of three brothers of the Cubitt family of Honing Hall to die serving in the 1/5th Norfolks, and Captain Evelyn Beck MC, who had saved so many lives by his decisive actions during the attack on Anafarta Ova where his brother Alec did not survive. It is tragic so many brothers had also fallen *together* in this single action; there were Austin and Charles Rudram of Mundesley, Frank and Joe Hardiment of Wicklewood, Sergeants Joseph and Edgar Fisher of Honingham, Bertie and Archie Hastings of Cromer, Thomas and Charles Creasey of West Runton and Cliff and Horace Bird from the neighbouring village of East Runton, their brother Arthur also died of

Serjeant Archie Hastings 1/5th Norfolks (Cromer) killed in action 19 April 1917.

Drummer Bertie Hastings 1/5th Norfolks (Cromer) missing, presumed died of wounds 19 April 1917.

wounds sustained in the battle. After the Second Battle of Gaza they were all dead. It was rare in a single action in either world war for so many brothers serving together in British county battalions to fall together, even on the first day of the Somme.

Among the hundreds of wounded was Private Bob Overman whose surviving letters have helped provide a very human narrative to accompany the exploits of the 1/5th Norfolks in this book. Evacuated to No.17 British Military General Hospital, Alexandria he appeared to be making a recovery, but he died from sudden heart failure as a result of his wounds on 14 May 1917. Company Quartermaster Serjeant William Burton, 1/5th Norfolks, wrote a letter of condolence to Bob's parents:

> *Poor old Bob was only one of many of the 1/5th who laid down their lives on that ill-fated day. After surviving the Gallipoli affair, it was awfully hard luck coming to grief in the Holy Land. Bob was always one of the smartest men in the Company and could be relied on always as a steady and reliable man.*

Bob was buried with full military honours at Hadra Military Cemetery, Alexandria.

Decorations for the Second Battle of Gaza for the 1/4th Norfolks were Military Crosses for Captain H. Joste Smith (RAMC attached 1/4th Norfolks), Lieutenant Ralph William Thurgar (posthumous), Second Lieutenant John Howlett Jewson, Second Lieutenant Guy Havat Wood and Military Medals for Corporal Frederick G. Rickwood, Corporal I.H. Paget (RAMC attached 1/4th Norfolks) and Private Walter

Bugler William Amis, 1/5th Battalion (Cromer) taken prisoner of war at Gaza April 1917 died of malaria Nigdi Hospital, Turkey 21 October 1917.

Self. The War Diary for the 1/5th Norfolks records the immediate awards of Military Crosses to Temporary Captain Murray Barclay Buxton and Lieutenant Arthur Cecil Blyth and a Distinguished Conduct Medal for Lance Sergeant Tom Walker. A number of Military Medals were also awarded subsequently to members of the battalion for their bravery in the field.

The surviving members of the 1/4th and 1/5th Norfolks formed a composite battalion with 1/8th Hants under Lieutenant Colonel Oliver Miles Torkington, late of the Scottish Rifles. On 21 April 1917 the 1/8th Hants were taken from the composite battalion and reorganisation of the 1/4th and 1/5th Norfolks began again. The 54th Division commander, Major General Stuart Wellwood Hare, sent an effusive letter of appreciation dated 29 April to all the battalions of 163 Brigade via their Brigade Commander, Brigadier Tom Ward:

> *My Dear Ward – Under present circumstances one has not a chance of seeing a Brigade or even a unit together to speak to them. I would, therefore, be much obliged to you, if you would tell all ranks in your Brigade...how deeply I appreciate the truly splendid work they did. The handling of the Brigade itself and of all the units in it, seems to have been worthy of the men the commanders had to lead, and I cannot say more than that. All ranks, those who fell and those who survived, acted up to the very highest traditions of the British Army and I do not believe any troops in the world could have done more, or shown greater gallantry or better discipline.*

Between 1 May and 16 May 163 Brigade was relieved by 74th Division and was in reserve at Sheikh Abbas. During this time they received 'in the field' training and reinforcements to rebuild the battalions. The 4/5th Norfolk Composite battalion was dissolved on 2 June. Lieutenant Colonel Torkington remained in command of the 1/4th Norfolks and Lieutenant Colonel Gerald Marmaduke de Langport Dayrell, late Bedfordshire Regiment (known among the mess and the men as 'Gentleman Gerald') took command of the 1/5th Norfolks.

The months of June and July 1917 mostly remained quiet with the battalions manning posts in the space from the Gaza–Cairo road where it seemed like a constant round of digging trenches and sandbag filling. Snipers were troublesome and the occasional shell that fell on our lines caused a few casualties.

One of the corporals of 1/5th Battalion showing the 163 Brigade shoulder insignia.

In late July divisional signs were adopted by 54th Division, their symbol was to be an umbrella blown inside out in recognition for successful raid carried out by the 1/5th Bedfords, 162 Brigade, 54th Division on the most advanced of the redoubts guarding Gaza that had been named Umbrella Hill earlier in the month. The units in 163 Brigade were issued coloured cloth shoulder badges in the shape of triangles worn point upwards, equally divided in the centre and coloured red and yellow.

August remained quiet; the whole of 54th Division was put into quieter lines and reinforcements drafted in to bring it back up to strength once again. With the exception of an attempted raid by the Turks, which was easily repulsed by artillery, it was a quiet time. No casualties, but a little excitement was caused with the capture of two Turks in a fig grove by the 1/4th Norfolks. But things would not remain quiet forever. The 1/4th and 1/5th Norfolks were reorganised and returned to the front line again with the 1/5th Suffolks on 26 August. On 2 September 1917 Captain George Fisher, 1/4th Norfolks, was killed while on patrol in a thick fig grove that was subsequently called Fisher's Wood and old Greshamian, Lieutenant Robert Henry Partridge, 1/5th Norfolks was accidentally killed on 4 September. As a whole though 54th Division and the campaign in Palestine were steadily being reinvigorated.

General Edmund Allenby had arrived to take over as GOC Egyptian Expeditionary Force on 27 June 1917. Allenby would later confess he felt he had been let down by being transferred from the Western Front to the Middle East, so he was determined to revive the operations there by aiming for decisive victories and set about organising specialised training for his men. By October 1917 the majority of the old senior commanders had been removed and both the 1/4th Norfolks and 1/5th Norfolks were nearly up to strength again; the weather was cooler and their training was taken up a gear. The men of the Norfolks would recall the new regime of tougher training as they were put through model trenches and practice attacks with runners and signallers being used for communications.

The battalions were also reorganised into rifle sections, Lewis gun section etc. right up to when the Norfolks' 163 Brigade relieved 156 Brigade in mid-October when they occupied a Gaza sub-sector with their old brigade comrades in the 1/8th Hants on the extreme left flank to the sea. The 1/4th Norfolks were in the centre, from Hereford Ridge to Cairo Ridge and the 1/5th Norfolks on the right occupying Samson's Ridge.

On 31 October Beersheba was captured by British infantry and Australian light horsemen with 1,000 prisoners and on 1 November 1917 General Allenby was ready to attack Gaza again. During the evening 163 Brigade moved up to the start position but took no part in the first phase of the operation. At 2.30am on 2 November D Company of the 1/4th Norfolks, attached to the 1/5th Suffolks for carrying purposes, attacked with the 1/8th Hants and, despite coming under heavy shelling and cloaked in smoke, they reached their objective trench. Meanwhile the main body of the 1/4th Norfolks had formed in support at 2.15am on the rear of the 1/8th Hants. The machine guns and light trench mortar were at the rear of C Company under Second Lieutenant Collier who was killed shortly after the advance commenced. As the battalion advanced at 3am it was hit by the enemy barrage, which had sailed over the 1/8th Hants, and sustained heavy casualties. At 3.55am, when the 1/4th Norfolks should have passed through the 1/8th Hants to attack their objective of Crested Rock, they were held up by hand-to-hand fighting in El Arish and, although they successfully occupied the trenches they attacked, they found it impossible to locate themselves in the battle and the objective of Crested Rock was, by then, unobtainable.

The 1/5th Norfolks had formed up at 2.50am on the left rear of the 1/8th Hants but the 1/5th Norfolks also lost direction, arrived in the wrong area and got caught in the barrage at 3.30am. It was too late to correct their direction and the result was confusion, but Captain Gardner and Lieutenants Cumberland, Catherall and Pallett went forward with small bodies of men and managed to penetrate Island Wood, Gibraltar and even Crested Rock, but wounded and lacking the necessary support Captain Gardner and the lieutenants were forced to retire at Island Wood. The fighting had been confused, the brigade consolidated the trenches they had reached but the attack had fallen considerably short of its objectives. Second Lieutenants John Thomas Collier, William Stanley Giles (attached to the 1/4th Norfolks from the Royal Warwickshire Regiment) and 23 other ranks of the 1/4th Norfolks lay dead and there were over 110 wounded. The 1/5th Norfolks suffered officer losses of Second Lieutenant William Shaw killed, two missing and eight wounded; the other ranks also had 29 killed, 9 missing and 136 wounded, 6 of whom died shortly afterwards.

The battle, however, was far from lost and the courage of the men of the Norfolk Territorial battalions under such trying circumstances did not go unrecognised. Second Lieutenant Ernest Cumberland was awarded the Military Cross, Serjeant Frederick Holmes and Private Harry Taylor both received Distinguished Conduct Medals for their courage and steady command during this action and Corporal (acting serjeant) Allen Ducker, Corporal George W. Warren, Lance Corporal (acting corporal) Ernest Lee and Private Archie Fuller all received Military Medals for their bravery.

The 163 Brigade continued to consolidate over the next few days and slowly but surely pursued the enemy out of the ground it was holding, until 7 November when they concentrated at Marine View and the pursuit of the now retreating enemy was taken over by 52nd Division. The battalions then began salvage operations. On 8 November all Turkish positions on the Gaza–Beersheba line had been captured. The brigade (leaving the 1/4th Norfolks behind) advanced to Sheikh Hassan where the men bathed, rested and the battalions reorganised. On 11 November 1917 Major General Hare GOC 54th Division sent out a special Order of the Day:

> *Now that the third battle of Gaza has been fought and won, I wish to congratulate the division on the part that they played in it. The gateway between Egypt and the Holy Land is one of the historic battle grounds of the world and the 54th Division has shown fighting qualities worthy of this scene of countless battles.*

Serjeant Allen Ducker, 1/5th Battalion (Honing) awarded the Military Medal for Bravery in the Field during the assault on Gaza, November 1917.

When soldiers returned to the area of Sheikh Abbas, where hundreds of men of the 1/4th and 1/5th Norfolks had been mown down during the Second Battle of Gaza, their bodies still lay where they fell. A burial party was detailed to the area for some time and several officers from all the battalions of 163 Brigade came to help identify the bodies. It was found most of their identity tags had been taken from their bodies (Private Maystone had written home from Gallipoli about how Turkish snipers had rifled the bodies of the dead to take their identity tags as trophies), but named articles of clothing, kit and personal effects that were still found about their persons helped to identify many of them.

Captain Fair and Captain Wolton commented in their *History of 1/5th Battalion, The Suffolk Regiment: 'All were laid to rest in a common grave after an impressive service. We felt then that their lives had been sacrificed in a gallant attempt to capture a position that was impregnable by day. Truly it was said: 'The best of our grand old Territorial Brigade lie here.'*

On 14 November 163 Brigade left Sheikh Hassan on an 11-mile march to Herbieh, en route for Jaffa. On 16 November they left Herbieh and onwards they marched on good roads through a beautiful land of orange groves, green hedges and red-tiled houses with whitewashed walls, just like those many of the lads had seen depicted on the colour plates of artistic views of the Holy Land in their Sunday School books. On 20 November the 1/4th and 1/5th Norfolks were on outpost duty on the high ground east of Bariyeh, between Jerusalem and Jaffa. Here the heavens opened up and the rains lashed down testing a number of their worn bivouacs to destruction.

The 1/4th and 1/5th Norfolks relieved the mounted division on outposts at Annabeh on 22 November, soon moving to Mideh, where on 24 November an enemy cavalry patrol was spotted entering Nalin. After an hour, three patrols, each of them with a

Gaza War Cemetery before its wooden crosses were replaced with Imperial War Graves headstones. 'The best of our grand old Territorial Brigade lie here.'

Lewis gun and signallers were dispatched to clear the place with Second Lieutenants Guy Wood and Jack Lewell commanding the advance platoons. They made their ground and held it, but under heavy fire. At 5pm the three patrols returned with the news that one of their number was missing believed killed and Second Lieutenant Lewell and five other ranks wounded.

The nearby attack on Silta saw it held by Second Lieutenant Bill Gordon of the 1/5th Norfolks with his own men and some of the Royal Scots. The Turks attacked with 200-300 men who started throwing grenades. In the face of such numbers and grenade explosions Gordon withdrew, consolidated and led two counter-attacks, but sadly these were unsuccessful. Reduced to fifty men, two Lewis guns and very little ammunition, they were finally forced from the outskirts of the village to retire to Ramleh where they were bombed by three or four enemy aircraft on 27 November. One soldier was killed and eight wounded, three of whom subsequently died of wounds. A number of the mules from the transport section were also killed and injured.

On 1 December 163 Brigade took over from 162 at Deir Turief where, with minor moves of location and carrying out patrols, it remained until 9 December when Jerusalem surrendered. General Allenby entered on foot as a mark of respect to the Holy City on 11 December. Jerusalem was a significant gain, but the campaign was not over, for also on 11 December a 1/4th battalion patrol under Lieutenant D.A. Walters ascertained the enemy were still holding the feature known as Stone Heap Hill and those adjacent in force. Both the 1/4th and 1/5th Norfolks were on the left of the forward line facing the enemy as they made a determined attack on Zephiziyeh Hill, which was held by about fifty men of C Company of the 1/4th Norfolks under Captain Sir Thomas Berney. They were hard-pressed and it was due to Berney's coolness and personal courage that he held the position against superior numbers and owing to his accurate estimate of the situation, the counter-attack was made at the right moment.

Captain Sir Thomas Berney, C Company, 1/4th Battalion commanded and held the heights of Zephiziyeh Hill during the attack on 11 December 1917.

B Company under Captain Walter Flatt made a most gallant counter-attack, clearing enemy trenches with fixed bayonets. The Turks gave way at once and, sent to flight, were pursued down the hill and through the sangers by Flatt and his men. Flatt personally led the charge down the hill and proceeded to attack them himself with the bayonet until he was wounded after a grenade exploded near him and he was knocked unconscious. When he recovered consciousness, he returned under heavy fire to give information about Captain Berney's situation. Lieutenant G.H. Dean, acting on the orders of Captain Flatt, led a portion of the company round the side of Zeiphy Hill and by vigorous attack drove off the Turks. He subsequently joined Serjeant Bloomfield who was supervising the machine guns and inflicted considerable casualties upon the enemy. After Captain Flatt was wounded Serjeant Hector Wilson led the remainder of the men up over the top of the hill and forced the few remaining Turks to beat a hurried retreat. Captain Flatt concluded his report on the action with a single sentence: '*Work, while clearing the trenches, was sharp and bloody*.'

The 1/4th Norfolks, however, had also suffered heavily. Captain Tom Jennings and Second Lieutenant Alfred Wood were killed, along with 12 other ranks and the heroic Captain Flatt, along with Captain Norman Smith (medical officer attached from 2nd East Anglian Field Ambulance), and Second Lieutenant William Gowing were all wounded (the latter two died of their wounds). Thirty-six other ranks were also wounded, five of them also died later and one man was reported wounded and missing. Special commendations for gallant conduct in the command of the situation on the hill were recorded to Captain Sir Thomas Berney and to Captain Walter Wortley Flatt for their dogged pursuit of the enemy, for which they were each awarded the Military Cross.

Captain Berney was also keen to mention in his report the good example and steadiness of Second Lieutenant Giles. Serjeant McCabe, the only senior NCO left in C Company, who took over duties of company serjeant major in the heat of the attack, was also praised for his good example and steadiness, as was Serjeant Jarvis and Corporal Reginald Addy, who had shown bravery in his patrol work and carried out the duties of platoon commander after his officer was wounded; he was awarded a Military Medal.

Special mention was also recorded of the Lewis machine gunners, Corporal Leonard Bindley, kept his gun and team under control and went back under heavy shell fire to company HQ to report the situation. The report of the action in the 1/4th Norfolks War Diary states:

His disregard for his own safety in the performance of his duties and his skilful handling of the Lewis Gun, prove him to be an NCO of exceptional value. Lance Corporal Edward Painter, Private Francis Merryweather for their gallantry and devotion to duty on the day, not forgetting Private Arthur McNaughton who operated his Lewis gun until he was the only man left. When his gun became damaged, he went along the trench under fire some sixty yards to get another gun which he bought back and continued to fire until he was hit three times.

Corporal Bindley and Private McNaughton were both awarded the Military Medal for bravery in the field.

On 15 December 1917 the Norfolk battalions attacked Stone Heap Hill. The 1/4th Norfolks was to lead with A and C companies under Captains Henry Back and Bernard King, with the 1/5th Norfolks under Major William Campbell (attached from the Suffolk Regiment) in support. The attack began at 8am, the start point was a cactus garden about 1,600 yards to the south-west of the hill. The left of the battalion was directed on the spur, the centre and right extending across the valley of a water course. At once they encountered machine-gun fire from Stone Heap Hill and Sanger's Hill on their right flank. Hurrying across the open space in front of them they reached their objective almost at a charge. The support companies swung round the saddle of the hill to take out the enemy firing onto the right flank, and effectively cleared the area as the 1/5th Suffolks silenced the guns on Sanger's Hill. The enemy was dislodged and driven northwards.

Consolidating their gains, the Norfolk battalions received orders in the afternoon to storm a further small hill about 700 yards from Stone Heap Hill, overlooking Et Tireh village. For this purpose, two fresh companies from the 1/5th Norfolks under Lieutenant Buckley were sent up from brigade reserve. Despite fire from three sides, the advance was covered by an effective barrage and they held their ground until evening. This battle had, however, proved to be another costly one for the 1/4th Norfolks with the deaths of Second Lieutenant Barnabas 'Barney' Davenport (attached from the Royal Warwickshire Regiment) and 11 other ranks. Lieutenants Sydney Knowles and Cecil Hole (also attached from the Royal Warwicks) were wounded along with 65 other ranks out of the 6 officers and 219 other ranks engaged in the attack. The 1/5th Norfolks also sustained 2 killed and 8 wounded.

Captain Bernard King was specially commended for his leadership during the attack, Serjeant Stephen Beal was also mentioned for single-handedly capturing an enemy machine gun; he was also praised for his courage in attending to his wounded men under fire. Particularly brave conduct during the combat was also noted from Lance Serjeant George Wardropper and Privates Bates and King. Private Frank Andrews saw a number of his comrades lying wounded in the open and, despite high explosive shells and shrapnel continuing to fall and rifle fire, he went out, applied dressings and carried them 150-200 yards to a less exposed place. In one instance he carried a man from B Company on his back for 200 yards. Several lads owed their lives to Private Andrews that day. The two companies of the 1/5th Norfolks also suffered 2 other ranks killed and 7 wounded in the attack.

The 1/4th Norfolks were relieved on Stone Heap Hill on 16 December and returned to bivouac at Deir Turief, then on to man Olive Tree Post and Fork Post at Yehudiyeh, which were shelled on 21 and 22 December. Fortunately, only one soldier was wounded. The 1/4th Norfolks were withdrawn from the front line on 23 December and were able to spend Christmas Eve on fatigues and managed to have a small celebration of Christmas Day near Kefr'Ana and, as the War Diary states, *'No work was done.'* However, they got to exercise it off with company route marches on Boxing Day.

Meanwhile the 1/5th Norfolks had been sent to man lines at Wadi Kereikak where general trench routine and repairs were the regular order of the day. On 22 December Lieutenant Colonel Dayrell relinquished command of the 1/5th Norfolks and command was taken over by Major William Campbell from the Suffolk Regiment. The battalion was then withdrawn from the line and moved into billets at Wilhelma on 23 December. There the battalion was reorganised and they celebrated Christmas.

The opening months of 1918 were spent by the battalions in Palestine. It began wet and it rained so hard that drainage operations had to be carried out, but general training carried on. On 25 January Major Campbell left the 1/5th Norfolks to join the 1/5th King's Own Scottish Borderers and Major Charles Worsley Vincent, 1/8th Hants, assumed command on joining for duty on 21 January. February began so wet that training was impeded and sometimes proved impossible. When the rains subsided training continued again from 8 February and as the weather picked up divisional football and brigade sports competitions were held. The latter was more fun-orientated with such competitions as wrestling on mules, a donkey race and even a Gretna Green race. After less than a month in command Major Vincent rejoined his unit on 13 February and Major L. Sinclair Thomson, Suffolk Regiment, assumed command of the 1/5th and remained in post for the rest of the war.

The battalion returned to front line service relieving the 1/11th Londons at posts in the Jiljulieh, a few miles north of Jericho on 16 February. The 1/4th Norfolks returned the same day and relieved the 1/5th Suffolks at Ras El Ain and El Mirr. It was a quiet time, more for training than fighting; there were inter-battalion sports, a concert by the divisional band one evening and some officers and men had home leave to the UK, others used their leave to explore some of the Holy Land.

However, an effusive letter about one such leave trip and the life being enjoyed by a certain soldier of the Norfolks attached to the staff on the Palestine front was published in the *Yarmouth Mercury* in April 1918. In response 'a few bloaters' (the affectionate name for lads from Great Yarmouth, named so after the cured herring the town was

54th (East Anglian) Division Christmas card celebrating the capture of Jerusalem, December 1917.

famed for), from the 1/5th Norfolks wrote a reply that certainly showed they were not all enjoying the 'land of milk and honey'. It gives an authentic insight into the lives of our soldiers during the opening months of 1918:

In the letter referred to above you are told that each man daily received 1lb. bread, plenty of fresh meat, jam, rice and fresh fruit in season. Well, we don't. We get twelve ounces of bread and 1 biscuit a day a week, and fresh meat, I suppose he means bully beef, or perhaps he refers to the rokies we get in the stew, and plenty of jam, that's 1lb. tin between 6 or 7 men; fresh fruit, that's 1 lime or 2 spotted apples a man every other day, or 1lb. tin of fruit between 10 men. Sometimes we get so much it is impossible to dish out, so they have to toss up to see who shall take the lot...

The boys here do one hour's tent sentry every night, up at 3.30, fall in at 4.30, march two miles, start digging and arrive home again about 8.30, sometimes later, covered in dust and slightly wet with perspiration. It's true they have the rest of the day off, till 5.30 and then bathing parade, but what rest can you get during the day? Just imagine being tormented with flies, ants and other insects and trying to get to sleep in a temperature of 112 degrees (in the tents) dripping wet with perspiration. He tells you he enjoys his walks over the hills. Well, if he had done the training climbing the hills and making attacks in marching order, I suppose he would have been dead by now....

You start a long march and during the march your throat gets clogged up with dust, you are wet through with perspiration, lips and mouth parched, and a full water bottle on your pack, not daring to drink too much in case you can't get any at the next stopping place...The last operation we took part in was in April. We marched eight miles the first day, resting till night-time in the sun. We got into our one and only blanket to rest, but we awakened about 11.00pm to find it raining in torrents and our beds swimming in water. Then about 3.00am, still raining a little, we marched off for 17 miles in shirt sleeves, again resting in the sun for the remainder of the day, getting into our wet blankets for the night. Up again at 3.00am and march off for another 17 miles, and this time stopping three days or so, and no tents. Then we marched back in two days, doing about 20 miles each day and here we are, all merry and bright, and still smiling...PS – We have no complaints as regards to rations or work, because we are still alive and we consider we're laughing.

The men knew there would still be at least one more battle to conclude the campaign. In April, practice attacks were carried out along with company and battalion training. The 1/4th and 1/5th Norfolks trained, while in the Fejja area the 1/5th Norfolks served on outpost duty with 1/4th Norfolks at Warley Wood and 1/5th Norfolks at Cats House mid-month and then on to Orange Post from late April. A special memorial service for those who fell in action at the Second Battle of Gaza was held by the Norfolk Territorial battalions on the anniversary, 19 April.

In May 1918 some of the companies took part in a tactical exercise with the 54th Division Platoon Leaders School, but other than the usual round of manning trenches and reinforcing trenches there were some periods of rest. An evening of entertainment provided by the 2/1st East Anglian Field Ambulance concert party on 13 May offered a welcome respite from the daily routine.

On 23 May the 1/5th Norfolks moved to lines at Mejdel Yaba. Shortly after midnight on 29/30 May an enemy patrol approached posts held by A Company, 1/5th Norfolks, under Captain William James. They were sent packing by a swift retort of rifles and Stokes mortar fire and one of their number was captured. A second patrol tried a second attack and they were also given short shrift and withdrew. Such was life into June, with occasional enemy patrols being effectively dealt with by rifle fire and artillery and men of the Norfolk Territorial battalions patrolling in their own right.

On the night of 8/9 June 1918 Captain Jewson MC led C and D companies of the 1/4th Norfolks on a raid up Bureid Ridge and returned without loss. Encouraged by this, a 'driving raid' on Kayak Tepe led by A Company 1/4th Norfolks under Captain Stanley Steel and Second Lieutenants Andrew Camilleri and Raymond Funnell set out on the night of 18/19 June. Although the enemy look out whistles rang out from the hill and warned all that the attacking force had been spotted, the men of the Norfolks carried on, but Lieutenant Camilleri was wounded early in the advance when they met heavy machine-gun fire. Onwards they pressed and the 1/4th Norfolks took the first lot of enemy sangars in fierce hand-to-hand fighting where Lance Corporal Duke claimed five enemy by his bayonet alone. Turning right against the next sangar, A Company were faced with barbed wire. A number of men drew their cutters but only Serjeant Jobson succeeded in cutting a gap. Now the men were under heavy fire from machine guns on Jervis Tepe and from a party of enemy who had deployed to the rear by Wadi Rabah. Captain Steel was killed outright and soon only one officer, Second Lieutenant Funnell, remained unwounded and made the decision that the men would simply be mown down as they tried to cut the wire so ordered the move down Kayak Tepe and ordered covering artillery fire. Company Serjeant Major Charlie Covell and a small party formed the rear guard and Serjeant Frederick Rickwood MM did sterling work recovering the wounded, succeeding in bringing in all but two.

On 27 June 1918 the Norfolk battalions were moved to the rail head at Ludd under orders to entrain for Kantara. The intention had been to withdraw 54th Division from Palestine to send them to France. This was cancelled at the last moment and they were turned back to the lines at Surafend. A short period in support followed and then the 1/4th Norfolks were sent to Jaffa where two weeks rest and recuperation by the sea was a very much appreciated respite for the troops.

August opened with the brigade horse and hound show followed by continuous training, for the rest of the month each battalion was given brigade and battalion schemes of attack with orders attached.

General Allenby began his final advance on 19 September 1918. It was impressed upon all battalions in 163 Brigade that rapid movement and adherence to clearly delineated objects were essential if the operation was to be successful. Commanding officers were expected to take risks in following up the general line of the advance. The front of the Corps would, after a general wheel, be on a north-south line from Wadi Deir Ballut to the Tul Keram–Messudeih road.

At 2am on 19 September the 5th Norfolks (less C Company) and 1/8th Hants (to whom C Company had been attached in support) were to head the attack with the 1/4th Norfolks and 1/5th Suffolks behind. As the men set off, the enemy barrage passed over them, killing about twelve men (half of them claimed by one shell). As the battalion moved Captain Cyril Walker, the adjutant, was wounded. When a pause in the barrage occurred, the men were able to stop, take some food and drink and bring up the machine guns. At 11.45am the brigade was ordered to take the high ground at Kh. Sirisia. Captain James led the attack with A Company and two platoons from D and they were soon engaged with about fifty enemy on a hill; meanwhile Second Lieutenant

Lovell pushed forward with his Lewis gunner to the ridge in an attempt to keep down the enemy fire. Working his way around the hill, Lovell eventually occupied it and, discovering Captain James wounded, found himself in command of the company, which he decisively brought up by the wadi on to the ridge and the enemy retreated.

The advance now moved eastward and continued until stopped by darkness. The men were badly fatigued and thirsty, but Mesha was occupied before the dawn by B and half of D companies under Captain Blyth, a location they held until relief by C company (who had been refreshed after receiving a supply of water) on 20 September and thus ended the last major engagement of the Norfolk Territorial battalions in the Great War. Second Lieutenant J.G. Lovell (attached to the 1/5th Norfolks from the Northampton Regiment) was awarded the Military Cross and Military Medals were awarded to three men from the two companies that valiantly occupied Mesha, namely Privates Alfred Gay and Albert Hart of D Company, and Private Edward Arbon of B Company, 1/5th Norfolks.

The general advance had proved a great success, the right flank of the Turkish Army was penetrated and the enemy soon collapsed and many prisoners were captured. In this victory the 54th Division captured Kefr Kasim. A long march now followed through Palestine, keeping to the coastal plain the whole way north, until Haifa was reached. After a brief rest, the march resumed through Syria, via Tyre, Sidon, Athlit and Beirut, which was reached on 1 November 1918. After taking part in a triumphal march through the city past Lieutenant General Sir Edward Bulfin, Commanding XXI Corps, the

Men of 1/4th Battalion halt by the roadside during the advance to Beirut, 1918.

division continued its march to Junieh, about 20 miles to the north where the battalions made camp at Minas. Here they received the welcome news of the Armistice and they returned to Beirut where a camp was pitched in pine woods near the city. In one last act of recognition, Major General Hare, commanding 54th Division presented medal ribbons at a parade of 163 Brigade on 22 November.

Four days later, on 28 November 1918, the Norfolk Territorials boarded HM Transports *Ellenga* and *Hunslet* in Beirut harbour. On 29 November they arrived at Port Said and on 30 November at Kantara with 23 officers and 584 other ranks in the 1/4th Norfolks and 30 officers and 461 other ranks in the 1/5th Norfolks. From here the Territorial battalions were returned to Egypt and the demobilization camp at Helmieh, near Cairo, where they were tasked with erecting a new camp for reinforcements at Luna Park. On 17 November it was a Thanksgiving Day for Victory and a general holiday and the celebrations did not end there. On 20 December the Norfolk Territorial battalions, along with the rest of 54th Division, marched through Old Cairo and past the EEF Commander-in-Chief General Allenby, in Opera House Square. The streets were strung with bunting, the bands played and the men stepped out, heads up and shoulders back. It was a fitting end to the active service for all the regiments, even though some Egyptians seemed to think the British forces had been driven back out of Palestine.

Most of the men of the Norfolk Territorial Battalions were not released for demobilization until early January so they had one last Christmas in Egypt. The 1/4th Norfolks enjoyed games and a good Christmas dinner but the 1/5th Norfolks ended up having to celebrate on Boxing Day because they were on divisional duties on 25 December. Lieutenant Colonel Harvey, 1/4th Norfolks, was to recall his bitter disappointment that he had not been allowed to rejoin his battalion on active service again on account of his age and that his battalion never returned home as a unit.

Drums and A Company 1/4th Battalion, marching past General Allenby, Cairo 20 December 1918.

One of the platoons from the Norfolk Territorial Battalion, Cairo 1918. The overseas service chevrons and wound stripes on the forearms of many of these men tell their own story.

The 1/5th Norfolks did not return as a battalion either, but rather they were gradually drafted away and the men returned home piecemeal during demobilization. The only remnant to return to Britannia Barracks was a cadre of six men under the command of Captain Frederick Hooker on 7 November 1919.

The last soldiers to be decorated with the Distinguished Conduct Medal in the Norfolk Regiment Territorial Force battalions were true stalwarts. For the 1/4th Norfolks, it was Regimental Quartermaster Serjeant W. Bale of Diss who had served in the battalion since 1915, through Gallipoli, Egypt, Syria and Palestine. His citation, published in the *London Gazette* of 11 March 1920, states: '*He has always shown courage and determination in bringing up the battalion's rations and water up to the front line under heavy fire. By his energy and sense of duty he has earned the respect and confidence of all ranks.*'

For the 1/5th Norfolks, it was Serjeant William Grigglestone of Gorleston who was recognised for both his bravery in service and a particular action, his citation states: '*He has always acted with conspicuous courage in action. During the operations on 19 September 1918, near Mesha, he led his platoon with great skill and disregard of personal danger and by his initiative turned a flank of a machine gun post that was threatening to hold up the advance of the enemy.*' (*London Gazette 2 March 1920*). Grigglestone went on to spend a lifetime in the Norfolk Regiment, saw it made the Royal Norfolk Regiment in 1935 and was still serving as 1 Royal Norfolk Regimental Serjeant Major in the Second World War when he was known to the men as simply 'Old Griggo'. His total years with the regiment spanned 1911-1944.

Chapter 9

Reserve Battalions

'And when they're trained and ready
For the front and they embark
You will hear the people shout
There's the lads from Halton Park'

Anon

The 2/4th Battalion, The Norfolk Regiment (T.F.)

In August 1914 orders were issued to County Territorial Force Associations by Lord Kitchener, the Secretary of State for War, to maintain the Territorial Force at Home Stations at the full strength of its establishment, by raising new units to replace the Territorial units which volunteered for general service with the expeditionary forces. The role of the new units was:

1. To supply drafts for overseas units
2. To continue recruiting up to the establishment for home defence, the personnel being enlisted under two classifications viz: for general service overseas, and for home defence only.

The 4th Battalion (Reserve) (later known as 2/4th Battalion), The Norfolk Regiment (TF) was raised in September 1914 by Major Edward Mornement TD, who was promoted to lieutenant colonel in October 1914 to command the unit. Headquarters were at their 'parent' battalion HQ at the Drill Hall on Chapelfield. The unit chiefly recruited from south and east Norfolk and Norwich. With all other available barracks and suitable temporary barracks filled with first line troops, the men of 4th Norfolk Reserve were billeted in the homes of the inhabitants of the city, the householder being paid a subsidy of 2s 6d per soldier.

In those early months the ranks of the battalion were swelled to over 700 rank and file, mostly ex-servicemen enlisted from the National Reserve and ex-Militia men posted to the 4th Norfolk Reserve. This battalion was the first of the Norfolk Reserve Battalions to complete its establishment and moved to divisional HQ at Peterborough in November 1914.

In January 1915 the battalion was moved to Lowestoft under orders to co-operate with OC Naval Base (Captain A.A. Ellison). Although the battalion had been referred to as the 2/4th, it was only fully and formally retitled 2/4th Battalion, The Norfolk

Volunteers for 4th Battalion recruited from the Attleborough area, September 1914.

Regiment (TF) at this time. Under direction of loaned naval petty officer gunners, every man in the 2/4th Norfolks was trained to a high degree of proficiency on the 12-pounder naval field guns and naval machine guns as part of their defence work in the port. The battalion also provided personnel to man the naval searchlights and serve on the No.2 Armoured Train.

New recruits for the 4th Battalion Reserve leaving Thorpe Station, Norwich for Peterborough, 1914.

Parade of 2/4th and 2/5th battalions in the Market Place, Peterborough, 1914.

In July 1915 the battalion was divided into:

(A) General Service (G.S.) category
(B) Home Service of lower medical categories

The GS category retained the title of the 2/4th Norfolks and moved to Bury St Edmunds, while the lower grade men remained to form the 61st Provisional Battalion (TF) and continued to garrison Lowestoft, later moving to coastal defence duties in sectors along the Suffolk coast. In November 1916 the 61st Provisional Battalion was renamed the 11th Battalion, Norfolk Regiment (TF) and transferred to Guildford in December 1916. They moved to Colchester in March 1917 and disbanded the following December.

From Bury the 2/4th Norfolks moved to Harrogate in July 1916; moves to and from Doncaster via Thoresby over the ensuing months until March 1917 saw the 2/4th Norfolks relocated again, this time to occupy Sobraon and Meanee barracks respectively in Colchester. The remaining A1 and B1 category men were transferred to overseas units. Those who remained in the battalion were low grade fitness, many of them ex-wounded and sick soldiers. The absence of able-bodied men saw the battalion's function as a training reserve battalion cease and it was finally disbanded by order of the Army Council in July 1917 and remaining personnel sent to 4 (Reserve) Battalion.

The 2/5th Battalion, The Norfolk Regiment (TF)
Under the expansion scheme of the Territorial Force a reserve battalion of 5th Norfolks was raised in East Dereham at the HQ of the 1/5th Norfolks in October 1914. Captain

The 1916 draft for the front from C Company, 2/4th Battalion, Killinghall Camp, Harrogate, Yorkshire.

Woodwark was appointed OC Depot and was given two junior officers, second lieutenants St George and R.G. Cubitt to assist him. Major H. Ellis Rowell was gazetted lieutenant colonel with command of the new 2/5th Norfolks.

Although most had no real uniforms, just printed arm bands, no rifles or equipment, their zeal in drill, exercise and training were remarkable and their fine, uniformed band under Bandmaster Dines was a great asset. But the uniform situation for the men became critical to the development of the unit. Sir Aylwin Fellowes, the chairman of the Norfolk Territorial Force Association, visited the HQ and upon seeing for himself gave leave for the OC to buy boots and what uniform could be procured for the troops – and the association would pay the bills. The only khaki uniform and most of the greatcoats which could be procured were second-hand and even with this in hand, when the battalion was ordered to proceed to Peterborough on 5 December 1914 a number of men still had to march with their comrades wearing their civvy coats and caps.

Lieutenant Colonel Herbert Ellis Rowell, Commanding Officer, 5th Battalion Reserve, later retitled 2/5th Battalion.

New recruits for 5th Battalion Reserve in East Dereham Market Place, October 1914. Supplies were running low and many men were awaiting parts of their uniforms to arrive.

Issuing caps to the men of the 5th Battalion Reserve in front of Battalion Headquarters, Quebec Street, East Dereham 1914.

'Lynn Athletic' Football team 2/5th Battalion, Peterborough, February 1915.

In early January 1915 a fully-uniformed recruiting march was staged across the principal towns of Norfolk by the band and a hand-picked cadre of men under two or three officers and NCOs. The result was a fine body of recruits that brought the battalion up to strength and organised into four strong companies under Captains T.B. Hall, G.J. Bracey, H. Smith and Hubert Durrant.

The battalion was quartered in Peterborough until May 1915 when it proceeded to Cambridge. Major Woodwark, the adjutant, left to take over command the 2/4th Norfolks and Captain Geoffrey John Bracey became adjutant in his stead. The men of the 2/5th Norfolks marched to Bury St Edmunds in late July 1915 and after five days there moved to camp at Thetford. In August 1915 the battalion moved to undertake trench construction for the defence of London scheme at Brentwood in Essex. While in Brentwood, second lieutenants Hordle, Herbert W. St George, C.E. Durrant, Cecil Rowell, Douglas Hervey, Arthur Blyth, Geoffrey Shakespeare, Noel Hemsworth, A. Leslie Shutes, Robert Partridge, Kenelin Lyall and Richard Plaistowe were the first junior officers to leave the 2/5th Norfolks for Gallipoli where they took the place of the officers of the 1/5th Norfolks lost in the action of 12 August.

By winter the remainder of the 2/5th Norfolks had returned to Bury and were eventually absorbed into the 2/4th Norfolks and a small cadre of 2/5th Norfolks maintained their home defence role until the winter of 1917.

3/4th and 3/5th Battalions, The Norfolk Regiment (T.F.)

Formed in early 1915 at Norwich and East Dereham respectively, the Dereham battalions were raised under the command of Colonel George Francis Addison Cresswell CVO VD.

Officers and senior NCOs of 3/5th Battalion at Halton Park 1916. Many of these men would soon be in Egypt and would proceed with 1/5th Battalion into Palestine in 1917.

'Holyboys 1/5th Norfolks back from Suvla Bay' returned sick or wounded from Gallipoli recovered and with 3/5th Battalion at Halton Park, 1916.

'The Old ANZACs' returned soldiers of $1/5^{th}$ Battalion with the $3/5^{th}$ Battalion at Halton Park Camp, 1916. Some of them are already wearing their Wolseley helmets in anticipation of a return to their battalion.

Both battalions were quartered in their 'home' depot city and town until August 1915 when they were moved to Windsor Great Park. In the first week of October 1915 they moved again to Halton Camp near Tring in Hertfordshire; from there both battalions sent out many drafts to the $1/4^{th}$ and $1/5^{th}$ Norfolks in the Middle East. It was also to the $3/4^{th}$ and $3/5^{th}$ Norfolks that many of the men who had been evacuated home from Gallipoli reported, ready to join the next batch of reinforcements for their old battalions.

In February 1916 Colonel Fletcher took over command and the battalions were formally designated the $3/4^{th}$ and $3/5^{th}$ (Reserve) Battalions. On 1 September 1916 the $3/4^{th}$ Norfolks absorbed $3/5^{th}$ Norfolks and joined the East Anglian Reserve Brigade. By November 1917 the battalion was at Crowborough, Sussex and saw out the final months of the war in Hastings.

Chapter 10

Legends and the Truth: What Happened to the Men Who Fell on 12 August 1915?

'I lived for war and by war. War was my life.'
Sir Ian Hamilton (1853-1947)

In the immediate aftermath of the attack of 12 August 1915, 163 brigade commander, Brigadier Capel Brunker was returned to the UK. Officially he was not removed from command, although some officers believed this was the case. Lieutenant Colonel Harvey of the 1/4th Norfolks noted Brunker was evacuated to England at the close of the fighting in a state of collapse.

The problems had begun when IX Corps Commander, Lieutenant General Stopford, had failed to capitalise on the element of surprise achieved by the successful landings of his troops back on 6 August. He did not push his troops on to take the hills beyond the beaches and through his procrastination gave the Turkish commanders the time they needed to deploy thousands of reinforcements to the area. When the advances were finally ordered they failed in the face of vastly superior numbers of enemy troops. Stopford, however, did not hesitate to blame the 53rd Division for the failure of the attack on Scimitar Hill on 10 August. The root of the problem, he believed, was that they (and 54th Division) were made up of battalions of Territorial Force soldiers. In his *Gallipoli Diary* (Vol. II) General Hamilton wrote of the communication he received from Stopford on 11 August:

> *At 4.30 p.m., a letter from Stopford anent the failure of the 53rd Division—depressing in itself, but still more so in its inferences as to the 54th Division. He says these troops showed 'no attacking spirit at all. They did not come under heavy shell fire nor was the rifle fire very severe, but they not only showed no dash in attack but went back at slight provocation and went back a long way. Lots of the men lay down behind cover, etc. They went on when called upon to do so by Staff and other Officers, but they seemed lost and under no leadership—in fact, they showed that they are not fit to put in the field without the help of Regulars...'*

Hamilton also recorded that Stopford said of 54th Division:

> *I am sure they would not secure the hills with any amount of guns, water and ammunition assuming ordinary opposition, as the attacking spirit was absent; chiefly*

> *owing to the want of leadership by the Officers. Ignoring our Kavak Tepe scheme, he goes on then to ask me in so many words, not to try any attack with the 54th Division but to stick them into trenches.*

Stopford went on to describe the 53rd and 54th Divisions as *'sucked oranges, the good in them having been drafted away into France and replaced by rejections'*. General Hamilton was not impressed, especially as such comments were coming from a man he had to apply pressure upon to act on more than one occasion, a man who was insulting experienced and capable officers Hamilton trusted and knew of old. Hamilton was also under pressure from Kitchener, who had expressed his concerns about the slow progress of the operations. Hamilton wanted to press on with the offensive. Stopford pointed out Anafarta Ova was riddled with snipers who could impinge on the success of the operation and Hamilton agreed to a drive to flush out the snipers on 12 August to clear the way for an attack on 13 August. The 53rd Division had been badly cut up, so Major General Inglefield offered 163 Brigade of 54th Division for the task.

Hamilton despatched his chief of staff, Major General Walter Braithwaite, to Suvla on 12 August to discuss the planned advances and was empowered to cancel them if necessary. Stopford explained to Braithwaite that the logistics of supporting a break-out from Suvla to the hills at that time would have been beset with difficulties and they agreed to cancel the advance on 13 August, regardless of the outcome of the attack that afternoon. Hamilton could not stomach Stopford any longer, he wrote in his diary: *'Ought I have resigned sooner than allow generals old and inexperienced to be foisted upon me.'* He telegraphed Kitchener stating the IX Corps generals were 'unfit' for command and Stopford was dismissed by Hamilton on 15 August.

Stopford was condemned in the press for his vacillation of purpose during the campaign. At the Gallipoli Enquiry he was criticised for failing to keep abreast of developments ashore and for not being more proactive in getting his troops moving, but the rebuke was mild and he was defended from other criticisms that had been levelled against him by Hamilton. However, neither Stopford nor Brunker were given a field command again. Historians often debate the 'what ifs' and 'buts' of Gallipoli, but they all agree that Stopford should not have been given a field command of fighting troops in the first place.

After the action of 12 August 1915 most of the dead of the 1/5th Norfolks, and indeed the other battalions in the attack, lay on ground defended and held by Turkish forces that would not be taken and held again for such a period that the bodies could be searched for and recovered during the Gallipoli campaign. Neither British authorities nor Graves Registration Units would be able to gain access to the ground until after the end of the war. It was also proving very slow and problematic for the International Committee of the Red Cross Prisoners of War Agency, and even for diplomatic channels, to find out if men had been killed or taken prisoner during the campaign.

After initial checks had been carried out among the British wounded or through diplomatic channels with Turkish authorities in the immediate aftermath of the attack of 12 August, the families of those who were unaccounted for were simply notified by telegram or letter dated around 21 August that their loved one was 'Missing'.

HM King George V in the uniform of a Field Marshal, 1914.

The impact on families and local communities was profound. All along the coast of Norfolk and just inland, from King's Lynn to Great Yarmouth, everyone seemed to know someone who was lost, be they a family member, friend or neighbour. One of the sharpest losses was felt in Dersingham, a village with a population of 1,450 people where 217 local men had gone to serve their king and country. A number of the Dersingham lads, all of whom had been members of the Sandringham Company, were posted missing after the action of 12 August 1915; five of them would subsequently be declared dead. Around 25-27 August the first of the wounded from the action who had been evacuated from the peninsula were brought back by hospital ships to a variety of hospitals for treatment and convalescence around Britain. Then letters started coming home speaking of the costly action and the questions of what had happened to loved ones posed to official channels quickly gathered momentum, not least on the Sandringham Estate.

On 1 September 1915 King George V sent a telegram to Sir Ian Hamilton, General Officer Commanding the Mediterranean Expeditionary Force: *'I am most anxious to be informed as to the fate of men of 5th Battalion Norfolk Regiment as they include the Sandringham Company and my agent Captain Frank Beck.'*

General Hamilton replied by telegram the same day:

> *I greatly regret to inform your Majesty that up to the present I have no news of the fate of the men of the 5th Norfolk Regiment beyond the fact that 14 officers and about 250 men are missing, including Sir H. Beauchamp the Commanding Officer and Captain F.R. Beck and Lieut. A.E.A. Beck. General Inglefield reported to me personally that the Battalion and their leader were filled with ardour and dash and on coming into contact with the enemy, pressed ahead of rest of brigade into close broken country when he entirely lost touch of them and at the time he could not tell me anything more. I have called for further information and will on receipt wire your Majesty at once.*

On 2 September 1915 King George V sent a telegram from Windsor Castle to Frank Beck's brother Arthur in the estate office at Sandringham:

> *I telegraphed to Sir Ian Hamilton for news of your brother and the Sandringham Company. In reply he says he is unable to ascertain any particulars except that their*

Brigadier reported that the battalion and its leader on coming into contact with the enemy keenly dashed forward ahead of the Brigade into difficult country and entirely lost touch with the General. Further enquiries are being made on receipt of which I will at once let you know. I heartily sympathise with all the families who are left in suspense, but I am proud that the battalion has fought so splendidly.

George R.I.

Hamilton followed up asking the 54th Division Commander, General Inglefield, to investigate, but little solid information as to the fate of the men of the 1/5th Norfolks could be ascertained at that time. Hamilton had known Inglefield during the South African War when he was brigade major and assistant adjutant general to General Smith-Dorrien. He trusted him, considered him a '*good straight fellow*' and even after the failure of the attack had recorded in his diary on 13 August: *'Inglefield was a practised old warrior, and would not let him down.'* Of the 54th Division, he wrote '*taking these Territorials as they are; a scratch lot; half strength; no artillery; not a patch upon the original Divisions as I inspected them in England six months ago; even so, they'd fight right enough and keen enough if they were set fair and square at their fence.*' Inglefield had commanded the 54th Division since June 1913, knew the calibre of the officers and men of the 1/5th Norfolks and he rightly defended them to the hilt. It is also worthy of note he was retained as commander of 54th Division until April 1916.

His reply to Hamilton was written on 3 September 1915:

On 12 August, the 163rd Infantry Brigade was ordered at short notice to clear the village of Anafarta Ova of Turks who were reported not to be in strength. The movement was to be completed by dusk and was preparatory to a forward movement of the whole Division on the following morning.

The Brigade moved off in the afternoon from a position distant about 2 miles from Anafarta Ova, the 5th Norfolk Regiment being on the right. The opposition was much stronger than expected but it was apparent at the outset that the 5th Norfolk Regiment was not, at any rate at first, so strongly opposed as the other battalions of the Brigade and there is little doubt it lost touch before long and, pressing forward over broken country where communication was difficult, soon became separated from the Battalion on its alert.

What happened after that is not known and no information is forth-coming from the present Battalion Commander.

The Battalion had only been one or two days on shore and as the weather was very hot and the advance rapid the men suffered considerably from a craving thirst, caused by the dryness of the atmosphere in this climate. As a result, exhaustion soon set in and later this exhaustion became acute.

The weaker men fell back or failed to keep up with those in front and many of these found their way back to their former camp in the night or on the following day.

They, however, knew nothing of what happened to the rest of their Battalion and even now the Battalion Commander can give no information as to the advance of the firing line after it had covered a distance of about half a mile.

This I regret is all the information I can give.

16 Officers and some 250 men have disappeared and the present Battalion Commander, Major Barton, assures me that no information as to any of these can be obtained.

I deeply deplore the loss the regiment has sustained.

I feel however absolute confidence that Col. Sir H. Beauchamp and those with him bore themselves gallantly, whatever may have been their trials in their endeavours to accomplish the task assigned them.

General Inglefield

Despite genuine attempts at finding an answer the situation remained unclear. Enquiries poured into the Norfolk Territorial Force Association, Mayors were approached by their townsfolk and concerns were expressed by families from across the social strata of the county to those in authority as they sought to find out what had happened to their loved ones. On 28 September 1915 the issue was formally raised as a question in the House of Commons. Sir Robert Price, MP for East Norfolk, asked Harold Tennant the Under Secretary of State for War whether he had any further information about the number of men of the 1/5th Norfolks missing since 12 August and whether it was now possible to state whether any and which of them are prisoners of war?

The Under Secretary replied:

Of about 200 men reported missing, up to date only seven have been reported to the War Office as prisoners of war. It is possible that some of the others who are recorded as missing may be in direct communication with their relatives but I cannot give any figure for these men. Every effort has been made to obtain from the Turkish Government full lists of the prisoners of war in their hands but so far these efforts have not been successful.

General Hamilton himself was recalled to London on 15 October. He was replaced by Lieutenant General Sir Charles Monro and plans for an evacuation began soon afterwards. The last British troops left the peninsula on 8 January 1916. Hamilton was undoubtedly a brave old soldier, but his tactics and overall strategy were also from an older age of soldiering. He was never offered another field command.

Sir Ian Hamilton's third Gallipoli despatch, dated 11 December 1915, was published in the *Supplement to the London Gazette* on 6 January 1916. Clearly the pressure for answers was still weighing upon him when he spoke of the attack on Anafarta:

The 54th Division (infantry only) arrived and were disembarked on August 11th and placed in reserve. On the following day – August 12th – I proposed that the 54th Division should make a night march in order to attack at dawn on the 13th, the heights Kavak Tepe – TekeTepe. The Corps Commander having reason to believe that the enclosed country about Kuchuk Anafarta Ova and the north of it was held by the enemy, ordered one brigade to move forward in advance and make good

Kuchuk Anafarta Ova, so as to ensure an unopposed march for the remainder of the division as far as that place. So that afternoon 163rd Brigade moved off, and, in spite of serious opposition, established itself about the A. of Anafarta (118m 4 and 7), in difficult and enclosed country.

In the course of the fight, creditable in all respects to the 163rd Brigade, there happened a very mysterious thing. The 1/5th Norfolks were on the right of the line, and found themselves for a moment less strongly opposed than the rest of the brigade. Against the yielding forces of the enemy Colonel Sir H. Beauchamp, a bold, self-confident officer, eagerly pressed forward, followed by the best part of his battalion. The fighting grew hotter, and the ground became more wooded and broken. At this stage many men were wounded or grew exhausted with thirst. These found their way back to camp during the night. But the Colonel, with sixteen officers and 250 men, still kept pushing on, driving the enemy before him. Amongst these ardent souls was part of a fine company enlisting from the King's Sandringham estates. Nothing more was ever seen or heard of any of them. They charged into the forest and were lost to sight or sound. Not one of them ever came back.

The combination of an entire company of men from the king's estate being involved in *'...a very mysterious thing'* instantly seduced the newsman's eye and stories of the 'disappearance' of the Sandringham Company hit the headlines from the day after. The story kept rolling as the king, during visits to hospitals, asked soldiers returned from Gallipoli if they had heard anything of the Sandringham Company and his agent Captain Frank Beck. One of them was 19-year-old Private William Arnold Doggett, 1/4th Norfolks, who was in a Leeds hospital having been evacuated from the peninsula after suffering shrapnel wounds. To His Majesty's enquiries he could only relate that he thought Captain Beck had probably been killed. It was clear the king had reluctantly come to the same conclusion, his face marked with sadness he agreed that Doggett was probably right. Doggett himself was killed at the Second Battle of Gaza in 1917.

In late October 1915 men of the 1st Newfoundland Regiment made it as far as the farm buildings of Anafarta. In his book *Trenching at Gallipoli* (1916), battalion member John Gallishaw wrote:

The block house we held stood just in the centre of the line that the Fifth Norfolks had charged into early in August and from which not one man had emerged. The second or third day we occupied it, a detachment of engineers was sent to make loopholes and prepare it for a stubborn defence. In the wall on the left they made a large loophole. The sentry posted there the first morning saw about twenty feet away the body of a British soldier, partly buried. Two volunteers to bury the body were asked for.

Half a dozen offered, although it was broad daylight and the place the body lay offered no protection. Before anyone could be selected, Art Pratt and young Hayes made the decision by jumping up, taking their picks and shovels and vaulting over the wall of the block house. They walked out to where the body lay. It had been torn in

The War Budget,
January 20th, 1916.

"The Mystery of the Norfolks"

The Norfolks belonged to the division which dashed up the heights of the Gallipoli Peninsula from Suvla Bay. The order was given that Anafarta must be taken by dusk. Headed by Capt. Frank Beck, His Majesty's estate agent at Sandringham, the men, most of them from the King's estates around Sandringham, "charged into the forest and were lost to sight and sound. Nothing more was ever heard or seen of any of them. . . . Not one of them ever came back." So runs Sir Ian Hamilton's report on their charge.

Artist's depiction of 'The Mystery of the Norfolks' published in The War Budget, *20 January 1916.*

pieces by a shell the previous afternoon. At first a few bullets tore up little spurts of ground near the two men but as soon as they reached the body, this stopped. The Turks never fired on burial parties... When the Turks saw the object of the little expedition, they allowed Art and Hayes to proceed unmolested. They watched them dig a grave beside the corpse and when they had finished, with a shovel they turned the body into it. Before doing it, they searched the man for personal papers and took off his identity disk. These bore the name 'Sergeant Golder, [sic] *Fifth Norfolk Regiment'.*

Serjeant John Lee Goulder, 1/5th Battalion (Aylsham), killed 12 August 1915.

The men of the 1st Newfoundland had, in fact, discovered the body of well-liked Aylsham Serjeant John Lee Goulder, 1/5th Norfolks. They erected a small cross over the grave bearing the inscription:

'IN MEMORY OF
SERGEANT J GOLDER
FIFTH NORFOLK REGIMENT
KILLED IN ACTION'

It is not clear if the family of Serjeant Goulder were ever informed of the discovery of his body or its burial. Tragically his two other brothers, Robert Christopher 'Dick' Goulder and Clare Horsley Goulder, died on the Somme the following year, both serving in the 8th Norfolks.

Other news of the action did reach home and, despite detailed and specific letters from NCOs and men of the 1/5th Norfolks who survived the action being published in local newspapers, the national press failed to pick up on them and the story of the 'disappearance' of the Sandringham Company became the stuff of legend.

For families left in the limbo of not knowing what had happened to their fathers, husbands, brothers or sons the pain was only too real. As weeks passed appeals appeared in the local press. Typical was this one which appeared in the *Yarmouth Mercury*:

Mrs Beck of 76, Bell's Marsh Road, Gorleston, some weeks ago received an official intimation from the War Office that her son Pte. L. Beck of the 5th Norfolks, D Company, has been reported missing since August 25th since which nothing more has been heard of him. Pte Beck left England with the M.E.F. on 29 July and was last heard of from the Dardanelles, and his mother is naturally anxious to know

THE GALLANT 5th NORFOLKS

65 OF THE YARMOUTH MEN IN THE DARDANELLES.

Lce-Cpl. A. Turby (missing). Lce-Cpl. H. F. Leggett (missing). Pte. A. Durrant (missing). Scout J. C. Bushell (missing). Pte. Reginald Blyth (missing).

Sergt. G. Cleveland (killed August 15th 1915). Pte. C. Milligan (in hospital). Pte. W. Groom (missing). Pte. S. Grice. Co.-Sergt. Maj. B. S. Parker (wounded).

Pte. Robert Denton, 4th Norfolks (wounded). Pte. Arthur Parker. Pte. Ernest G. Parker. Pte. Bert Reyner. Pte. Wm. Moss (invalided home).

Bugler P. Pearce (wounded). Sig. A. Hellenburgh (missing). Pte. C. Moseley. Corpl. G. Catchpole. Sergt. A. Rivett.

Pte. Thos. E. McSteen (wounded). Pte. Ernest Kerrison (wounded). Pte. Daniel C. Colby (died of wnds., Alexandria). Pte. T. H. Holmes (in hospital at Alexandria). Drmr. John Askwood (seriously ill).

Pte. H. G. Hacon (missing). Corpl. S. Bracey (missing). Pte. C. H. Westgate (missing). Pte. F. G. Beckett (missing). Pte. S. Bowles (missing).

Pte. Fred. C. Saville. Pte. Stanley Smith. Pte. W. Datey. Pte. V. C. Buckingham. Pte. Sidney Baker.

Pte. H. E. Darnell (wounded). Pte. F. R. Lykes (wounded). Pte. A. Rouse (killed August 25th 1915). Pte. G. A. Browne (wounded). Pte. T. Dodson (missing).

Pte. L. Fuller. Pte. A. Palmer. Pte. H. Allenbury. Pte. Layton. Pte. A. J. Marjoram.

Pte. W. J. Seaman. Pte. W. Kemp. Pte. M. Harbord. Pte. W. D. Jay. Scout W. Ellett (wounded). Lce.-Cpl. A. Howes.

Some of the 65 lads from Great Yarmouth and district killed, injured or posted missing after the attack on Anafarta Ova published in the Yarmouth Mercury *16 October 1915.*

> *what trouble has overtaken him. It is thought therefore some of his chums may see this in print and be able to write to Mrs. Beck giving some details of her son's movements up to the time of his disappearance.*

Some families received letters from those who had seen their comrades fall beside them. Some of these spoke of seeing them receive a 'mortal' wound, the worst was feared but their pal, although wounded, was in hospital. Sadly, these were very much the exception to the rule. The family of 19-year-old Joe Bentley, 1/5th Norfolks, received this letter from fellow B Company soldier, Corporal Donald Foster of King's Lynn:

> *You will no doubt have seen by the papers that our battalion has been in action, and unfortunately we have not come out of the ordeal without some casualties and it is with the greatest regret and sorrow that I have to tell you that Joe was killed. He at the time of fighting was side by side with Jack and a piece of shell hit him in the head. I cannot possibly describe my feelings as I give you this sad news, but trust that you will find room in your hearts to forgive me for breaking the news to you.*

Joe's body was never recovered, or if it was it was unidentified. Many families of the missing were hit with financial difficulties. Some even faced eviction as army pay was stopped and there would be no widow's pension until decisions were made by the authorities about the fate of their loved ones. It should be remembered that this was happening before the British Legion (formed 1921) and there were only a limited number of charities which families of servicemen could turn to in such times of need. A great deal was done at a local level by religious groups led by hard-working rectors and ministers at the churches and chapels the men had attended before the war. A number of the officers in the 1/4th and 1/5th Norfolks also worked in or came from families in the legal profession and many of them also helped those in need to press their case through legal channels.

For most of the families of the missing their wait would be at least a year before they received an official notification 'in accordance with the decision of the Army Council' that the soldier had 'died on or since' 12 August 1915 and military pensions were usually awarded to next of kin and dependants soon after. A widow with one child would usually be awarded a pension of 18s 9d, or a widow with three dependent children 26s 3d. This was a little less than the average weekly wage for a working man and careful budgeting was required if they were going to manage. Some widows married quickly afterwards to try and ensure their young families would not have to live on the breadline, others managed on their own.

The War Office, however, was still not issuing certificates of death and this caused problems with estates of the deceased, so a compromise was offered as explained in this letter to the family of T/Captain Edmund Gay via Purdy & Holley Solicitors of Aylsham (Tom Purdy's family firm) in August 1919:

I am commanded by the Army Council to inform you that, as the latest official report regarding this Officer is to the

Private Joe Bentley, 1/5th Battalion (South Lynn), killed in action 12 August 1915 aged 19.

Captain Edmund Gay, 1/5th Battalion, missing, presumed killed in action 12 August 1915.

effect that he was missing, in the Gallipoli Peninsula, on the 12th day of August 1915, this Department is not in a position to issue a formal certificate of death.

Looking, however:-

(1) To the length of time that has elapsed since this Officer was officially reported missing, during which period no further information has been received concerning him,

(2) To the fact that his name has not appeared in any list of prisoners of war received from the Turkish Government,

The Army Council are regretfully constrained to conclude, for official purposes, that Captain Gay is dead, and that his death occurred on, or since, the 12th Day of August, 1915.

I am to add that the Army Council have, unfortunately, no doubt as to the death of this Officer, and to explain that their action, as set forth above, is notified to those concerned, upon application for a certificate of death.

What happened to the bodies of the officers and men of the 1/5th Norfolks and if there was any way of determining exactly what had happened to them remained elusive.

Queen Alexandra

Princess Marie Louise would recall *'It is difficult for those who did not experience the agony of two World Wars fully to grasp the tragedy we lived through – scanning those terrible lists of dead, missing and wounded each day in the newspapers 1914-1918.'* The whole royal family were stricken by grief, but King George V would add *'The public may only get one report, but I have to know everything – bad news, as well as good from the various fronts, nothing can be kept from me.'* After all his enquiries, both official and unofficial His Majesty had to resign himself to the fact his agent and a number of the Sandringham Company were missing and in all probability would not be coming back.

Among all the royal family it was Queen Alexandra who would not give up trying to find out the fate of Frank Beck and the valiant men who had pushed forward the attack. After the death of King Edward VII, his son, King George V had continued to keep York Cottage as his country home and Queen Alexandra remained in Sandringham House where she closed off the late king's room, leaving everything in place as if he had been alive. The dowager queen had already taken a step back from public life as her son assumed the throne, but she still devoted a great deal of time to charitable causes, especially those associated with hospitals and welfare. Sadly, her increasing deafness and the pressure of work for so many charitable causes in wartime took its toll and Queen Alexandra retreated to a more solitary life at Sandringham from 1915 where she felt her deafness was far less of a disability within her own household.

Queen Alexandra retained a small, loyal retinue around her, every one of them familiar faces she had known and trusted for many years, three of whom she rapidly

HE whom this scroll commemorates was numbered among those who, at the call of King and Country, left all that was dear to them, endured hardness, faced danger, and finally passed out of the sight of men by the path of duty and self-sacrifice, giving up their own lives that others might live in freedom.

Let those who come after see to it that his name be not forgotten.

Pte. Ernest Edward Bussey
Norfolk Regt.

Memorial Scroll for Private Ernest Edward Bussey, 1/5th Battalion killed in action 12 August 1915 age 20, sent to his parents Walter and Mary Bussey of Melton Constable.

became utterly dependent upon. Her closest friend and constant companion was the Hon. Miss Charlotte Knollys, her Lady of the Bedchamber. Miss Knollys, known to all in the royal family of Edward VII's generation as 'Chatty', and to the family of George V as 'Miss Charlotte', was the only woman not related to the queen who was allowed to call her 'Alix'. Charlotte Knollys (sister of the king's private secretary) became very much the interpreter of the queen's wishes and administrator of her domestic and business affairs. She personally dealt with much of the queen's social correspondence, sometimes as many as a hundred letters a day.

The queen's other companion was her daughter, Princess Victoria. The most studious of the royal daughters, Victoria had always been loved by the people on the Sandringham Estate for her unaffected manner; she had a kindly word for even the humblest cottager, she gave lovely presents of books and needlework to people on the estate and she had caused quite a stir shortly before the war when she paid an informal visit to Cromer and was spotted partaking of a bun in a confectioner's shop. Princess Victoria had dutifully stayed with her mother instead of marrying. During the war she accompanied Queen Alexandra on most of her visits and went out to visit camps and hospitals in France and England in her own right.

Queen Alexandra's most devoted servant was the distinguished old soldier General Sir Dighton Probyn VC. After years serving as treasurer and comptroller of the household for Edward while he was Prince of Wales, and as Keeper of the Privy Purse when he

HM Queen Alexandra (far right) with her closest companions and staff. Left to right Sir George Holford, the Hon. Miss Charlotte Knollys (standing), HRH Princess Victoria (seated) and General Sir Dighton Probyn 1910.

became king, when King Edward died in 1910, Probyn, then aged 77, was probably looking forward to a well-earned retirement, but when he was asked by the dowager queen to act as her comptroller he unquestioningly agreed to serve her. Dighton Probyn was an impressive man with a huge white beard down to his chest. Sadly, in later life gout had contracted the muscles of his neck to the degree he was unable to lift up his head, an affliction, Probyn would jest, which was a judgement on him for having said he would not give a rap for any man who would not look him in the eye, and now all that he could do was to see the holes in women's stockings! Dighton Probyn lived at Park House on the Sandringham Estate; day to day he dealt with much of Queen Alexandra's official correspondence and was always close to hand as courtier, friend and confidant.

As the reports of soldiers being missing began to be received Queen Alexandra personally visited the families of members of the Sandringham Company on the estate and its villages and visited the school with Princess Victoria to enquire of the headmaster how the children were coping. The Duke of Windsor recalled Queen Alexandra during the war: '*With all her queenly dignity my grandmother had a wonderful way with people. The warmth and understanding of her approach to human problems left no doubt as to the sincerity of her solicitude.*'

Dighton Probyn wrote at her behest to Walter Page the US Ambassador to Britain on 27 October 1915 to see if more information could be obtained via the American Embassy in Constantinople:

Dear Mr Page

I write by direction of Queen Alexandra to beg of Your Excellency's assistance in a matter in which Her Majesty is deeply interested.

There is a certain Captain F.R. Beck, for whom Her Majesty has a very great regard, having known him personally for some 50 years – ever since his childhood.

For considerably over 20 years he has been Agent at Sandringham, having succeeded his father in that Office. Long before the war broke out he, at the suggestion of King Edward, who was anxious to help their Territorial movement, raised a company of men on the Sandringham Estate, and that company was eventually drafted into the 5th Norfolks...

This regiment landed at Suvla Bay on the 9th of August last. They went into action on the 12th of August, and from that day nothing has been heard of them...For my part, having known Capt. Beck intimately since his childhood, I never thought there was a chance of his being alive after I heard he was missing, as I felt he would be too gallant a man to surrender, and that he would only possibly have been induced to do so to save the lives of others, not his own. Now however, on reading General Inglefield's despatch, and the cutting from local papers, the hopes of Capt. Beck's numerous friends and admirers have been raised and amongst these sanguine people Queen Alexandra ranks the highest.

Her Majesty desires me to say she begs you kindly to do all you possibly can through your Embassy at Constantinople to ascertain if Captain F.R. Beck and his nephew, Lieut. Alec Beck are amongst the prisoners there...

> *I have taken upon myself to promise Queen Alexandra that Her Majesty may rest assured you will do all in your power to obtain for her the information she is so anxious to get about her valued friend and servant.*

Page replied in early December stating the Turkish Foreign Office had replied to his enquiries that they had no trace of Frank nor Alec in Turkish hands. Probyn thanked him for his efforts and reply, but sadly even Sir Dighton was of the opinion that they were not prisoners '*there can be no hope for them and we must, I am afraid, feel certain they have been murdered or at any rate given up their lives somewhere for their King and country'*.

As the war rolled on Queen Alexandra continued to pour over casualty lists and the great Sandringham house parties were no more. She became more reclusive and clung on with growing fervour to her memories and the things she held dear. Lady Nora Wigram, wife of King George V's assistant private secretary was invited by the queen to visit Sandringham House in October 1917. In a letter to her mother she described how the queen showed her around:

> *She kept on saying, 'The King used to sit there' or 'The King used to do this' and one pictured all the revels that used to take place. Finally, she took me to her own private sitting room – a truly marvellous room so crowded that one cannot turn round – a bewildering mass of photographs and every sort of treasure. I don't think I am exaggerating when I tell you there were over 200 things on her writing table; the only space left being taken up by her blotter...She loves all her little possessions, and kept showing them off.*

It was not surprising Queen Alexandra clung on to the past either; the losses of the war resonated with her own life again and again. Although he was not killed in war, she too had lost a son in his maturity, Prince Albert Victor, who died of the pneumonia he contracted as a result of a severe bout of influenza just one week after his twenty-eighth birthday in 1892. Just weeks before she had almost lost Prince George who had also been stricken with the same illness. She had also lost her brothers; King Frederick VIII of Denmark had died of paralysis in 1912 and King George of Greece had been assassinated in 1913.

Queen Alexandra's sister, Maria Feodorovna, the Dowager Empress of Russia was the mother of Emperor Nicholas II, a man who bore a remarkable likeness to his cousin, Queen Alexandra's son King George V. Cousin 'Nicky' had visited Sandringham when he was Tsarevich and he returned to the British Isles again with his family as Tsar in 1909. Nicholas and Edward then entertained each other's families and guests aboard their respective royal yachts during the Cowes Regatta in 1909. The overthrow of the Russian monarchy in 1917 and the execution of the Emperor Nicholas and his family by their Bolshevik guards in July 1918 shocked their relatives and the world.

The Dowager Empress Maria had refused to leave Russia, even after the overthrow of the monarchy in 1917. Only at the persuasion of her sister, Queen Alexandra, did she depart from Russia, escaping via the Crimea where she was whisked away on Royal Navy

Reverend Charles Pierrepont Edwards MC.

battleship HMS *Marlborough* to Britain in 1919. Empress Maria came to stay with her sister at Sandringham and Marlborough House. After the Russian Revolution there was little or no possibility of finding the bodies of the murdered Russian royals, but after the end of the First World War there was a chance the body of Captain Beck, his fellow officers and the men of the 1/5th Norfolks, who had been missing since 12 August 1915 might, at last, be found in Gallipoli.

The Reverend Charles Pierrepont Edwards MC, who was both present in the immediate aftermath of the action on 12 August 1915 and delivered a number of sermons to the 1/5th Norfolks while in the field, returned to the peninsula in 1918 as Officer Commanding Graves Registration Unit Gallipoli. The discovery of the bodies was described by another former Army Chaplain, Baptist Minister Reverend Leonard Egerton-Smith who was also working with the GRU in 1919:

> *For a long time all search for these men was fruitless. And quite by accident their bodies were discovered. A private attached to the GRU was purchasing local supplies from a farm situated far over in what was the enemy terrain and found a Norfolk badge. Further search revealed the remainder... I rode out to see their bodies brought in.*

Reverend Leonard Egerton-Smith.

In Pierrepont Edwards' report dated 23 September 1919, originally headed 'Not for publication', a copy of which was sent to Sandringham, he wrote:

> *What are almost certainly the remains of the officers and men of the 5th Norfolks who were missing after the action of the 12th August 1915 have now been discovered in a square 118.I. (Ref. 1/20000Map.)*

A faded photo but it is the earliest known photograph, taken by Rev. Leonard Egerton-Smith, of the 'forest' where the bodies of the 5th Norfolks who had advanced furthest were discovered.

> *The bodies were scattered over an area of about a square mile at an average distance of over 800 yards in rear of the Turkish front line and were lying most thickly round the ruins of a small farm. Up to date 180 bodies have been found, 122 of which have been identified by shoulder titles as belonging to the 5th Norfolks, such others as have been identified belong either to the 5th Suffolks or the 1/8th Hants. The bodies of three officers were found belonging to the Norfolks but it was impossible to identify them. I have ordered a special search to be made for Col. Beauchamp.*
>
> *Two identity discs were found, one belonging to Pte Cattor* [sic] *and the other to Pte Barnaby with 5th Norfolks but I cannot trace either of them in the card index. In fact there are no records of any men of this battalion here.*

In the newspaper accounts, Pierrepont Edwards related the story of how he discovered one of the bodies of the man who had '*taken cover behind a stone, and the large pile of empty cartridge cases around his skeleton showed that he had defended himself to the last*'.

In his final notes in his report the Reverend Pierrepont Edwards qualifies his findings further:

> *My reasons for supposing that the bodies discovered are those of the men who were missing after the action of 12th Aug. are as follows:-*
>
> *(1) In Sir Ian Hamilton's despatches it is stated that they were lost in a forest. The country in the vicinity of the place where the bodies were found is comparatively thickly wooded and is the only area in the Suvla sector which would in any way tally*

with the description. In addition, the farm would be on the frontage allotted to the battalion in the order of battle.

(2) The spot is half a mile behind the Turkish front lines and I have no record that it was reached on any subsequent occasion or that the three battalions, trace of which have been found, ever made an attack there again.

(3) According to one account Col. Beauchamp was last seen entering a farm in this area at the head of his men, and nothing further was heard of him. The Turkish occupier of this land has been interviewed and he stated that when he returned to the ruins of his farm after the evacuation it was covered by the decomposing bodies of British soldiers which he threw down a ravine in the immediate neighbourhood. It was in this ravine that many of the bodies were found and it would appear from this that a portion of the battalion were surrounded in the farm and annihilated.

Pierrepont Edwards' notes on the graves in Gallipoli to accompany his report state:

1. Almost every grave was desecrated and the Cross or other distinguishing mark destroyed or removed. In some cases the bodies had not be re-interred. This explains the difficulty in finding the graves of those known to have been buried. In the case of isolated graves it was frequently impossible.

2. 'Bodies' were only bones and all recognisable uniform decayed. A shoulder title, Regimental crest or badge of rank was often the only means of identification and in many cases even these were absent.

3. The Turk always robbed the dead of everything of value and made a practice of collecting discs. This accounts for the fact that so many are buried as unknown.

4. All remains have now been buried in Graves marked with wooden crosses. Most of these are carefully fenced in Cemeteries.

5. It is known that A Co. of the 1/5th Norfolk who were on the left of the line went off to silence guns that were causing heavy casualties. The Turkish farmer also stated that there were big numbers of bodies lying in the open – these had been thrown into a Dere (dry bed that becomes a running stream in rainy season) and so carried away. This is the ground for the opinion that the advance was caught by machine gun fire. Identifications were found in the order of the advance:-

Left	*Centre*	*Right*
5 Suffs.	*8 Hants.*	*5 Norfs.*

6. Both our and the Turkish front line trenches have been advanced since 12th August 1915. The remains were found on land which was never subsequently reached by British troops and buried with the Church Service on 7th Oct. 1919 by me.

(Signed) C. Pierrepont Edwards

Chaplain Ter. Forces

54th Division

A faded photograph taken by Rev. Leonard Egerton-Smith of the removal of the bodies of the men of 5th Norfolks from their temporary graves. They were given permanent graves in Azmak Cemetery where they still lie today.

The recovered bodies of the officers and men of the 1/5th Norfolks who died on 12 August 1915 were initially buried in temporary graves near where they were found by the Graves Registration Unit. They were then removed and given a permanent place of burial in Azmak Cemetery, Suvla, Turkey, close to the area occupied by the battalion before the attack. The only two soldiers mentioned in the report were in fact 240436 Corporal John Augustus Barnaby and 1028 Private Walter Carter (no Catter is recorded as serving or dying with any regiment in Gallipoli) both served with the 1/5th Norfolks, both are recorded as 'Died 28 August 1915'. They are buried side-by-side in Azmak Cemetery, Suvla, Grave Ref. I.C.6 and I.C.7 respectively.

The date of 28 August 1915 is misleading, the battalion was not in action nor did they sustain any casualties on 28 August as they made their way to the reserve lines. The 'missing' casualties of the 1/5th Norfolks were mostly described in the official records of the War Graves Commission and published in *Soldiers Died in the Great War 1914-19* as either 'Died 28 August 1915' or 'Died 21 August 1915', the reason being that on those dates it was officially assumed, not having heard from Turkish authorities that the man was a prisoner of war and because his body had not been recovered at the time, that he was 'Missing'. Their families had to wait considerably longer for official confirmation that they might assume their husband or son was dead. Most of the casualties of the 1/5th Norfolks of 12 August 1915 have now been amended and appear with the correct date on the CWGC website, but a few like Barnaby and Carter remain unchanged.

It should not be forgotten that other attacking units in the brigade also suffered striking losses in the attack of 12 August 1915. Officers in the 1/8th Hants and 1/5th Suffolks had also been horrified when they heard the plans for the action relayed to them. When Captain Clayton Ratsey, 1/8th Hants, heard the plan of attack he simply said '*My God we'll all be killed.*' They too had not been issued any proper maps of the area. The 1/8th Hants lost eight officers and nearly half its battalion, killed, injured or missing during the attack. Among their missing who were never to return was 29-year-old Captain Clayton Ratsey and his brother Captain Donald Ratsey. Some 301 men of the 1/8th Hants who died on that day are commemorated by the Commonwealth War Graves Commission on the Gallipoli peninsula. Only one body was ever recovered and identified, that of Rifleman Bertie Wray; he has a grave at Hill 10 Cemetery, all the others are named on the Helles Memorial to the Missing.

The 1/5th Suffolks were on the left of the line of the brigade attack. In their *History of 1/5th Battalion, The Suffolk Regiment* Captain Fair and Captain Wolton confirm Lawrence stated: '*We had just half an hour in which to plan and issue orders for an advance against an enemy whose position was not known.*' Lieutenant Colonel H.M. Lawrence DSO OBE who was the adjutant of the 1/5th Suffolks at the time of the attack on 12 August 1915 wrote:

> *There was just time to let company commanders know this and what battalions would be on the flanks to be kept connected with. From the very start anxiety was felt at having to go out into the blue leaving the left flank exposed to rifle and MG fire from the high ground on the flank, which at once made itself felt.*

The 1/5th Suffolks lost 12 officers, including Lieutenant Colonel William Armes, the 'father of the battalion' who had worked so hard to bring it up to a high standard, and 178 other ranks killed, wounded or missing. Fair and Wolton continue:

> *Only three men were afterwards reported prisoners, so all these Officers, NCOs and men must be presumed to have been killed. It is thought that these fine men were the foremost and the quickest to advance and, in their keenness, had bravely rushed forward in isolated parties and without adequate support. They seem to have completely disappeared. No one came back who could give an account of what had happened to them.*

The 1/5th Suffolks were fortunate to have around 100 men turn up among the evacuated wounded, but there were still 75 missing officers and men; 73 of them are now named on the Helles Memorial to the Missing. Only two of them, Major Robert Kendle and Private Thomas Ince, were found and identified and were buried in Azmak Cemetery near where the unidentified soldiers of the 1/5th Suffolks, 1/8th Hants and 1/5th Norfolks that were found on the battlefield were also interred in a common grave.

Conclusion

The 'mystery of the vanished battalion' may well have been consigned to history had it not been revived in the mid-1960s by an account signed by three Australian veterans. They claimed to have witnessed a dense cloud some 220ft in height and 200ft in width straddling a dry creek bed near Hill 60 on 21 August 1915, and how '*A British regiment, the First Fourth Norfolks of several hundred men, was then noticed marching up this sunken road or creek towards Hill 60. However, when they arrived at this cloud, they marched into it without hesitation, but no one ever came back out.*'

The cloud, according to the account, then slowly but surely joined the others hovering around the area, moved northwards and, in the space of three-quarters of an hour, had disappeared from view. You will notice the date they claimed to have seen the cloud was 21 August 1915, not 12 August 1915, the unit 'identified' in the account was the 1/4th Norfolks not the 1/5th Norfolks and the area described was not Anafarta Ova. But as the tale was retold and 'investigated' in subsequent magazine articles and books of the UFO and mystery genre that picked up on the story, it rapidly became entwined with the old tales of the 'vanished battalion' and the Sandringham Company.

There was undoubtedly a lot of dust that could be kicked up by troops during actions on the peninsula; the tinder dry bushes would easily ignite and plumes of smoke could fog a battlefield in a cloud-like way, but the rest just doesn't add up. However, interest in the action of 12 August 1915 was reignited and because the national media never seemed to pick up on the accounts written by soldiers of the 1/5th Norfolks who had actually been present at the action when the battalion had supposedly disappeared that had been published in the local press in the days, weeks and months after the stories of the disappearance first broke in 1916, nor had they bothered to track down and interview any of the remaining veterans who had survived the action that were still around in the 1960s, 70s and 80s. Consequently, for many, the question still remained of what had actually happened to 'the vanished battalion'.

After over thirty years of research in both public and regimental archives, and having had privileged access to many private collections, every one of the letters, published and unpublished, that the author has seen written by members of the 1/5th Norfolks who returned from the fighting of 12/13 August 1915, every diary written at the time, every memoir written in retrospect, plus the findings of both the official and confidential report of Reverend Pierrepont Edwards, corroborate the story that the men of the 1/5th Norfolks, led by their colonel, had pushed too far into enemy territory and fought until there were small pockets of them holding out in the natural ditches and gullies of the landscape and in a small farm.

Pierrepont Edwards interviewed the Turkish occupier of the land who said that after the British had evacuated the peninsula he had returned to the farm where he found the decomposing bodies of the British soldiers '*which he threw down a ravine in the immediate neighbourhood. It was in this ravine that many of the bodies were found and it would appear from this that a portion of the battalion were surrounded in the farm and annihilated.*'

A more modern, darker twist to the legend emerged in a story told by a single veteran, Gordon Parker, a former signaller in the Royal Engineers who had been attached to 54th Division during the Gallipoli campaign. Parker claimed to have encountered Pierrepont Edwards years after the war. During their conversation it was hardly surprising that the subject of Gallipoli, the campaign in which they had both served, came up. Parker claimed Edwards had spoken of the discovery of the '*mass grave containing the remains of many of the Norfolks*' and told him '*that every man had been found shot in the head'*. Furthermore he added how Pierrepont Edwards had embarked on something of a '*personal crusade to find the truth of what befell a group of men for whom he had great regard'*.

Parker's claims were repeated in Nigel McCrery's book *The Vanished Battalion: One of the Greatest Mysteries of the First World War Finally Solved* (1992). They also featured in the documentary based on the book, were reflected in the BBC Drama *All the King's Men* and the national press coverage that surrounded them, some reportage going so far as to suggest a 'war crime' may have been committed – all stuff as 'newsworthy' as latching onto Hamilton's despatch and suggesting an entire battalion had 'disappeared' back in 1915.

Despite all of this media attention and subsequent research by historians, reporters, professional and amateur researchers there has never been any further corroborating evidence presented to support Parker's claims. Nor has evidence emerged of Pierrepont Edwards' 'personal crusade' in the wake of his alleged discovery of many men being shot in the head: no further confidential report, no newspaper appeal for information, no private nor any official letters in pursuance of his investigations. Pierrepont Edwards was a brave padre, decorated for his gallantry in the field, as a parish priest he had become known as 'The Fighting Parson' for his open expression of his political views years before the outbreak of the war. He never forgot the men or the losses he saw in Gallipoli; he ensured the altar rail in the church of St Peter & St Paul at West Mersea where he was rector for nearly fifty years, was carved with a dedication to the memory of the fallen of the men of 54th Division who died in the Great War. He was not afraid of speaking up in public nor was he afraid of upsetting others if he believed he had good reason to pursue his cause. Surely, something would have been found by now.

What has emerged during research for this book is a letter from Lance Corporal Robert Tiptod, one of the last defenders of the farm, published in the *Yarmouth Mercury* of 2 October 1915:

> *...we kept making small rushes and now we were within rifle fire. It was awful to hear them whistling past you and seeing poor boys dropping, but we kept going and our objective was a small Turkish village which was strongly fortified. We had now got within 200 yards of a farmyard and had orders (when everybody had got their wind) to charge this place and what a charge this was. We yelled and ran for it all we were worth sticking every Johnny Turk as we came to them. We held this place for about three hours, waiting for reinforcements which never came, and as the enemy were far superior in numbers and had about 50 machine guns playing havoc with us, to*

> *our sorrow we had to retire. But what a time we had. I do not think one flinched a nerve...I do not think I shall forget it as long as I live. With shells bursting everywhere and bullets whizzing all around you it is like hell.*

No massacre occurred at the farm, just heavy casualties, no wonder the owner returned to find it strewn with the bodies of the defenders. Tragically, however, if enquiries had been made in 1919 to find witnesses to what happened there, like many of his comrades who survived the action of 12 August, Lance Corporal Robert Tiptod had been killed at their next major action at the Second Battle of Gaza in 1917. Each of the remaining pockets of the forward advance of the 1/5th Norfolks on 12 August was overwhelmed and the few who survived at that point had one of three fates. Some were simply 'annihilated' as stated by Pierrepont Edwards in his report of 1919, a handful were taken prisoner and others managed to retreat back to safer lines and thanked God and providence that they got away with their lives.

We should not forget that the British, French and ANZAC forces were invading Turkey and Turkish troops were defending their home country as ardently as Britain would have done if we had been invaded by enemy forces; I don't think we would have had very much sympathy for the invaders either. I have interviewed hundreds of combat veterans from the First World War up to the present day and after extensive research across a huge number of manuscripts, published and oral history accounts, I am convinced any combat soldier from any nation from either World War would agree there were times and attacks where taking prisoners, no matter how compliant, wounded or not, was simply not an option, or was not an option that would be contemplated by some of the soldiers involved in the fighting in a particular moment in a particular raid, attack or battle.

The reports submitted to the War Office by the chaplains attached to the Graves Registration Unit during the final consecration and dedication of the cemeteries of Gallipoli, who oversaw the last phase of the recovery of bodies, their removal to their final resting places and committal, contextualise why the bodies of the fallen of the 5th Norfolks were left where they fell without burial. In his final report written in Constantinople in 1920 the Reverend Cyril de Normanville, who had worked alongside Egerton-Smith as officiating Roman Catholic Chaplain wrote: '*The Turks have little or no respect for their own dead and they have no cemeteries either, there are a few by their hospitals, and hence we could not expect them to be careful guardians of our own.*'

In his own final report, the Reverend Leonard Egerton-Smith concurred: '*It was no concern of the Turk to inter those who were "lying out" where they fell in scrub and gully. Christian or Moslem, he left them alone.*' There is no mention of a single suspicion of anything other than the men simply being casualties of war in the entire report.

The losses during the attack on Anafarta Ova were terrible but there was no massacre of the men of the 1/5th Battalion, The Norfolk Regiment on 12 August 1915. Private Fred Cann of A Company, 1/5th Norfolks, sums it all up pretty well in his letter home to his parents in Gorleston received early in September 1915: '*We went out during the advance too far and got surrounded, and had to make the best of our way back, when I think of it, it is really marvellous that any of us are alive today.*'

The precise circumstances of how Captain Frank Beck died remain unknown. The last recorded sighting of him was mentioned in a letter from Private John Dye printed in the *Lynn News* of 8 January 1916 who stated he saw Captain Beck 'in a kind of sitting position under a tree with his head leaning over on to his right shoulder' and it is, in all probability, where he died. Subsequently a few of Captain Beck's personal effects were recovered. First his cheque book and pocket book simply described as 'found on the plain near Anafarta' were returned to Sandringham. There was no clarification if they had been removed from his body or just found lying among the detritus after the battle.

Then in 1921 the gold watch presented to Frank Beck by Dighton Probyn came to light. The British Military Representative in Smyrna had received information the watch was in the possession of former Turkish General Musta Bey in Constantinople. Bey, who had been commanding the Turkish troops in the sector where the 1/5th Norfolks had attacked, was demanding £150 in money and safe conduct from Constantinople to Smyrna in exchange for the return of the watch. After wrangling, the matter was finally resolved by the personal intervention of Mustafa Kemal, the first president of modern Turkey. The watch was forwarded to General Charles Harington, Commander of the Occupation Forces in the Black Sea and Turkey, to returned it to Dighton Probyn along with a few other personal effects from Captain Beck. The watch was eventually returned with a further inscription bringing the story to date by Dighton Probyn who presented it on her wedding day to '*To my old friend's eldest child, his daughter Meg Beck, hoping it may be kept as an heirloom in the Beck family for years to come April 26th 1922.*'

Remembrance

In 1918 there were very few could claim they had served through the entire campaigns and battles of Gallipoli, Egypt and Palestine with the Norfolk Territorial battalions. Most of those who did make it home had returned as wounded or sick. Many of them suffered physically and mentally for the rest of their lives. Most of those who could return to their old line of work on the land, in factories, on the railways or in business did so, but times were tough and some struggled to find employment in the 1920s. Most of them just got on as best they could, worked where they could, settled down, married, raised a family and never wanted to talk about the war again.

Many of those whose letters have helped to tell the story of the Norfolk Territorial Battalions in this book sadly did not return from the war. Among those who did make it back were Major Tom Purdy TD (1873-1960) who retired a lieutenant colonel and returned to his family business of solicitors in Aylsham where he continued to help the members of his old battalion and their dependants in their fight for war pensions. Captain Cedric Coxon TD (1889-1968) did much to help his fellow sick and injured prisoners while in captivity. On his return to England he completed his training and served many years as a dentist in King's Lynn. Both Purdy and Coxon became senior officers in the local Home Guard companies during the Second World War.

Captain John Howlett Jewson MC TD DL (1895-1975) who had survived Gallipoli and was one of the few officers to remain uninjured after the Second Battle of Gaza,

'Good Old Norfolk' one last parting photo of lads from the Norfolk Territorial Battalions, Cairo, Egypt 1918.

rejoined his family timber business after the war and served in the Territorial Army throughout the inter-war year, rising to become commanding officer of the 4th Battalion, The Royal Norfolk Regiment TA. Lieutenant Colonel Jewson oversaw their mobilization in 1939 and led them through the darkest hours of invasion scares in 1940. Captain Murray Buxton MC was wounded and returned to Britain from Palestine. After the war he became a chartered civil engineer living in Surrey with offices in London. He was killed in an air raid on Westminster, London on the night of 14/15 October 1940 aged 51.

The man who made the most significant name for himself on civvy street was the original 1/5th Norfolks Medical Officer, Dr Robert McDonald Ladell (1881-1965). Wounded during the attack on Anafarta Ova, his leg never healed properly and had to be amputated nearly 30 years later during the Second World War. During the inter-war years Dr Ladell became one of Britain's first licensed psychologists. He wrote a number of books, including volumes on how to overcome stammering, cure blushing and even a volume to help parents explain the facts of life to their children. He had numerous papers published, made some valuable contributions to *The Psychologist* and other medical journals, including some interesting articles on perceptions of war which he felt strongly should be divested of all glamour and prestige, the first step being to remove verbal camouflage. Ladell wrote: *'What we mean now by war is organised murder and we should say so.'*

"LEST WE FORGET"

MEMORIAL SERVICE

TO THE MEN OF THE

5th Battalion Norfolk Regiment

who fell at Suvla Bay,

HELD ON THE ANNIVERSARY DATE,

FRIDAY, AUGUST 12th, 1921,

at King's Lynn.

6.30 p.m.—All Service and Ex-Service men "Fall In" Tuesday Market Place.
7.0 p.m.—Service on the Walks' Football Field.

THE SOLDIER.

If I should die, think only this of me :
That there's some corner of a foreign field
That is for ever England. There shall be
In that rich earth a richer dust concealed ;
A dust whom England bore, shaped, made aware,
Gave once her flowers to love, her ways to roam,
A body of England's, breathing English air,
Washed by the rivers, blest by suns of home.

And think this heart, all evil shed away,
A pulse in the eternal mind, no less
Gives somewhere back the thoughts by England given ;
Her sights and sounds ; dreams happy as her day ;
And laughter, learnt of friends ; and gentleness,
In hearts at peace, under an English heaven

Rupert Brooke

Service sheet for the Memorial Service to the men of the 5th Battalion who fell at Suvla Bay held at The Walks, King's Lynn, 12 August 1921.

The majority of the men of the 1/4th and 1/5th Norfolks who died in the First World War have no known grave; their names appear instead on either the Helles Memorial on the Gallipoli Peninsula or on the Jerusalem Memorial, Israel and Palestine. The greatest concentration of those who do have graves and memorial headstones are the 223 officers and men from both Norfolk Territorial battalions buried at the Gaza War Cemetery. One of the first memorial services to the men of the 1/5th Norfolks who died at Suvla Bay to take place in Norfolk was held on The Walks' Football Ground, King's Lynn on the anniversary of the battle, 12 August 1921. In the years after the end of the First World War the men of both the 1/4th and 1/5th Norfolks raised their own old comrades associations, held annual reunion dinners and did their best to help those who had served in the battalion if they fell on difficulties, suffered illness or hard times. Many of them, along with other ex-servicemen, their families, the families of soldiers who did not return, friends, local councils, church communities and caring local people helped to raise money for war memorials to be erected in memory of their local war dead. On Remembrance Sundays the old comrades would don their medals and gather once more to pay their respects to their pals who did not return.

Across the county of Norfolk there are numerous war memorials that record the names of their village, town or parish fallen, many of these memorials include the names of their local men – friends, family members and neighbours who fell while serving in the territorial battalions of The Norfolk Regiment.

Unveiling of the Sandringham War Memorial by HM King George V on 17 October 1920.

The Memorial Window to Captain Frank Beck MVO and his men at West Newton Church, dedicated at a special service on Sunday, 9 January 1921.

The Sandringham War Memorial was unveiled by HM King George V on the afternoon of 17 October 1920. Inscribed '*This cross was erected by King George V and Queen Mary to honour the memory of the Officers and Men of the Sandringham Company, 5th Battalion, The Norfolk Regiment and those on the Estate who fell in the Great War*,' it bears the names of all 77 men from the king's estate who fell during the First World War. Also present at the unveiling were Queen Mary, Queen Alexandra, Princess Mary, Prince Henry and Princess Victoria.

A magnificent window in memory of Captain Frank Beck and the men of the Sandringham Company who fell on 12 August 1915 was dedicated at West Newton Church, which was crowded to overflowing for the service on Sunday, 9 January 1921. Beneath the window is a brass plaque in memory of Frank's widow, Mary Plumpton Beck (1871-1938) who, like many other wives and sweethearts of those who were posted as missing after the action, refused to wear black. They never gave up hope until the bodies were discovered by the War Graves Registration Unit in 1919.

Throughout the 1920s and 30s more war memorials were erected across the county and the children of King George V, who had spent so many happy years of their youth growing up at York Cottage on the Sandringham Estate, now grown to maturity, unveiled some of the most significant. HRH Princess Mary, famed for her brass gift tin presented to soldiers on active service Christmas 1914, unveiled the King's Lynn war memorial on 26 January 1921. HRH Prince Henry (later the Duke of Gloucester) performed that same duty at Great Yarmouth on 7 January 1922 and at the old 5 Norfolk Battalion Headquarters town of East Dereham on 22 October 1922.

Unveiling of the King's Lynn War Memorial by HRH Princess Mary on 26 January 1921.

HRH Prince Henry unveiling East Dereham War Memorial on 22 October 1922.

In the years after the First World War Queen Alexandra was troubled by a constant ringing in her ears and failing memory after suffering a burst blood vessel in her eye which left her blinded for some time. She became a recluse, only occasionally seen in public being chauffeured in her car through the streets of King's Lynn. The death of Dighton Probyn in June 1924 left the queen without the man who had come to be her rock. Queen Alexandra died on 20 November 1925, aged 80. Her devoted, constant companion Charlotte Knollys was beside herself with grief. She was given her flat on South Audley Street, London by King George V but was lost without Alix. Charlotte Knollys died in 1930 aged 95. Princess Victoria never married and her last years were plagued with ill health and depression; she died on 7 December 1935 aged 67. King George V had been suffering

HM Queen Alexandra c1923.

Returned veterans of the First World War from Worstead at a Norfolk Regiment gathering at the Regimental Cottages Norwich in the 1920s. Fred Frostick stands third from right on the back row.

The identity tag worn by Private Fred Frostick $1/5^{th}$ Battalion throughout the Gallipoli campaign, including the day of the attack on Anafarta Ova.

with illnesses related to his heavy smoking for a number of years of his later life, deeply affected by the death of his favourite sister, died at his beloved York Cottage at Sandringham a month later.

The last major First World War Memorial to be opened in the county was for the City of Norwich which commemorates the 3,455 war dead of the city. It was decided an ordinary soldier should unveil it. A number of worthy candidates were nominated, but it was former Private Bertie Withers who had served in the $1/4^{th}$ Norfolks and had been severely wounded at the Second Battle of Gaza leaving him permanently disabled, who was given the honour of unveiling the memorial in front of a crowd of thousands on 8 October 1927.

The last surviving member of the $1/5^{th}$ Norfolks present at the action of 12 August 1915 was Private Freddie Frostick (1893-1992) who lived out many years of his life working as a gardener in Worstead and North Walsham. He marched every Remembrance Sunday proudly wearing his trio of First World War medals into great old age. He never forgot his comrades nor how lucky he was to survive.

A Sulva Bay commemoration service at Great Yarmouth War Memorial in the 1920s.

Appendix 1

Roll of the Original Members of the Sandringham Company

This unique roll is based on the signatures of E Company, 3rd Volunteer Battalion, The Norfolk Regiment, 'The Sandringham Company', in the book presented as a gesture of thanks to Lieutenant Stephen Coxon, 3rd Volunteer Battalion, The Norfolk Regiment on 15 June 1906 for his help establishing the Sandringham Company:

Captain Frank R. Beck
Lieutenant Anthony Knight

Colour Serjeant J. Walter Jones
Serjeant Frederick W. Bland
Serjeant George Boughen
Serjeant Thomas H. Cook
Serjeant. Harry L. Saward

Batterbee, G
Batterbee, H
Benstead, A
Bird, J
Bridges, F
Boughen, George
Bunn, F
Bunn, H R
Collison, F
Colman, P
Cook, C
Cooke, F
Cox, C E
Crisp, G
Crisp, J
Crowe, R
Curson, R
Daw, A
Dawes, A
Deaves, George
Dick, William
Dickson, George
Dunger, A
Dye, G
Dye, J
Dye, W
Finch, F
Ford, A J
Foster, W
Godfrey, E
Godfrey, Robert
Green, A
Grimes, B
Grimes, S
Hammond, R
Hanslip, J W
Harlow, H H
Harrod, G
Hodges, W
Hipkin, W
Houchen, H
Hubbard, Charles E
Hudson, E S
Hudson, J
Jex, A
Johnson, J
Kingston Rudd, A.
Lines, A
Lines, P
Lines, W
Magners, B
Mallet, R
Marshall, Cecil
Martin, Hubert C.
Mitchell, F
Morgan, F
Mottram, Maurice
Myer, J
Patrick, R
Primrose, G R
Pugh, W M
Riches, George
Ringer, J
Ringer, W
Rix, A R
Rix, H W
Rudd, O
Sayer, E
Sayer, G

Sharpen, F P A
Smith, S
Smith, W
Threadkell, R

Whitby, E
Walden, M
Webb, H L
Wells, G E

Wills, F
Woodhouse, F
Woodhouse, J
Yallop, J

Appendix 2

Roll of Honour
The Attack on Anafarta Ova

This roll identifies 300 known officers and men lost from the 1/5th Norfolks during the action of 12–13 August 1915:

22 Officers (14 killed, 6 wounded, 2 PoW)

283 Men (142 killed, 127 wounded, 14 PoW)

Killed

Officers

ADAMS, Second Lieutenant, ROBERT age 34. Son of Boyce and Sara Adams, Hanley, Stoke on Trent, Staffordshire. Helles Memorial, Turkey.

BECK, Lieutenant, ALBERT EDWARD ALEXANDER, MC age 34. Son of Edward William and Emily Mary Beck, of Home Close, Stoke Holy Cross; husband of Noel Harriette Rosetta Crotch (formerly Beck), of Seething. Helles Memorial, Turkey.

BECK, Captain, FRANK REGINALD MVO age 54. Husband of Mary Plumpton Beck of Dersingham. Agent to HM The King, Sandringham. Helles Memorial, Turkey.

BURROUGHES, Second Lieutenant, RANDALL age 19. Son of Francis George and Anne Kathleen Julia Burroughes, of 120, Mount St., Grosvenor Square, London. Helles Memorial, Turkey.

CUBITT, Captain, EDWARD RANDALL age 30. Son of Mr E.G. Cubitt, J.P., and Christabel M. Cubitt, of Honing Hall. Husband of Janet Catherine Cubitt, of 'Butlers', Hatfield Peverel, Essex. Helles Memorial, Turkey.

CUBITT, Lieutenant, VICTOR MURRAY age 27. Son of Mr E.G. Cubitt, J.P., and Christabel M. Cubitt, of Honing Hall. Helles Memorial, Turkey.

GAY, Captain, EDMUND, D Coy. age 32. Son of the late Edward and Ellen Gay (nee Waterfield), of Aldborough Hall; husband of Margaret Gay of Manor House, Wickmere. Helles Memorial, Turkey.

MASON, Captain, ARTHUR HUMPHREY age 32. Son of R. Harvey Mason and Jane Charlotte Mason, of Necton Hall, Swaffham. Helles Memorial, Turkey.

OLIPHANT, Second Lieutenant, MARCUS FRANCIS age 29. Son of the Rev Francis George and Mrs Elizabeth Oliphant of Bale Rectory, Melton Constable. Helles Memorial, Turkey.

PATTRICK, Captain, ARTHUR DEVEREUX age 32. Son of the late Alderman Thomas Pattrick and Mrs Pattrick of St. Augustine's, King's Lynn. Husband of Alice Isobel Mary Gibson Hoff. Helles Memorial, Turkey.

PROCTOR-BEAUCHAMP, Lieutenant Colonel, Sir HORACE GEORGE CB age 58. 6th Bart. Son of Sir Thomas Proctor-Beauchamp, 4th Bart., and the Hon Lady Beauchamp (nee Waldegrave), of Langley Park, Norwich. Helles Memorial, Turkey.

PROCTOR-BEAUCHAMP, Second Lieutenant, MONTAGU BARCLAY GRANVILLE. age 22. Eldest son of the Rev Sir Montagu H. Proctor-Beauchamp, 7th Bart., and Lady Proctor-Beauchamp (née Barclay), of Ebley Court, Stroud, Gloucestershire. Helles Memorial, Turkey.

WARD, Captain (Adjutant) ARTHUR EDWARD MARTYR age 37. Son of the Rev John Martyr Ward, of Gressenhall Rectory, Norfolk; husband of Audrey Ward, of High Elms, Compton, Berkshire. Helles Memorial, Turkey.

WOODWARK, Major, ERNEST REGINALD age 37. Son of Mrs Agnes E. Woodwark and the late Alderman G.S. Woodwark, JP of King's Lynn. Helles Memorial, Turkey.

Other Ranks

ALLEN, Private, GEORGE, 1136. Born and enlisted Aylsham. Son of James and Sarah Allen, of Edgefield Rd., Saxthorpe. Helles Memorial, Turkey.

ATTOE, Private, HUBERT ERNEST age 19. Born Briston. Enlisted East Dereham Son of Mr and Mrs Joseph Attoe, of Reepham Rd, Briston. Helles Memorial, Turkey.

BAKER, Private, SIDNEY, 2206 age 21. Born and enlisted Great Yarmouth. Son of Isaac and Lavinia Baker, of 12A, King St., Great Yarmouth. Helles Memorial, Turkey.

BALLS, Private, HORACE, 2245, D Coy. Age 20. Born and enlisted Norwich. Son of Edward C. Balls, of Hungate St., Aylsham, Norfolk. Helles Memorial,Turkey.

BARBER, Private, JOHN HORACE, 2622 age 18. Born Walsingham. Enlisted East Dereham. Son of William and Phoebe Barber, of Helhoughton. Helles Memorial, Turkey.

BARKER, Private, GEORGE HERBERT, 2308. Born Honingham. Enlisted East Dereham. Son of James and Elizabeth Barker of Honingham. Helles Memorial, Turkey.

BARNABY, Corporal, JOHN AUGUSTUS, 240436 age 25. Enlisted East Dereham. Son of Mr John and Mrs Georgina Barnaby, of 33, South Everard St, King's Lynn. Azmak Cemetery, Suvla, Turkey.

BARNES, Private, RICHARD, 1877. Born Wood Dalling, enlisted Aylsham. Son of Richard and Hannah Barnes of Wood Dalling. Helles Memorial, Turkey.

BEART, Serjeant, ERNEST WILLIAM, 2185 B Coy. age 25. Born Downham Market, enlisted East Dereham. Son of the late Mr C.E. and Mrs M. Beart, of Tacna, North Foreland, Isle of Thanet. Helles Memorial, Turkey.

BECK, Private, LEONARD EDWARD, 3133, D Coy. age 25. Son of James S. and Mary M. Beck, of 76, Bells Marsh Rd., Gorleston. Helles Memorial, Turkey.

BECKETT, Private, FREDERICK GEORGE, 1758. Born Great Yarmouth. Enlisted Great Yarmouth 1914. Resided 2, Station Terrace, Great Yarmouth. Helles Memorial, Turkey.

BELDING, Private, FREDERICK ERNEST, 2416, B Coy. age 31. Born Hunstanton. Enlisted Dereham. Son of the late Mr Rawston and Mrs Eliza Jane Belding, of 'Thetis', Victoria Avenue, Hunstanton. Helles Memorial, Turkey.

BENTLEY, Private, JOSEPH WIILLIAM 'JOE' 3411 age 19. Born South Lynn. Enlisted East Dereham. Son of Joseph and Eliza Bentley of 7, Saddlebow Road, King's Lynn. Helles Memorial, Turkey.

BERESFORD, Serjeant, ROBERT WILLIAM, 293 age 28. Born and enlisted Holt. Son of Henry Beresford, of Shire Hall Plain, Holt; husband of Emily E. Beresford, of Weston Square, Holt. Helles Memorial, Turkey.

BIRCHAM, Private, WILLIAM, 1549. Born Brampton, enlisted Buxton, Norfolk. Son of John and Eliza Bircham of The Common, Brampton. Helles Memorial, Turkey.

BLYTH, Private, REGINALD HENRY, 1692. Born and enlisted Great Yarmouth. Son of Arthur and Sarah Blyth of No.21 Row 117, Great Yarmouth. Helles Memorial, Turkey.

BOND, Private, WILLIAM JAMES, 2418 age 20. Born West Newton. Enlisted East Dereham. Son of Julia Riches (formerly Bond), of Alexandra Cottages, West Newton, King's Lynn, and the late John William Bond. Helles Memorial, Turkey.

BOWLES, Private, SIDNEY ROBERT, 2757 age 20. Born Great Yarmouth. Enlisted Great Yarmouth 4 August 1914. Son of Mr W. and Mrs C. Bowles, of 15, North Market Road, Great Yarmouth. Helles Memorial, Turkey.

BRAND, Lance Corporal, CHARLES AGNEW, 3081, C Coy. Age 25 Enlisted September 1914. Husband of Charlotte Brand, of 9, Coniston Square, Great Yarmouth. Helles Memorial, Turkey.

BRIDGES, Private, LEONARD ARTHUR, 3335. Born Flitcham. Enlisted East Dereham. Grandson of William and Susan Bridges of Church Lane Cottages, Flitcham. Helles Memorial, Turkey.

BRITTON, Private, ALFRED ROBERT, 2968. Enlisted East Dereham. Son of John and Maria Britton of Lynn Road, Roydon near King's Lynn. Helles Memorial, Turkey.

BULLIMORE, Private, CECIL ERNEST, 1432 age 21. Born Westwick, enlisted Norwich. Son of George and Emma L. Bullimore, of Rose Cottage, Westwick, Norwich. Helles Memorial, Turkey.

BUSHELL, Private, GEORGE JOHN CHARLES, (One of the Battalion Scouts) 1306 age 23. Born Wicklewood, enlisted Great Yarmouth. Son of William and Elizabeth Bushell, of 15, Harley Road, Great Yarmouth. Helles Memorial, Turkey.

BUSSEY, Private, ERNEST EDWARD, 1387 age 20. Born Briston. Enlisted Melton Constable. Son of Walter Henry and Mary Bussey, of 29, Colville Rd, Melton Constable. Helles Memorial, Turkey.

BUTCHER, Private, GEORGE WILLIAM REYNOLDS, 3436 age 32. Born Litcham. Enlisted East Dereham. Son of William and Hannah Butcher; husband of Edith Frances Butcher, of East Lexham. Helles Memorial, Turkey.

CARTER, Private, SIDNEY, 1555. Born Shouldham. Enlisted West Newton. Son of John and Sarah Ann Carter of Ling House, Anmer. Helles Memorial, Turkey.

CARTER, Private, WALTER, 1028. Born Wretton. Enlisted Stoke Ferry. Son of Henry and Adelaide Carter of Stoke Road, Wretton, Downham Market. Azmak Cemetery, Suvla, Turkey.

CHAMBERLAIN, Private, WALTER CECIL, 2520 age 18. Enlisted Aylsham. Son of Walter Chamberlain, of Fox Lake, Aylsham. Helles Memorial, Turkey.

CHAPMAN, Private, JOHN ARTHUR, 3780. Born Moulton St Mary's, enlisted East Dereham. Husband of Emma Chapman, father of Reginald, Mabel and Florence of Gunthorpe. Helles Memorial, Turkey.

CHRISTOPHERSON, Private, CLIFFORD BUNTING, 2988 age 19. Enlisted East Dereham. Son of Fred and Mary Ellen Christopherson, of Swaffham. Helles Memorial, Turkey.

CODLING, Private, HARRY HENRY WILLIAM, 1879 age 20. Born Hindolveston. Enlisted Aylsham. Son of William Thomas Codling, of Hindolvestone. Helles Memorial, Turkey.

COWEN, Lance Serjeant, WILLIAM CHARLES, 1129 age 21. Born St Margaret's, Lynn and enlisted King's Lynn. Son of David and Fanny Cowen, of 2, Miller's Court, Bridge St., King's Lynn. Helles Memorial, Turkey.

COX, Private, EDGAR SAMUEL, 1376 age 22. Born Wolferton, enlisted Sandringham. Son of Mrs. Sarah Cox of Wolferton. Helles Memorial, Turkey.

CRAKE, Private, BERT, 2522, B Coy. Age 19. Enlisted East Dereham. Son of Thomas and Elizabeth Crake, of The Ship Inn, Bridge St., King's Lynn. Helles Memorial, Turkey.

CRANMER, Serjeant, ERNEST, 77 age 46. Born and enlisted East Dereham. Son of Mrs E. Cranmer, of London Rd., East Dereham; husband of Sarah Cranmer, of 2, Wellington Rd., East Dereham Helles Memorial, Turkey.

CRASKE, Private, VICTOR CYRIL, 1447. Born and enlisted Sheringham. Son of William and Mary Craske of Whitehall Yard, Windham Street, Sheringham. Helles Memorial, Turkey.

CROWE, Private, CHARLES, 2524 age 22. Born Roydon. Enlisted East Dereham. Son of Frederick and Susannah Crowe, of Roydon, King's Lynn. Helles Memorial, Turkey.

CURTIS, Private, WILFRED SIDNEY, 2312, A Coy. age 20 Born Colton. Enlisted East Dereham. Son of Henry and Agnes Curtis, of 46, Hall Drive, Honingham. Helles Memorial, Turkey.

DEACON, Private, JAMES LOUIS, 3383. Born Norwich. Enlisted East Dereham. Brother of Mrs Blanche Bolton, of 161, Rupert St., Norwich. Helles Memorial, Turkey.

DODSON, Private, SAMUEL DANIEL, 2210 age 25. Born Great Yarmouth, resided 73, Howard Street, Great Yarmouth, enlisted 4 August 1914. Son of Samuel and Harriet Dodson. Helles Memorial, Turkey.

DOUGHTY, Private, DONALD ERNEST, 2273 age 20. Born Downham, Enlisted East Dereham. Son of William and Frances Doughty. Helles Memorial, Turkey.

DOVE, Corporal, ROBERT GEORGE, 819 age 27. Born Harleston, Norfolk. Originally joined E (Sandringham) Company in 1909. Husband of Mrs Agnes Florence Dove, 1 Langham Cottages, Park Road, Hunstanton. Helles Memorial, Turkey.

DURRANT, Private, ARTHUR, 2472. Resided 9, St Mary's Lane, Great Yarmouth. Enlisted Great Yarmouth on 31 August 1914. Son of Mrs.Annie Maria Durrant of 1, Market Road Place, Great Yarmouth. Helles Memorial, Turkey.

EASSOM, Lance Corporal, ARTHUR, 2654. Born Wansford, Northamptonshire. Enlisted East Dereham on 7 September 1914. Son of William and Martha Eassom, 30, Stibbington, Wansford, Northamptonshire. Helles Memorial, Turkey.

EGLEN, Private, ISAIAH, 2652 age 35. Born Worthing, Norfolk. Enlisted East Dereham. Son of Mrs Hannah Eglen of 25, Dereham Road, Worthing. Helles Memorial, Turkey.

EMMERSON, Acting Corporal, ERNEST, 2129 age 26. Born and Enlisted at Dersingham. Son of John and Mary Ann Emmerson, of Excelsior Villa, Dersingham. Helles Memorial, Turkey.

FENTON, Lance Corporal, FRANK, 1411 age 22. Born and enlisted Thornham. Son of Mr and Mrs Purling Fenton, of Church St., Thornham. Helles Memorial, Turkey.

FIELD, Acting Corporal, HERBERT JOSEPH, 2490. Born Norwich. Enlisted at Great Yarmouth on 31 August 1914. Son of Mr James and Mrs Christiana Field, 22, St Benedict's Street, Norwich. Helles Memorial, Turkey.

FORSYTHE, Private, ROBERT EDWARD, 1881 age 21. Born Finchley, Middlesex, enlisted Great Yarmouth. Son of Mr J. Forsythe, of 19, High St., Gorleston. Helles Memorial, Turkey.

FOX, Private, ALBERT LEVI, 1950 age 19. Born Raynham. Enlisted Fakenham. Son of William and Annie Fox, of West Raynham. Helles Memorial, Turkey.

FRANKLIN, Private, HARRY, 2865 age 24. Enlisted Great Yarmouth on 28 August 1914. Resided 1, Gordon Road, Great Yarmouth. Son of William and Lucy Mary Franklin, of Fanners Green, Great Waltham, Chelmsford. Helles Memorial, Turkey.

FRANKLIN, Private, HERBERT THOMAS, 1571. Born and enlisted Swaffham. Son of Mrs. Beatrice Mary Symonds, 'Melford', Chestnut Avenue, Oulton Broad, Suffolk. Helles Memorial, Turkey.

FRANKLIN, Private, LEONARD, 1706 age 22. Born Watlington, enlisted Downham Market. Killed in action 12 August 1915 age 22. Brother of Mr H. Franklin, of 10, Russell Place, Bentinck St., King's Lynn. Helles Memorial, Turkey.

FUTTER, Private, ARTHUR ROBERT, 4298 age 26. Enlisted Great Yarmouth in March 1915. Son of Isaiah and Esther Futter, of 10, Priory St., Gorleston. Helles Memorial, Turkey.

GALLANT, Private, WALTER AUGUSTUS, 2192. Born Great Yarmouth. Enlisted Great Yarmouth, August 1914. Resided 5, The Conge, Great Yarmouth. Son of Walter and Alice Gallant of Great Yarmouth. Helles Memorial, Turkey.

GEDGE, Private, BERTIE BARTLEY, 2473. Born St. Nicholas Great Yarmouth enlisted Great Yarmouth. Son of Mrs Emily Gedge of No.6, Row 47, Great Yarmouth. Helles Memorial, Turkey.

GOREHAM, Private, WILLIAM, 1600 Born and enlisted Fakenham age 20. Son of William and Louisa Goreham of White Horse Street, Fakenham. Helles Memorial, Turkey.

GOULDER, Serjeant, JOHN LEE, 2179 age 32. Born Aylsham, enlisted Aylsham. aged 32. Son of John and Mary Goulder of Pound Road, Aylsham. Helles Memorial, Turkey.

GREENWOOD, Private, JOHN BECKETT, 3327 age 27. Enlisted East Dereham. Son of Matthew and Maria Greenwood, of Reymerston, Attleborough. Helles Memorial, Turkey.

GREEVES, Private, GEORGE, 3296 age 22. Born Brancaster. Enlisted East Dereham. Son of Francis and Mary Ann Greeves of Yaxham. Helles Memorial, Turkey.

GRIFFIN, Corporal, GEORGE, 1768 age 21. Born and enlisted Gayton. Son of Frederick and Mary Griffin, of 1, Blacksmith Row, Gayton, King's Lynn. Helles Memorial, Turkey.

GRISTON, Private, GEOFFREY JOSEPH, 2575 age 18. Born Norwich, resided North Walsham, enlisted East Dereham 1914. Son of William and Alice Griston of Church Street, North Walsham. Helles Memorial, Turkey.

GROOM, Corporal, ARNOLD, 1118 age 30. Born and enlisted Fakenham. Son of Mr and Mrs John Groom, of Coker's Hill, Walsingham, Norfolk; husband of Mary Ann Groom, of Wells Rd., Fakenham. Helles Memorial, Turkey.

GROOM, Private, WALTER, 2765. Born Wells-next-the-Sea. Enlisted East Dereham. Son of the late James and Sophia Groom of Burnt Street, Wells-next-the-Sea. Helles Memorial, Turkey.

GRUMMITT, Private, GEORGE ERNEST, 2673 age 32. Born Lowestoft, Suffolk. Enlisted East Dereham. Son of George and Catherine Grummitt. Husband of Tabitha Grummitt, of Neatherd Moor, East Dereham. Helles Memorial, Turkey.

HACON, Private, HERBERT GEORGE, 2576 age 17. Enlisted Great Yarmouth September 1915. Son of William G. and Rose Alice Hacon, of 37, Lichfield Rd., Great Yarmouth. Helles Memorial, Turkey.

HALL, Private, BERTIE, 1702 age 22. Born Hilgay, enlisted Downham Market. Son of Mrs A. Hall, of 10, Mile Bank, Haims Farm, Downham, Norfolk; husband of Violet Lucy Hall, of Ely Rd., Hilgay. Helles Memorial, Turkey.

HALLS, Private, ROBERT HENRY, 2491 age 26. Enlisted Great Yarmouth. Son of Mr R.H. and Mrs A.E. Halls, of 36, South St., Cambridge. Helles Memorial, Turkey.

HARBAGE, Private, THOMAS WILLIAM, 2579 age 21. Enlisted East Dereham. Son of Mrs Jane Harbage, of 22, Queen St., King's Lynn, and the late Thomas Hirons Harbage. Helles Memorial, Turkey.

HELLENBURGH, Private, ARTHUR ROBERT, 1564 age 19. Born St Nicholas, Great Yarmouth, enlisted Great Yarmouth. Son of the late Arthur and Patience Hellenburgh of No.19, Row 138, Great Yarmouth. Helles Memorial, Turkey.

HERON, Private, FREDERICK GEORGE, 3022 age 21. Enlisted East Dereham. Son of George and Sarah Heron, of Vicar St., Wymondham. Helles Memorial, Turkey.

HEY, Private, CHARLES WILLIAM, 3503. Born Great Dunham. Enlisted East Dereham. Son of James and Harriet Hey of Great Dunham. Helles Memorial, Turkey.

HOLMAN, Private, HARRY (Henry), 1441. Born Fordham, enlisted Downham Market. Son of George and Susan Holman of Hilgay Road, Fordham. Helles Memorial, Turkey.

HOWELL, Private, ERNEST, 3031 age 23. Born Dersingham. Enlisted East Dereham. Son of George and Elizabeth Howell, of 5, Manor Road, Dersingham. Helles Memorial, Turkey.

HOWELL, Acting Corporal, HENRY WILLIAM GEORGE, 1898 age 32. Born and enlisted East Dereham. Son of Henry Edwin and Emma Howell, of 7, Beresford Rd., Lowestoft. Helles Memorial, Turkey.

HUBBARD, Private, HARRY, 2152 age 19. Born Wereham. Enlisted Downham Market. Son of Harry and Elizabeth Hubbard, of 16, Windsor Terrace, Downham Market, Norfolk. Helles Memorial, Turkey.

HUMPHREY, Private, WILFRED LYAL, 2683 age 21. Enlisted East Dereham. Son of Frederic and Rose Alice Young Humphrey, of St Ann's Street, King's Lynn. Helles Memorial, Turkey.

HUMPHREY, Private, WILLIAM JOHN, 1523. Born Grimston, enlisted Flitcham. Son of Mary A. Humphrey. Helles Memorial, Turkey.

HUNTER, Lance Corporal, CHARLES, 321 age 25. Born North Pickenham, enlisted Hillington. Died 12 August 1915 age 25. Son of Henry and Emma Jane Hunter of Flitcham.

JOHNSON, Lance Corporal, RUSSELL CHARLES, 2212. Born Gorleston. Enlisted Great Yarmouth. Son of Charles Walter and Emma Maria Johnson of 253, Southtown Road, Gorleston, Great Yarmouth. Helles Memorial, Turkey.

KERRISON, Private, FREDERICK ROBERT JAMES, 1751 age 19. Born Walworth, Surrey, lived at Dersingham. Enlisted August 1914. Son of Frederick and Louisa Kerrison, of Fox Farm, Carleton Rode. Helles Memorial, Turkey.

LEGGETT, Lance Corporal, HENRY FRANCIS, 2348 age 20. Born and enlisted Great Yarmouth. Son of Henry George and Christiana Leggett, of 28, Northgate St., Great Yarmouth. Helles Memorial, Turkey.

LINES, Private, ROBERT, 2880 age 21. Born West Runton. Enlisted East Dereham. Son of John Robert and Blanche Jarvis Lines of 8, Spring Cottages, West Runton. Helles Memorial, Turkey.

LONG, Private, Herbert, 1688 age 20. Born Blakeney, enlisted Wells. Son of William and Elizabeth Long of High Street, Blakeney. Addenda Panel HELLES Memorial, Turkey.

LOVETT, Private, JESSE ERNEST, 2177 age 27. Born and enlisted East Dereham. Son of Frederick and Sarah Lovett, of 49, Commercial Rd., East Dereham. Helles Memorial, Turkey.

LYON, Private, ERNEST ARTHUR, 1969 age 23. Born South Lynn, enlisted King's Lynn. Son of Edmund Thomas and Edith Annie Lyon, of 10, Windsor Row, Windsor Rd., King's Lynn. Helles Memorial, Turkey.

MANNING, Private, WILLIAM, 1573. Born Rougham, enlisted Swaffham. Son of the late William and Mrs Leah Manning, Lynn Pit, Lynn Street, Swaffham. Helles Memorial, Turkey.

MARSTERS, Private, ERIC, 2442 age 18. Born Castle Rising. Enlisted East Dereham. Son of Matthew and Sarah Marsters of Castle Rising. Helles Memorial, Turkey.

McDONALD, Lance Corporal, FREDERICK, 2267 age 26. Born Great Yarmouth. Enlisted Great Yarmouth 4 August 1914. Husband of Annie McDonald, of 14, Coronation Terrace, George Street, Great Yarmouth. Helles Memorial, Turkey.

McLEAN, Lance Corporal, PERCY DOUGLAS, 2583, B Coy. age 19. Born King's Lynn. Enlisted East Dereham 4 September 1914. Son of Joseph Thomas and Florence McLean, of 32, South Everard St., King's Lynn. Helles Memorial, Turkey.

MEDLOCK, Private, ERNEST, 1764, B Coy. age 22. Born and enlisted Gayton. Son of Fredrick George and Emma Medlock, of 7, Marsh Lane, Gaywood. Helles Memorial, Turkey.

MEGGITT, Signaller, RICHARD DRING, 1622 age 21. Son of Edward and Charlotte Meggitt, of 5, Johnson Square, Albert St., King's Lynn. Helles Memorial, Turkey.

MILLER, Private, GEORGE STANLEY, 2867 age 29. Born St Nicholas, Great Yarmouth, enlisted Great Yarmouth. Son of the late James and Eliza Miller of Great Yarmouth. Helles Memorial, Turkey.

MISSIN, Private, JOSEPH, 2173, A Coy. age 22. Born Southery, enlisted Downham Market. Son of James William and Jael Missin, of Ten Mile Bank, Downham. Helles Memorial, Turkey.

MURRELL, Private, WALLACE 'Walley', 2976 age 25. Born Letheringsett. Enlisted East Dereham 14 September 1914. Son of Harriett Murrell, of Albert St., Holt. Helles Memorial, Turkey.

NEEDS, Lance Serjeant, GEORGE WILLIAM, 711 age 28. Born King's Lynn. Enlisted West Newton into E (Sandringham) Company in November 1908. Son of Mr and Mrs Henry Needs, of 26, Alfred Rd., Cromer. Helles Memorial, Turkey.

NURSE, Private, ROBERT WALLACE, 2130 age 22. Born North Heigham. Enlisted Dersingham 23 March 1914. Son of Robert Nurse, of 19, Centre Vale, Dersingham, King's Lynn. Helles Memorial, Turkey.

PAGE, Private, WALTER, 1484 age 20. Born St Nicholas, Great Yarmouth, enlisted Great Yarmouth 1914. Son of Mrs Catchpole, of 17, High Mill Rd., Southtown, Great Yarmouth. Helles Memorial, Turkey.

PARMENTER, Lance Corporal, WILLIAM RICHARD, 2198. Born Stratford, Essex, enlisted Great Yarmouth on 5 August 1914. Resided 12, Alderson Road, Great Yarmouth. Helles Memorial, Turkey.

PAYNE, Private, WILLIAM THOMAS, 2843 age 29. Enlisted East Dereham 1914. Son of Mr William and Mrs Charlotte Payne, of 4, Ivy Cottages, Hans Place, Cromer. Helles Memorial, Turkey.

PHILLIPS, Lance Corporal, FRED ERNEST, 2025 age 21. Born Icklingham, Suffolk, enlisted Sandringham. Son of Thomas and Annie E. Phillips, of West End, Costessey. Helles Memorial, Turkey.

PIKE, Private, LACEY, 2588, A Coy. age 19. Enlisted East Dereham. Son of Walter and Susannah Pike, of Church Farm Cottage, Antingham, North Walsham. Helles Memorial, Turkey.

PLAICE, Private, BERTIE, 2715 age 20. Enlisted East Dereham. Son of Robert and Mary Plaice, of Westgate St., Shouldham, King's Lynn. Helles Memorial, Turkey.

PORTER, Lance Corporal, HAROLD CHADWICK, 2550 age 19. Born Great Yarmouth. Enlisted Great Yarmouth. Son of Robert Herbert and Annie Porter of 58, South Quay, Great Yarmouth. Helles Memorial, Turkey.

RANSOM, Private, HERBERT CHARLES, 2193, A Coy. Age 20. Born and enlisted Great Yarmouth. Son of Arthur Herbert Ransom, of 177, Stafford Rd., Southtown, Great Yarmouth. Helles Memorial, Turkey.

REED, Private, ROLAND WALTER WILFRED, 4183 age 16. Born Northwold. Enlisted East Dereham. Son of William and Annie Reed of Little London, Northwold. Helles Memorial, Turkey.

REEVE, Private, CHARLES, 2723. Enlisted East Dereham. Son of James and Anna Reeve, Brisley Road, North Elmham. Helles Memorial, Turkey.

REYNOLDS, Private, FREDERICK JAMES, 2722 age 35. Born West Acre. Enlisted East Dereham. Son of the late Mr Frederick and Mrs Lydia Reynolds of High House Farm Cottages, West Acre. Helles Memorial, Turkey.

RINGER, Private, ROLAND EDWARD, 1559 age 23. Born West Newton, enlisted Sandringham. Son of Mr William and Mrs Rose Mary Ringer, of Victoria Cottages, West Newton. Helles Memorial, Turkey.

RIX, Private, HERBERT WILLIAM, 3487 age 25. Son of Mr and Mrs Levi Rix, of Whitwell Common, Reepham. Helles Memorial, Turkey.

RIX, Private, WALTER GEORGE, 1895 age 20. Born Cambridge. Enlisted East Dereham. Son of Walter George and Annie H. Rix, of Dogger Lane, Wells. Helles Memorial, Turkey.

ROBINSON, Serjeant, THOMAS, 1262 age 24. Born Cromer. Enlisted Cromer 1911. Son of Mrs Phillis Robinson. Helles Memorial, Turkey.

RUDD, Private, GEORGE, 1379 age 21. Born Hardley. Enlisted Aylsham. Son of Henry and Alice Rudd, of 16, Little Paddock St., Norwich. Helles Memorial, Turkey.

RUTLAND, Private, ARTHUR EDWARD, 2104 age 18. Born South Lynn. Enlisted King's Lynn. Son of Arthur Robert Rutland, of 1, Kirby St., King's Lynn. Helles Memorial, Turkey.

SELF, Acting Corporal, THOMAS, 1424 age 29. Born Worstead enlisted Westwick. Son of Tom and Harriett Self, of East Ruston, Norfolk; husband of Harriet Self, of 7, Bacton Rd., North Walsham. Helles Memorial, Turkey.

SHICKLE, Lance Corporal, LEWIS FRANK, 2398 age 22. Born Hockering. Enlisted East Dereham 31 August 1914. Son of Lambert and Alice Shickle of North Tuddenham. Husband of Mrs. Ivy C. Shickle of 12, Theatre Street, East Dereham. Helles Memorial, Turkey.

SIMPSON, Company Quartermaster Serjeant, WILLIAM CHARLES, 442 age 37. Born and enlisted North Walsham. Husband of Isabella Simpson, of near Church Plain, Vicarage St., North Walsham. Helles Memorial, Turkey.

SMITH, Private, FRANK HENRY, 2399 age 22 Enlisted East Dereham August 1914. Son of Walter George and Elizabeth Smith, of Riverside Cottage, Flordon. Helles Memorial, Turkey.

SMITH, Private, FREDERICK WILLIAM, 2731 age 22. Enlisted East Dereham, September 1914. Son of Mr T.W. and Mrs E. Smith, of Primrose Cottage, Saddlebow Rd., King's Lynn. Helles Memorial, Turkey.

SMITH, Serjeant, GEORGE THOMAS, 2459 age 29. Enlisted East Dereham, September 1914. Husband of Catherine Emily Smith, of 5, Windsor Rd., King's Lynn. Helles Memorial, Turkey.

SMITH, Private, SIDNEY OCTAVIOUS, 2729 A Coy. age 21. Enlisted East Dereham 7 September 1914. Son of Mr William Lucius and Mrs Maria Smith of 65, Buckingham Terrace, King's Lynn. Helles Memorial, Turkey.

SPOONER, Private, GEORGE, 3473 age 20. Born Bintree. Enlisted East Dereham. Son of Edward John and Sarah Ann Spooner, of Long Yard, Bintree. Helles Memorial, Turkey.

SPRECKLEY, Private, FREDERICK ALAN, 2412 age 19. Enlisted East Dereham. Son of George and Agnes P. Spreckley, of 45, Norfolk St., King's Lynn. Helles Memorial, Turkey.

STEVENS, Private, SIDNEY JAMES, 2598 age 21. Born King's Lynn. Enlisted East Dereham. Son of Robert and Mary Stevens, 115, Church Street, King's Lynn. Helles Memorial, Turkey.

TAYLOR, Lance Corporal, THOMAS GILES, 3349 age 20. Born King's Lynn. Enlisted East Dereham. Son of Thomas and Naomi Taylor, Estuary Bank, North Lynn. Helles Memorial, Turkey.

THEOBALD, Lance Corporal, MAURICE JEREMIAH, 26 age 33. Born Langford. Enlisted East Dereham Husband of Comfort Theobald, of 11, Commercial Rd., East Dereham. Helles Memorial, Turkey.

THOMPSON, Private, ARTHUR ERNEST, 2389 age 23. Born Hethel. Enlisted East Dereham. Son of May and Sarah G. Thompson, of Cavick House, Wymondham. Helles Memorial, Turkey.

TIPPLE, Lance Corporal, ROBERT JAMES, 1649 age 20. Born and enlisted Thornham. Son of William and Ellen Anne Tipple, of Thornham, King's Lynn. Helles Memorial, Turkey.

TRENOWATH, Lance Corporal, WILLIE, 2413, B Coy. age 25. Enlisted East Dereham. Son of Mr Thompson and Mrs Ada Edith Trenowath, of 110, High St., King's Lynn. Helles Memorial, Turkey.

TUBBY, Lance Corporal, ALFRED, 1519, A Coy. Age 19. Born Great Yarmouth. Enlisted Great Yarmouth 4 August 1914. Son of Alfred J. and Annie Tubby, of 15, Ferry Lane, Southtown, Great Yarmouth. Helles Memorial, Turkey.

TUCK, Lance Corporal, WILLIAM RANDALL, 2284 age 23. Born Nordelph. Enlisted East Dereham. Son of William Henry and Ellen Grace Tuck, of The Homestead, Stoke Ferry. Helles Memorial, Turkey.

TURNER, Serjeant, BENJAMIN ROBERT, 869. Born and enlisted Aylsham. Son of Benjamin Herbert and Mary Turner of Hungate Street, Aylsham. Helles Memorial, Turkey.

WAGG, Private, BERTIE, 1904 age 20. Born and enlisted Hunstanton. Son of Alfred and Phoebe Wagg, of Dorset House, Park Road., Hunstanton. Helles Memorial, Turkey.

WAKE, Corporal, HEZEKIAH WALTER, 240037 age 27. Born Helhoughton. Enlisted East Rudham. Son of Hezekiah and Mary Ann Wake of Sculthorpe. Helles Memorial, Turkey.

WALDEN, Private, MORRIS MALLETT, 2385 age 27. Born Dersingham, enlisted East Dereham. Son of William and Sarah Walden of Sherbourne Road, Dersingham. Helles Memorial, Turkey.

WALKER, Private, WILLIAM, 2842 age 24. Enlisted East Dereham, September 1914. Son of Mr H.W. and Mrs A.E. Walker, of Roydon, King's Lynn. Helles Memorial, Turkey.

WELLSMAN, Private, CYRIL, 2749 age 19. Enlisted East Dereham 12 September 1914. Son of Mrs Alice Wellsman of 54 London Road, King's Lynn. Helles Memorial, Turkey.

WESTGATE, Private, AMBROSE HENRY, 1565, C Coy. age 18. Born and enlisted Great Yarmouth. Son of Mrs Louisa Elizabeth Fairhead, of No.17 Row, 113, King Street, Great Yarmouth. Helles Memorial, Turkey.

WHITBY, Corporal, ALBERT WATSON, 1884 age 24. Born and enlisted Great Massingham. Son of George and the late Elizabeth Ellen Whitby of Great Massingham. Helles Memorial, Turkey.

WILSON, Lance Corporal, WILLIAM JOHN, 2752 age 21. Enlisted East Dereham. Son of Robert and Rose Anna Wilson, of 'Westacre', High House Farm, Castle Acre. Helles Memorial, Turkey.

WINTER, Lance Corporal, ERNEST WILLIE READ, 2616 age 24. Born King's Lynn. Enlisted East Dereham. Son of Albert Read Winter and Laura Louisa Winter, of Crown Road, East Dereham. Helles Memorial, Turkey.

WOOLNER, Private, LESLIE GEORGE, 1837 age 20. Born Hethersett. Enlisted Melton Constable. Son of John and Harriet Woolner, of Kitchener Road, Melton Constable. Helles Memorial, Turkey.

Wounded and Prisoners of War

Wounded

Officers

Culme-Seymore, Lieutenant Arthur Granville
Knight, Captain Anthony
MacDonald Ladell, Captain Robert (Medical Officer)
Oliphant, Lieutenant Trevor
Pelly, Second Lieutenant A. Roland
Purdy, Major Thomas Woods

Men

Allison, Private Frederick H. 3613
Allison, Private G. V. 1689
Atkins, Private W. R.
Bailey, Private Ernest A. 160 (Sculthorpe)
Bell, Private Harry 2141

Bircham, Private Sidney 2813
Bird, Private Arthur 3382
Bowers, Private Horace W. 2631 (King's Lynn)
Bracey, Corporal Sidney C. 2338 (Gorleston)
Bridges, Private Charles H. 4239
Brittain, Serjeant Frank 122 (King's Lynn)
Brooks, Private Frederick 1711 (Dumpling Green, Dereham)
Brown, Private John 1638 (Scarning Gatehouse)
Brown, Private Percy J. 2386
Browne, Private Gordon A. 3035 (Great Yarmouth)
Bullock, Private Bertie 704
Bunn, Private Cornelius C. 4342 (King's Lynn)
Burton, Lance Serjeant William J. 2639
Busby, Private Benjamin 1891
Callaby, Private. James 1885
Cleveland, Serjeant, George Alfred Bell, 1755. (Gorleston) (DoW 15 August 1915)
Colby, Daniel C. (DoW 12 September 1915)
Colman Private Edward 1880
Crowe, Corporal Robert John (Sandringham)
Darby, A/Sgt. Robert J. 2244
Dawson, Private Ernest J. 3648 (King's Lynn)
Dawson, Private John 4338
Day, Private Albert W. 1496
Dye, Private John H. 3053
Eggett, Private Harold 1511
Eke, Private Ernest C. 2015
Ellett, Private Wilfred 7655 (Great Yarmouth)
Fayers, Private Charles 4297
Fellowes, Private Reginald 2429 (Yaxham)
Fickling, Serjeant Alfred 765 (King's Lynn)
Francis, Private Albert W. 2665 (King's Lynn)
Franklin, Private Frederick 2424 (Gayton Thorpe)
Frost, Private William F. 3321 (Ryburgh)
Gardner, Private Ernest 2211
Garwood, Private Robert Charles 2497
Green, Acting Corporal, Bertie Ernest 2247. (Wymondham). (DoW 13 Aug 1915)
Green, Lance Corporal George William 2087
Green, Private William B. 2671
Grimes, Private Robert 2984
Hall, Corporal Herbert George Sidney 2333 (Dereham)
Hanton, Private Arthur 2474
Harbage, Lance Corporal John Davies 2537
Harbord Acting Lance Corporal Martin T. 1507

Hardy, Private Frank 1947 (King's Lynn)
Harrison, Private Clifford Last 3059 (Great Yarmouth)
Hart, Private Herbert 745
Hill, Private Victor A. H. 2359
Holmes, Private Thomas Harry 2188
Howard, Serjeant Bertie R. 2182 (Swaffham)
Howes, Lance Corporal A.
Hubbard, Private Daniel 2035 (Cromer)
Humphrey, Private Albert James 2853
Hutchinson, Private George E. 2686
Jackson, Private Percy 1771 (Gaywood)
Jakeman, Serjeant William Henry 1370. (Dersingham)
Jarvis Serjeant Christopher 456
Jarvis, Lance Corporal Reginald Frank 2687 (King's Lynn)
Jaye, Private William Leslie 2913.
Jones, Private Cecil R. 2005
Jones, Private E. (Happisburgh)
Keeler, Private. Elijah J. 2541 (Wickmere)
Kelf, Private Frank 4269
Kerrison, Private Ernest R. 2255
Killengray, Private Frank 1607
Kirby, Private Reginald 1501 (Cromer)
Lack, Private William 4252 (Downham)
Lacon, Private George 4304
Large, Private Reginald 1965 (Dereham)
Layton, Private George 4304 (Great Yarmouth)
Leeder, Private Norman 2006
Lines, Private George 3381
Lockwood, Private Julian E. 2366
Long, Private George 1647
Long, Private Samuel 3507
Lynes, Private Frederick R. 4236 (Great Yarmouth)
Marjoram, Private Albert 2036
Marjoram, Private Arthur S. 2892
Mason, Private H. C. 1726
Masters, Private Sidney S. 2444
Masterson, Private John F. 2910
McSteen, Private Thomas E, 3082 (Great Yarmouth)
Medlock, Private George 2701 (King's Lynn)
Meek, Private Cyril 1776 (Gayton)
Meggitt, Private Frederick C. 2703 (King's Lynn)
Melton, Private George 1557 (Dersingham)
Mennell, Private John S. 1933

Mitchell, Private Albert Edward 2038 (Dersingham)
Mitchell, Private A.J. 2038
Mumford, Drummer Horace J. 4206
Parker Company Quartermaster Serjeant Benjamin Sidney 537 (Gorleston)
Parker, Corporal Colin D.C. 1438
Pawley, Lance Corporal Charles 1669
Payne, Private William T. 2843 (Cromer)
Pearce, Private Robert Charles 3458 (Great Yarmouth)
Pearson Private Alfred 1943 (Denver Sluice)
Petrie, Private Gerald Douglas 2409
Phillips, Private Charles Barcham 2498
Platten, Lance Corporal Hubert G. 3415
Reynolds, Private. J.F. 3083
Rogers, Frank (King's Lynn) 2724
Rowe, Lance Corporal Walter 2725 (King's Lynn)
Saville, Private Frederick Charles 2380
Seago, Private Herbert 4314
Secker Private Frederick Charles 3302
Sheldrick, Private Thomas F. 4184 (Swaffham)
Shepherd, Private Cecil 4275
Smalley, Private F. W. 3012 (King's Lynn)
Smith, Private George 2520
Smith, Private Henry J. 2554
Smith, Private James 3036
Smith, Private Stanley I. 4270
Spurling, Private Edward 422
Strong, Private George R. 2758
Thompson, Private Ernest 2556
Thrower, Colour Serjeant Robert W. 1779
Trenowath, Private Harry 2799 (King's Lynn)
Tuddenham, Serjeant Walter S. 1873 (Hilgay)
Warren, Private Charles H. 2124
Ward, Private Percy 2259 (King's Lynn)
Williams, Private Frederick 2251
Williamson, Lance Corporal Thomas 1592

Prisoners of War
Two officers and fourteen men PoWs viz:

Officers
Coxon, Captain Arthur Cedric Meers – wounded – PoW Angora Internment Camp
Fawkes, Second Lieutenant William George Stewart – wounded – in the Djaal Red Crescent Hospital – then PoW Angora Internment Camp

NCOs and Other Ranks

Allen, Serjeant Alfred A., 1870 D Company (King's Lynn) – wounded – PoW Constantinople

Blott, Corporal William 2513 A Company (King's Lynn) – PoW Constantinople

Brown, Private Arthur E. 3357– wounded – PoW Constantinople

Ducker, Private Ephraim Charles 2860 (Honing) – wounded - PoW Constantinople

Fox, Lance Corporal Frank N. 1585 C Company – wounded - PoW Turkey

Grimes, Lance Corporal, William Charles, 322 C Company. (Born Congham, enlisted Hillington). Taken PoW 12 August 1915. Died whilst a prisoner of war 12 September 1915. Haidar Pasha Cemetery, Turkey.

Harnwell, Private, George, 2125. Taken PoW 12 August 1915. Died of wounds whilst a prisoner of war 21 August 1915 age 16. Son of George and Mary Elizabeth Harnwell, of Bridge Road, Downham West. Haidar Pasha Cemetery, Turkey

Hooks, Private Fred 3043 (Swaffham) – wound above eye – PoW Constantinople

Nobbs, Private Harry 2468 (A Company) – wounded – PoW Constantinople

Reeve, Private Alfred 2410. – wounded – PoW Constantinople

Stearman, Private Clifford. K. 3155. – wounded – PoW Constantinople

Swann, Drummer Donald C. 2120 (D Company) – wounded – PoW Constantinople

Thompson, Private Jesse Robert 2558 (Dereham) – wounds to back and leg. Died while prisoner of war 21 October 1916 age 24. Son of William and Fanny Thompson of East Dereham. Baghdad (North Gate) War Cemetery.

Webber, Private Arthur Thomas 3063 (Great Yarmouth) – wound to head.

Appendix 3

Roll of Honour of the Dead of $1/4^{th}$ and $1/5^{th}$ Battalions, The Norfolk Regiment Second Battle of Gaza 19 April 1917

Memorial plaque sent to the widow of Captain Evelyn Beck MC, $1/5^{th}$ Battalion, killed in action at the Second Battle of Gaza, 19 April 1917.

$1^{st}/4^{th}$ Battalion, The Norfolk Regiment

Officers

JEWSON, Major, WILLIAM HENRY age 42. Son of George and Mary Jewson, of Tower House, Bracondale, Norwich. Jerusalem Memorial, Israel.

MORGAN, Captain, WILLIAM VANSTONE age 29. Son of Benjamin Branford Morgan of 209, Unthank Road, Norwich. Jerusalem Memorial, Israel.

PAGE, Captain, SYDNEY DURRANT age 44. Son of John J.G. Page, of 'The Elms', Heigham Grove, Norwich. Gaza War Cemetery, Israel.

THURGAR, Captain, Ralph William MC. age 27. Son of William Augustus Thurgar of 'Eastcroft', Hemsby, Great Yarmouth. Gaza War Cemetery, Israel.

COLE, Lieutenant, FREDERICK JOHN. Son of Mr John Cole, Manor House, Lingwood, Norwich. Jerusalem Memorial, Israel.

LEVY, Second Lieutenant, JOSHUA. Son of Lewis and Sarah Levy of 9 Woodland Terrace, Borough Road East, Middlesborough. Gaza War Cemetery, Israel.

CHILVERS, Second Lieutenant, REGINALD CUTHBERT age 18. Son of John and Matilda Chilvers of Surbiton Hill SW. Jerusalem Memorial, Israel.

NCOs and Other Ranks

ABBOTT, Private, ERNEST ALBERT, 201060. Born Catton, enlisted Norwich age 22. Son of Joseph C. and Rosina Abbott, of 36, Knowsley Rd. Norwich. Jerusalem Memorial, Israel.

AGGAS, Private, SAMUEL FRANK, 201118. Enlisted Norwich 19 April 1917 age 20. Son of Florence Aggas, of Dolphin Bridge, Heigham St., Norwich. Jerusalem Memorial, Israel.

ATHERTON, Private, STANLEY WILLIAM, 200673 age 23. Son of Thomas and Alice Atherton of 74 Marlborough Road, Norwich. Jerusalem Memorial, Israel.

BALLS, Private, HORACE WILLIAM, 200806, A Coy. age 23. Son of William and Laura Balls, of Coston, Hardingham. Gaza War Cemetery, Israel.

BARBER, Private, GEORGE THOMAS, 200083. Born Heigham, Norwich enlisted Norwich. Son of William and Fanny Barber of Unicorn Yard, St Martin's Norwich. Jerusalem Memorial, Israel.

BARNARD, Private, ALBERT, 200905 age 20. Born Aylsham, enlisted Norwich. Son of Mr G.H. Barnard, of Oulton, Aylsham, Norfolk. Gaza War Cemetery, Israel.

BARNARD, Private, GEORGE ZACHARIAH, 200399 age 25. Born and enlisted at East Harling. Son of George and Eliza Barnard, of King St., East Harling, Attleborough. Jerusalem Memorial, Israel.

BARNARD, Private, ROBERT REGINALD, 200237, D Coy. Age 24. Born at Wymondham. Enlisted Norwich Aug. 1914. Son of Frederick and Elizabeth Barnard. Gaza War Cemetery, Israel.

BEATY, Private, GEORGE WILLIAM, 203439 age 20. Born King's Lynn, enlisted East Dereham. Son of John and Jessie Beaty of 27, Purfleet Street, King's Lynn. Jerusalem Memorial, Israel.

BEDWELL, Private, JOSEPH FRANCIS, 200172 age 20. Born Ditchingham, enlisted Homersfield. Son of Joseph and Elizabeth Bedwell of The Street, Earsham. Jerusalem Memorial, Israel.

BEETON, Private, REGINALD VICTOR, 201095 age 18. Enlisted Norwich. Son of Mr and Mrs Beeton, of 121, Armes St., Norwich. Jerusalem Memorial, Israel.

BELL, Private, LESLIE WALTER, 200436 age 24. Born Griston, enlisted Norwich. Son of Mr and Mrs G.A. Bell, of Watton Rd., Ashill. Gaza War Cemetery, Israel.

BENNELL, Private, ARTHUR JAMES, 201485 age 20. Born Bale, enlisted Norwich. Son of Robert Bennell, of Bale. Gaza War Cemetery Israel.

BIRCH, Private, HARRY, 201366 age 22. Born and enlisted Leek Staffordshire. Son of George and Annie Birch, of 3, South Portland St., Leek, Staffs. Gaza War Cemetery, Israel.

BLOOMFIELD, Private, HAROLD FRANK, 200683 age 19. Born Heckingham. Enlisted Norwich. Son of Gertrude Elsey of Cringleford, Norwich. Gaza War Cemetery, Israel.

BOND, Private, JOHN RICHARD, 203621 age 37. Born Sherton, Lancs., enlisted Lancaster. Son of Charles and Laura Fanny Bond, of 11, Beaumont St., Lancaster; husband of Mary Jane Bond, of 23, Beaumont St., Lancaster. Jerusalem Memorial, Israel.

BOOCOCK, Private, WILLIE, 202865 age 40. Born and enlisted Nelson, Lancs. Son of William and Nancy Boocock, of 15, Crawford St., Nelson; husband of Hilda Boocock, of 55, St. Mary's St., Nelson, Lancs. Jerusalem Memorial, Israel.

BORRETT, Lance Corporal, FREDERICK ARTHUR, 201963 age 29. Born Redenhall, enlisted Norwich. Son of James and Harriet Borrett, of Wortwell. Gaza War Cemetery, Israel.

BOWEN, Company Serjeant Major, DANIEL JOHN, 200082, A Coy. Age 28. Born Banham, enlisted Attleborough. Son of Thomas Bowen, of Doe Lane, Banham. Jerusalem Memorial, Israel.

BOWES, Private, STANLEY JOHN, 200915 age 17. Born Lenwade, enlisted Norwich. Son of the late John and Eliza Bowes. Jerusalem Memorial, Israel.

BRIGHTON, Corporal, TOM STANLEY, 200634. Enlisted Norwich. Son of the late Truman and Agnes Brighton, of Launceston, Cornwall. Jerusalem Memorial, Israel.

BROWN, Corporal, EDWARD FREDERICK, 201476. Born Old Catton, enlisted Norwich. Husband of Rose, father of Gwendoline. Jerusalem Memorial, Israel.

BROWN, Private, LEONARD, 201348 age 19. Born Hatfield, enlisted Hertford. Son of Walter William and Susan Harriet Brown, of 4, Friendly Terrace, Hatfield Heath, Harlow, Essex. Jerusalem Memorial, Israel.

BROWNE, Private, ERNEST ARTHUR, 201460 age 31. Born St John's Norwich, enlisted Norwich. Son of Benjamin Browne, of 7, Victoria Villas, Waltham Abbey, Essex. Jerusalem Memorial, Israel.

BUCKENHAM, Private, ERNEST EDWARD, 201440 age 19. Born Whaplode, Lincolnshire, enlisted Norwich. Son of George Buckenham of Leadenhall Farm, Holbeach, Lincolnshire. Jerusalem Memorial, Israel.

BUCKLE, Private, GEORGE, 200755. Born Tottington. Enlisted Norwich. Died of wounds. Son of Herbert and Amy Buckle of Hall Farm, Hunworth. Gaza War Cemetery, Israel.

BURKE, Private, MICHAEL, 203630. Born and enlisted St Helen's, Lancs. Jerusalem Memorial, Israel.

CADWALLADER, Private, Harry, 203297. Born Wolverhampton, enlisted Birmingham. Gaza War Cemetery, Israel.

CAREY, Serjeant, EDWARD JAMES, 200228 age 44. Born St Martin's-at-Oak, Norwich, enlisted Norwich. Son of Mr and Mrs E. Carey, of 174, Oak St., Norwich. Jerusalem Memorial, Israel.

CAREY, Serjeant, JOHN HERBERT, 201257, C Coy. age 32. Born at Bushey, Herts., enlisted Leighton Buzzard. Son of John Herbert and Henrietta Louisa Carey. Gaza War Cemetery, Israel.

CHADWICK, Private, HARRY, 202860. Born and enlisted Burnley, Lancs. Killed in action 19 April 1917. Gaza War Cemetery, Israel.

CHAPMAN, Private, ROBERT, 200917. Born St Stephen's, Norwich, enlisted Norwich. Husband of Rose Ann Chapman. Jerusalem Memorial, Israel

CHILDS, Private, RICHARD, 201358. Born Toddington, Beds, enlisted Bedford. Jerusalem Memorial, Israel.

CHILVERS, Serjeant, PERCY READ, 200284 age 26. Born Tottington, enlisted Norwich. Son of Mrs Alice Chilvers, of 'Shrublands', Brandon Rd., Watton. Jerusalem Memorial, Israel.

COCKADAY, Private, ALBERT EDWARD, 201347 age 21. Born North Heigham, enlisted Norwich. Son of Archibald and Laura Cockaday, of 4, Weston Square, Holt. Gaza War Cemetery, Israel.

CURSON, Private, STANLEY EDWARD, 200924 age 20, A Coy. Born Swanton Abbott, enlisted Norwich. Son of Robert and Annie Curson. Jerusalem Memorial, Israel.

DACK, Private, CHARLES, 200150 age 23. Born Deopham, enlisted Hingham. Son of Mr C. and Mrs C.E. Dack of Deopham. Jerusalem Memorial, Israel.

DAVIDSON, Private, WILLIAM, 203622 age 27. Born Runcorn, Cheshire, enlisted Warrington, Lancs. Husband of Ada Davidson of 16, Bentinck St., Runcorn, Cheshire. Gaza War Cemetery.

DAWSON, Corporal, WALTER, 200480 age 29. Enlisted Norwich. Son of George and Anna Read, of Ketteringham. Jerusalem Memorial, Israel.

DAYNES, Private, SAMUEL JAMES, 201451. Born Ranworth, enlisted Norwich. Son of James and Ellen Daynes of Heath Farm, Woodbastwick. Jerusalem Memorial, Israel.

DEWING, Corporal, ROBERT JOHN, 200707 age 30. Born Briston. Enlisted Norwich 4 August 1914. Son of William and Sarah Dewing, of The Street, Kelling. Jerusalem Memorial, Israel.

DOCKING, Private, HARRY JAMES, 200190 age 24. Born and enlisted Brandon. Son of Henry and Eliza Docking of 97 Thetford Road, Brandon, Suffolk. Jerusalem Memorial, Israel.

DOGGETT, Lance Corporal, WILLIAM ARNOLD, 200372 age 21. Enlisted Norwich. Son of Alfred and Blanche Doggett of 67, Glebe Road, Norwich. Jerusalem Memorial, Israel.

DRESH, Private, THOMAS JAMES, 201345. Born St. Luke's, Middx., enlisted St Pancras, Middx. Jerusalem Memorial, Israel.

DUNNETT, Private, PERCY ALFRED, 200462 age 20. Born Besthorpe, enlisted Norwich. Husband of Violet E. Darkins (formerly Dunnett), of Low Common, Deopham. Jerusalem Memorial, Israel.

EDWARDS, Private, SYDNEY ARTHUR, 200746 age 22. Enlisted Norwich. Son of Mr and Mrs A.W. Edwards of 145, Northumberland Street, Norwich. Jerusalem Memorial, Israel.

ELSEY, Serjeant, DAVID JOHN, 200005 age 30. Born and enlisted Diss. Husband of Keziah Elsey, of 5, Mission Rd., Diss. Jerusalem Memorial, Israel.

ELY, Private, ALEXANDER, 200326 age 40. Born St Martin's Norwich, enlisted, Norwich. Husband of Phoebe Alice Ely, of 8, Baldwin's Yard, Oak St., St. Martin's, Norwich. Jerusalem Memorial, Israel.

EVERITT, Private, Herbert, 203406. Son of William and Sarah Everitt of Chapel Yard, West Lynn. GAZA WAR CEMETERY, Israel.

FELTHAM, Private, JONATHAN EDWARD, 200733 age 27. Born Saxlingham, enlisted Norwich. Son of Jonathan and Margaret Feltham of Coltishall. Gaza War Cemetery, Israel.

FISHER, Private, CECIL HOWARD, 201155 age 19. Born Poringland, enlisted Norwich. Son of Howard and Florence Fisher of Stoke Holy Cross. Gaza War Cemetery, Israel.

FRANKLIN, Private, FREDERICK WILLIAM, 200336 age 38. Born Wymondham, enlisted Norwich. Husband of Maude Louisa Lister (formerly Franklin), of 174, Essex St., Crook's Place, Norwich. Jerusalem Memorial, Israel.

FROST, Private, GEORGE HENRY, 200533 age 31. Born Redenhall, enlisted Harleston. Son of Ambrose and Betsy Frost of Green Lanes, Starston. Jerusalem Memorial, Israel.

FROST, Private, WILLIAM, 201511. Born Lyng, enlisted Norwich. Husband of Ethel Frost. Jerusalem Memorial, Israel.

FUTTER, Private, JOSEPH, 203613 age 35. Son of Isaiah and Esther Futter of Gorleston. Gaza War Cemetery, Israel.

GATES, Lance Corporal, FREDRICK JOHN HARRY, 200484 age 21. Born at East Wretham enlisted Norwich. Son of George and Harriett Gates of Little Hockham. Gaza War Cemetery, Israel.

GIBBONS, Private, JOHN William, 200481. Born Wicklewood. Enlisted Norwich. Son of Walter and Alice Gibbons of Wickewood. Gaza War Cemetery, Israel.

GRAVER, Lance Corporal, WILLIAM HORACE, 200039 age 27. Born Heigham, enlisted Norwich. Husband of Lily Graver of 1 Freemans Buildings, Thorn Lane, Norwich. Jerusalem Memorial, Israel.

GREEN, Private, THOMAS, 203628 age 39. Born Cronton, Lancs., enlisted Warrington. Husband of Mary Green of 24, Lumley St., Garston, Liverpool. Jerusalem Memorial, Israel.

GURNEY, Private, ALBERT, 201278. Born Wheepley Hills, Bucks., enlisted Hertford. Jerusalem Memorial, Israel.

HAINES, Serjeant, GEORGE HENRY, 200874 age 24. Born Blakeney, enlisted Norwich. Son of George Edward and Dorothy Annie Haines, of Haddiscoe. Jerusalem Memorial L, Israel.

HAMBLING, Private, KENNETH BENTLEY, 201394 age 22. Born Thrapston, Northants, enlisted Mill Hill Middx. Son of Alfred John William and Eliza Fanny Hambling, of South Mimms, Middx. Jerusalem Memorial, Israel.

HARDIMENT, Private, EDGAR 'JOE', 201056 age 30. Born Wicklewood, enlisted Norwich. Son of Arthur and Phoebe Hardiment, of Chapel Lane, Town Green, Wymondham. Gaza War Cemetery, Israel.

HARDIMENT, Private, FRANK, 200669 age 22. Enlisted Norwich. Son of Arthur and Phoebe Hardiment, of Chapel Lane, Town Green, Wymondham. Jerusalem Memorial, Israel.

HARRIS, Private, HARRY, 203318 age 28. Born and enlisted Birmingham. Husband of Gertrude Harris, of 2/22, Long St., Sparkbrook, Birmingham. Jerusalem Memorial, Israel.

HARVEY, Private, THOMAS, 203313 age 41. Born Birdingbury, Warwick, enlisted Southam. Husband of Mary Jane Harvey of Birdingbury. Gaza War Cemetery, Israel.

HEWETT, Corporal, CECIL EDWARD, 200217, B Coy. Age 34. Born Honingham, enlisted Brook. Son of William and Rosetta Rebecca Hewett of Brooke. Jerusalem Memorial, Israel.

HEWITT, Private, JOHN, 201288 age 22. Born Deptford, Kent, enlisted St Albans, Herts. Son of Mr and Mrs W. Hewitt, of 4, Council Cottages, South Common, Redbourn, Herts. Jerusalem Memorial, Israel.

HILL, Lance Corporal, ROGER, 200597 age 25. Enlisted Norwich, September 1914. Son of Frank and Deborah Hill, of Marine View, Great Yarmouth. Gaza War Cemetery, Israel.

HINGLEY, Private, FRANK ALFRED, 202883 age 33. Born and enlisted Nottingham. Son of Thomas and Jane Hingley. Jerusalem Memorial, Israel.

HOWLETT, Lance Corporal, REGINALD COLEMAN, 200839 age 21. Enlisted Norwich. Son of Hezekiah and Rose Howlett of The Lodge, South Walsham. Jerusalem Memorial, Israel.

HULL, Private, GEORGE, 201424. Born and enlisted, Studham, Beds. Jerusalem Memorial, Israel.

HURRELL, Private, PERCY ROBERT, 200501. Enlisted Norwich. Son of Robert and Eleanor Hurrell of Deopham Green. Jerusalem Memorial, Israel.

JACKSON, Private, JOSEPH, 201419. Born Selby, Yorks, enlisted Watford, Herts. Jerusalem Memorial, Israel.

JENKINS, Private, WILLIAM HENRY, 203305 age 21. Born and enlisted Birmingham. Son of William and Sarah Ann Jenkins of Hawthorn Cottage, 3, Back 26, Cromwell St., Birmingham. Jerusalem Memorial, Israel.

JILLINGS, Private, WILLIAM 200793. Enlisted Norwich. Son of James Jillings. Jerusalem Memorial, Israel.

KETT, Serjeant, ARTHUR AYTON, 200468 age 31. Born Thorpe, Norwich. Enlisted Norwich, September 1914. Son of Henry and Martha Kett of Thorpe, St. Andrew. Gaza War Cemetery, Israel.

KIMBERLEY, Private, FRED, 202870 age 30. Born, Foulridge Lancs., enlisted Colne. Husband of Alice Kimberley of 37, Liverpool Avenue, Ainsdale, Southport. Gaza War Cemetery, Israel.

KIRBY, Private, GEORGE, 200102 age 21. Born Newton Flotman, enlisted Swainsthorpe. Son of George and Rebecca Kirby of Newton Flotman. Jerusalem Memorial, Israel.

KRANTZ, Serjeant, FRANK, 200417. Born Kensington, Middx., enlisted Norwich. Son of Theodore and Anna Krantz. Jerusalem Memorial L, Israel.

LAND, Private, EDWARD, 201043 age 27. Born Hellesdon, enlisted Norwich. Husband of Ethel Land, of 5, Boardered Entry, Ber St., Norwich. Gaza War Cemetery, Israel.

LAW, Private, FREDERICK L., 203333 age 31. Born and enlisted Birmingham. Son of Leonard and Elizabeth Law, of 19, Lozells St., Lozells, Birmingham. Jerusalem Memorial, Israel.

LAWS, Private, WILLIAM, 201162 age 35. Enlisted Norwich. Son of Mrs Amelia Laws, of 69, Nelson St., Norwich. Jerusalem Memorial, Israel.

LEE, Private, ALFRED JAMES, 201407. Born Hoddeston, Herts, enlisted Hertford. Jerusalem Memorial, Israel.

LINCOLN, Private, CHARLES, 200176. Born Rockland All Saints, enlisted Watton. Son of William and Lydia Lincoln of Scoulton. Gaza War Cemetery, Israel.

LISTER, Private, ARTHUR GEORGE, 200042 age 25. Born and enlisted Diss. Died of wounds 20 April 1917. Son of Agnes Smith (formerly Lister), of Denmark St., Diss, Norfolk. Deir El Belah War Cemetery, Israel.

LONG, Private, HENRY PERCIVAL 'HARRY', 200860. Born Great Yarmouth, enlisted Bedford. Son of Harry and Harriet Long of Bath Hill Terrace, Great Yarmouth. Jerusalem Memorial, Israel.

LOVICK, Private, ARTHUR ROBERT, 200973 age 28. Born St John's Sepulchre, Norwich, enlisted Norwich. Son of John and Caroline Lovick, of 11, Goldwell Rd., Norwich; husband of Mary Ann Lovick, of 54, Suffolk St., South Heigham. Jerusalem Memorial, Israel.

MARRISON, Private, HERBERT, 200880. Born St Barnabas, Norwich, enlisted Norwich. Son of Samuel and Elizabeth Marrison of 18 Globe Yard, North Heigham. Jerusalem Memorial, Israel. Although over 2,000 miles apart, his brother Acting Bombardier Percy Marrison, 106th Brigade, Royal Field Artillery, was killed in action in France on exactly the same day.

MARSHALL, Private, THOMAS WILLIAM, 202886. Born Hinderwell, enlisted Redcar, Yorks. Gaza War Cemetery, Israel.

MASON, Private, SIDNEY, 200489 age 20. Enlisted Norwich. Son of Fredrick and Eliza Mason of Great Hockham. Jerusalem Memorial, Israel.

MASON, Private, WILLIAM HENRY, 200086 age 21. Born St Edmunds, Norwich, enlisted Norwich. Son of Henry and Mary A. Mason, of 24, Rose Yard, St. Augustines, Norwich. Jerusalem Memorial, Israel.

MATTHAMS, Private, SYDNEY JOHN, 201414 age 21. Born Rayleigh, Essex, enlisted Southend. Son of Mr and Mrs R. Matthams, of 11, Hambro Villas, Hambro Hill, Rayleigh, Essex. Jerusalem Memorial, Israel.

MATTHEWS, Private, THOMAS, 203308 age 32. Born and enlisted Leamington, Warks. Son of Mr and Mrs Matthews, of 88, New St., Leamington Spa. Jerusalem Memorial, Israel.

McCANN, Private, WILLIAM THOMAS BRUNTON, 201311 age 28. Born Earsdon, enlisted Whitley Bay, Northumberland. Husband of Margaret Jane Reynolds (formerly McCann), of 2, Ash St., Hebburn Colliery, Co. Durham. Gaza War Cemetery, Israel.

McINERNEY, Private, EDWARD, 201353, A Coy. age 19. Born Isleworth, Middx., enlsted Kingston-upon-Thames. Son of Mrs A. Mclnerney, of 16, Smith St., Surbiton Hill, Surrey. Gaza War Cemetery, Israel.

McMILLAN, Lance Corporal, WILLIAM, 202863. Born Maxwelltown, Dumfries, enlisted Clitheroe, Lancs. Gaza War Cemetery Israel.

MEALE, Private, HEBER, 200488 age 34. Enlisted Norwich. Son of Josiah and Frances Meale, of Chandler's Hill, Wymondham. Gaza War Cemetery, Israel.

MOORE, Private, GEORGE WILLIAM, 202876 age 34. Born Hethersett, enlisted Norwich. Son of George and Maria Moore, of Hethersett; husband of Emma Moore of Rose Cottage, Hethersett. Jerusalem Memorial, Israel.

NEALE, Private, WILLIAM ERNEST, 200539 age 26. Enlisted Norwich. Son of Henry Neale, of 45, Wells Rd., Hockham. Gaza War Cemetery, Israel.

NEVILLE, Serjeant, FREDERICK CHARLES, 200709 age 27. Born and enlisted Norwich. Husband of Gertrude Neville, of 27, Sewell Rd., Norwich. Jerusalem Memorial, Israel.

NILAND, Private, MARTIN, 201302 age 42. Born Carraghariff, Roscommon, enlisted Nottingham. Husband of Martha Revell (formerly Niland), of Cliffe Villas, High Rd., Chilwell, Nottingham. Jerusalem Memorial, Israel.

NORGATE, Corporal, HARRY PERCY, 200056, C Coy. age 21 Born Horstead, enlisted Coltishall. Son of Edward and Emily Norgate, of 'Fern Lea', Horstead. Jerusalem Memorial, Israel.

NOURE, Private, MAHOMMED, 202890 age 33. Born Cape Town, enlisted London. Husband of Minna Noure, of 43, Frere St., Port Elizabeth, South Africa. Jerusalem Memorial, Israel.

NUNN, Private, ARTHUR WILLIAM, 200993 age 35. Born Stoke Holy Cross, Norwich. enlisted Norwich. Husband of Edith Nunn of 5, Black Swan Yard, Ber St., Norwich. GAZA WAR CEMETERY Gaza War Cemetery.

OLDHAM, Private, ALFRED ERNEST, 202891. Born Willesden, enlisted Mill Hill, Middx. Gaza War Cemetery, Israel.

ORVICE, Private, GEORGE ARTHUR GENTRY, 200700. Enlisted Norwich. Son of George and Harriet Orvice of 95 Northumberland Street, Norwich. Jerusalem Memorial, Israel.

OSBORNE, Private, GEORGE CHARLES EDWARD, 201032 age 20. Born Alburgh, enlisted Norwich. Son of Alfred and Harriett Osborne, of Alburgh. Jerusalem Memorial, Israel.

PALMER, Private, WILFRED NORMAN, 200848 age 20. Enlisted Norwich. Son of Herbert and Rosine Palmer of 67 Northcote Road, Norwich. Gaza War Cemetery, Israel.

PATTINSON, Company Serjeant Major, HENRY ROBINSON, 200010 age 35. Born and enlisted East Harling. Husband of Ida Pattinson of Kenninghall Road, East Harling. Jerusalem Memorial, Israel.

PAYNE, Private, GEORGE ALBERT, 201034, D Coy. Enlisted Norwich. Son of George Albert Payne, White Plot Farm, Feltwell, Norfolk. Jerusalem Memorial, Israel.

PEACHEY, Corporal, EDWARD, 200025 age 29. Born and enlisted Diss. Son of George and Harriet Alice Peachey, of Roydon Green, Diss. Gaza War Cemetery, Israel.

PICKLES, Private, WILLIAM, 202861 age 33. Born and enlisted Nelson, Lancs. Husband of Elizabeth Hannah Pickles, of 15, Moseley Hill Rd., Towneley, Burnley. Jerusalem Memorial, Israel.

POND, Private, HERBERT HORACE, 200585. Enlisted Norwich. Son of Herbert and Edith Pond of 24, Bishops Bridge Road, Pockthorpe, Norwich. Jerusalem Memorial, Israel.

POSTILL, Private, JOHN, 201395 age 20. Born and enlisted Hull. Gaza War Cemetery, Israel.

POWER, Private, FRANCIS JOHN, 200246 age 24. Born Lakenham, enlisted Norwich. Son of Emily Elizabeth Power. Jerusalem Memorial, Israel.

PYE, Private, JAMES ALBERT, 200900 age 26. Enlisted Norwich. Son of Mr and Mrs Richard Pye of Corpusty. Gaza War Cemetery, Israel.

RACKHAM, Private, REGINALD DENNIS, 200835. Born and enlisted Norwich. Lived at 34 Southwell Road, Norwich. Son of Valentine and Martha Rackham of Pretoria Cottage, Heacham. Jerusalem Memorial, Israel.

READ, Private, CHARLES ROBERT, 201021 age 25. Born Lakenham, enlisted Norwich. Husband of E.E. Alexander (formerly Read), of 4, St. Marks Cottages, Lakenham. Gaza War Cemetery, Israel.

READ, Private, HAROLD, 200586. Enlisted Norwich. His foster mother was Mary E. Abel. Gaza War Cemetery, Israel.

REEVE, Private, ARTHUR JOHN CLEAVERING, 200875 age 25. Born North Heigham, enlisted Norwich. Son of Arthur John and Jane Reeve of 59, Devonshire St. Norwich. Jerusalem Memorial, Israel.

RICHARDSON, Private, CHARLES, 202893. Born and enlisted Sunderland. Jerusalem Memorial, Israel.

ROBERTS, Private, WILLIAM THOMAS, 203299. Born and enlisted Birmingham. Gaza War Cemetery, Israel.

ROCK, Private, ALFRED, 203335. Born King's Bramley, Staffs., enlisted Coventry. Jerusalem Memorial L, Israel.

ROSE, Private, ROBERT, 200701 age 23. Enlisted Norwich. Son of Mr and Mrs J. Rose, of 14, Goose Lane, Waterloo Rd., Norwich. Jerusalem Memorial, Israel.

RUDD, Private, ARTHUR, 200628. Enlisted Norwich. Killed in action. Son of John Rudd, 21 Garden Terrace, Rose Valley, Unthank Road, Norwich. Jerusalem Memorial, Israel.

RUDMAN, Private, WILLIAM, 203315. Born Barking, Essex, enlisted Birmingham. Killed in action 19 April 1917. Jerusalem Memorial, Israel.

SADD, Private, JAMES PETER, 200126 age 22. Born Heigham, enlisted Norwich. Son of Walter Sadd of 310, Heigham St., Norwich. Jerusalem Memorial, Israel.

SANDERS, Private, HARRY WILLIAM, 201411. Enlisted St Albans, Herts. Gaza War Cemetery, Israel.

SARGEANT, Private, HARRY, 200504 age 34. Enlisted Norwich. Son of Henry and Sarah Sargent of Canns Lane, Hethersett. Gaza War Cemetery, Israel.

SAVAGE, Private, DONALD JOHN, 200425. Enlisted Norwich. Son of William and Eliza Savage of 13, Chalk Hill Road, Norwich. Gaza War Cemetery, Israel.

SAYER, Private, FREDERICK JOHN, 200614 age 21. Born Brook, enlisted Norwich. Son of George and Hannah Marie Sayer, of Brooke. Jerusalem Memorial, Israel.

SHACKSON, Private, JAMES HENRY, 201294. Born Clovelly, Devon, enlisted Tunstall, Staffs. Son of Charles and Mary Shackson, 63 The Village, Clovelly, Devon. Jerusalem Memorial, Israel.

SHAW, Private, JAMES, 200495. Enlisted Norwich. Jerusalem Memorial, Israel.

SLATER, Private, FREDERICK HUBERT, 200959. Born Honing, enlisted Norwich. Son of Richard and Thurza Slater of College Farm Cottages, Aldeby near Beccles. Gaza War Cemetery, Israel.

SMITH, Private, FREDERICK GEORGE, 200547 age 20. Enlisted Diss. Son of George and Emma Rebecca Smith, of South Lopham, Attleborough. Gaza War Cemetery, Israel.

SMITH, Private, HENRY ROBERT 'Harry', 200728. Enlisted Norwich. Husband of Susie, father of Reuben, Doris and Alice. Gaza War Cemetery, Israel.

SMITH, Private, WILLIAM, 201499 age 37. Born West Dereham, enlisted Norwich. Son of William Smith, of Downham West; husband of Jennie Smith of Bridge Rd., Downham West, Gaza War Cemetery, Israel.

STAGG, Private, BERTIE ROBERT JOHN, 200111 age 23. Born and enlisted Thetford. Son of William and Annie Elizabeth Stagg of 16, St. Nicholas St., Thetford. Jerusalem Memorial, Israel.

STEVENS, Private, CHARLES LEONARD, 200600 age 21. Born at Kettleburgh, Suffolk. Enlisted Norwich. Son of George and Harriett Stevens, of Mill St., Gislingham, Eye, Suffolk. Gaza War Cemetery, Israel.

STONE, Corporal, HENRY LOUIS, 201331 age 24. Born Willesden Green, enlisted Shepherd's Bush, Middx. Son of Henry and Mary Stone, of Frogmore, Kingsbridge, Devon. Jerusalem Memorial, Israel.

STURGEON, Private, SIDNEY MYLAND, 200039 age 21. Born Merton, enlisted Watton. Son of William Sturgeon of Home Farm, Thornhaugh, Peterborough. Gaza War Cemetery, Israel.

TAYLOR, Private, WILLIAM, 201315. Born Dersingham, enlisted Sheffield. Son of Enoch and Ann Taylor of Dersingham. Gaza War Cemetery, Israel.

WATTS, Private, ROBERT, 200861, A Coy. age 28. Born Worstead, enlisted Bradford, Yorks. Son of Jonah and Elizabeth Watts of Westwick, Norwich. Jerusalem Memorial, Israel.

WELLS, Corporal, FREDERICK CHARLES, 201256. Born Stoke, Suffolk, enlisted Ipswich. Gaza War Cemetery, Israel.

WICKETT, Private, DANIEL, 201375 age 40. Born Oldbury Worcs, enlisted Tipton, Staffs. Husband of Annie Wickett of 9, Tudor St., Coneygree, Tipton. Gaza War Cemetery, Israel.

WINTER, Private, FREDERICK WILLIAM, 201008. Born St Peter-par-Mountergate, Norwich, enlisted Norwich. Son of Robert and Eliza Winter of 1, Maidstone Road, Rose Lane, Norwich. Gaza War Cemetery, Israel.

YALLOP, Private, ALFRED, 200049. Born St Mile's, Norwich, enlisted Norwich. Son of Emma Yallop of 2, Lion and Castle Yard, Timberhill, Norwich. Jerusalem Memorial, Israel.

YOUNGMAN, Private, WILLIAM, 200123. Born Shotesham St Mary, enlisted Saxlingham. Son of John and Elizabeth Youngman of Market Lane, Shotesham. Jerusalem Memorial, Israel.

1/5th Battalion, The Norfolk Regiment

Officers

GRISSELL, Lieutenant Colonel, BERNARD SALWEY, DSO, Commanding Officer 1st/5th Bn., Norfolk Regiment. Age 37. Son of the late Thomas de la Garde Grissell, of Redisham Hall, Beecles, Suffolk; husband of Olive Grissell. Gaza War Cemetery, Israel.

BECK, Captain, ARTHUR EVELYN, MC age 31. Son of Edward William and Mary Beck, of Norwich; husband of Jennie Winifred Beck, of 'Winfield', Church St., Hunstanton. Gaza War Cemetery, Israel.

BIRKBECK, Captain, GERVASE WILLIAM. Died of wounds 20 April 1917 age 30. Son of Henry and Ysabel Birkbeck, of Westacre High House, Castle Acre, King's Lynn. Jerusalem Memorial, Israel.

CUBITT, Captain, EUSTACE HENRY, (Adjutant). 19 April 1917 age 28. Son of Edward George and Christabel M. Cubitt, of Honing Hall. Gaza War Cemetery, Israel.

GARDINER, Lieutenant, ERIC JOHN. Enlisted January 1916. Resided Wednesday Market Place, King's Lynn, son of Dr Arthur Gardiner MD, anaesthetist at King's Lynn Hospital and Margaret Wyndham Gardiner. Jerusalem Memorial, Israel.

PLAISTOWE, Lieutenant, RICHARD REEVES age 23. Born Islington. Son of Richard and Jane Plaistowe of 66 Southwood Lane, Highgate W. Gaza War Cemetery, Israel.

HERVEY, Lieutenant, DOUGLAS FREDERICK age 21. Died on 17 May 1917 from wounds, received on 19 April 1917. Son of M.W. and Ada Marian Hervey, of East Bilney all, East Dereham, Norfolk. Cairo War Memorial Cemetery, Egypt.

READ, Second Lieutenant, TERRENCE CAPON age 32. Died 22 April 1917 from wounds received on 19 April 1917. Son of A.W. Read, of 'Boscombe', 92, Christchurch Rd., Ipswich. Gaza War Cemetery, Israel.

NCOs and Other Ranks

ALLEN, Private, SAMUEL HENRY, 241068. Born West Lynn. Enlisted East Dereham. Son of Samuel and Martha Allen of West Lynn. Gaza War Cemetery, Israel.

ALLENBURY, Private, HARRY JEFFEREYS, 241563. Born Paddington, Middx, enlisted Norwich. Son of Annie Allenbury, he lived with his aunt and uncle at 6 Row 113, King Street, Great Yarmouth. Gaza War Cemetery, Israel.

AMES, Private, EDWARD, 241164 age 24. Born in Bradford, Yorks. Enlisted Norwich. Died of wounds 19 April 1917. Son of William and Alice Ames of 199, Nelson St., North Heigham, Norwich. Gaza War Cemetery, Israel.

AMIS, Drummer, WILLIAM WALTER, 240204. Born and enlisted Cromer. Taken Prisoner of War 19 April 1917. Died of malaria, Nigdi Hospital 18 August 1918. Son of William and Caroline Amis of Prince of Wales Road, Cromer. Baghdad (North Gate) War Cemetery, Iraq.

ANDERSON, Private, CHARLES, 241083 age 19. Enlisted King's Lynn. Son of Charles and Fanny Anderson of Chapel Yard, Pilot Street, King's Lynn. Gaza War Cemetery, Israel.

ASPIN, Private, JOHN, 242447. Born Darwen, Lancs, enlisted Blackburn. Gaza War Cemetery, Israel.

ATHERTON, Lance Corporal, EDWARD, 242456. Born and enlisted St Helen's Lancs. Jerusalem Memorial, Israel.

ATMORE, Private, WILLIAM, 240959. Enlisted East Dereham. Son of Christmas Atmore of Fiarstead, Gressenhall. Jerusalem Memorial, Israel.

BACON, Private, ERNEST WALTER, 240536 age 25. Enlisted East Dereham. Son of Walter and Ann Bacon, of East Dereham Gaza War Cemetery, Israel.

BAILEY, Private, GEORGE WILLIAM, 240973. Born Longham. Enlisted East Dereham. Son of Edward Bailey of East Hall Farm Cottage, Sedgeford. Jerusalem Memorial, Israel.

BANGER, Private, HENRY DAVERSON, 240908, D Coy. age 21. Enlisted East Dereham. Son of Michael and Madge Banger, of 7, Rodney Rd., Great Yarmouth. Jerusalem Memorial, Israel.

BARNES, Private, FREDERICK, 240157. Born Little Massingham. Enlisted Great Massingham. Son of Maria Barnes, Drivers Cottages, Great Massingham. Gaza War Cemetery, Israel.

BEALES, Private, ALFRED HENRY, 242535. Born Little Ellingham, enlisted Attleborough. Husband of Maria Beales. Jerusalem Memorial, Israel.

BECKETT, Company Serjeant Major, CHARLES, 240014. Born Mickleham, Surrey. Enlisted Dersingham. Son of Charles and Alice Beckett, of Chilton Gardens, Hungerford, Berks. Gaza War Cemetery, Israel.

BIRD, Corporal, CLIFFORD, 240548 age 23. Born East Runton. Enlisted East Dereham. Son of Arthur and Amanda Bird of 2 Garden Cottage, East Runton. Jerusalem Memorial, Israel. His brother Horace was killed on the same day.

BIRD, Serjeant, FRANK, 240129 age 31. Born West Runton, enlisted East Runton. Son of Walter and Mary A. Bird, of Inglewood Bungalow, East Runton, Cromer. Jerusalem Memorial, Israel.

BIRD, Serjeant, HORACE JOSEPH, 240546. Enlisted East Dereham. Son of Arthur and Amanda Bird of 2 Garden Cottage, East Runton. Jerusalem Memorial, Israel. His brother Clifford was killed the same day.

BLAKE, Private, John, 240167. Born Grimston, enlisted King's Lynn. Killed in action 19 April 1917 age 21. Son of Charles and Sarah Blake, of Keeper's Lane, Congham, King's Lynn. Gaza War Cemetery, Israel.

BLAND, Private, ARTHUR, 241070. Born Gayton. Enlisted East Dereham. Killed in Action 19 April 1917. Son of Walter Bland of East Winch Road, Gayton. Gaza War Cemetery, Israel.

BLISS, Private, REGINALD THOMAS, 240093. Born and enlisted Great Yarmouth. Resided 20 Rodney Road. Killed in action 19 April 1917 age 23. Son of Charles and Rosa Bliss. Gaza War Cemetery, Israel.

BOCKING, Private, HARRY, 240194. Born Sporle, enlisted Thornham. Son of Frederick and Hannah Bocking of East Hall Farm, Sedgeford. Jerusalem Memorial, Israel.

BOLTON, Private, CECIL JAMES, 240638. Enlisted East Dereham. Age 20. Son of Herbert and Jeanette Bolton of Cley-next-the-Sea, Norfolk. Jerusalem Memorial, Israel.

BONNETT, Corporal, RAYMOND, 240287. Born Oakham, Rutland, enlisted East Dereham. Killed in action 19 April 1917 age 23. Son of Thomas and Emily Bonnett, of Wereham Rd., Stoke Ferry. Gaza War Cemetery, Israel.

BROCK, Private, GABRIEL, 241113. Enlisted King's Lynn. Died of wounds 19 April 1917 age 24. Son of George and Sarah Brock of Rosedale House, Burkitt St., King's Lynn. Gaza War Cemetery, Israel.

BROOKS, Serjeant, WALTER CHARLES, 240347 age 24. Enlisted East Dereham. Killed in action. Son of Mr and Mrs Walter George Brooks of Catfield. Jerusalem Memorial, Israel.

BROWN, Private, FREDERICK WALTER, 240751, A Coy. age 26. Born at West Runton, enlisted East Dereham. Husband of Augusta Louisa Brown of Sea View Promenade, Sheringham. Gaza War Cemetery, Israel.

BROWN, Private, WILLIAM, 242340. Born Gorleston, enlisted Norwich. Son of William Brown. Lived at 15, Burnt Lane, Gorleston. Jerusalem Memorial, Israel.

BROWNE, Private, FRANK WILLIAM, 241058 age 22. Enlisted East Dereham. Son of Mr and Mrs A.F. Browne, of 173, Queen's Rd., Norwich. Jerusalem Memorial, Israel.

BUCK, Private, WALTER JOHN, 240373 age 21. Enlisted East Dereham. Son of Edward John and Rhoda Elizabeth Buck, of Beetley. Jerusalem Memorial, Israel.

BUDDS, Private, WALTER GLADSTONE, 240924, A Coy. age 22. Enlisted Great Yarmouth. Died of wounds 19 April 1917. Son of Maria Budds of 86, St. Nicholas Rd., Great Yarmouth. Jerusalem Memorial, Israel.

BULLEY, Private, WALTER, 242537 age 23. Born St James, Norwich, enlisted Norwich. Son of Frederick and Eliza Bulley of 41, Silver Road, Norwich. Gaza War Cemetery, Israel.

BUNN, Private, WILLIAM ALBERT, 240111 age 23. Born Dersingham, enlisted Sandringham. Son of Henry and Lucy Bunn, of Beech Drift, Dersingham. Gaza War Cemetery, Israel.

BUNNING, Private, WILLIAM HENRY, 241131 age 20. Enlisted King's Lynn. Son of Mrs. S.A. Bray, of 34, Sir Lewis St., King's Lynn. Gaza War Cemetery, Israel.

BURN, Serjeant, LESLIE CLAUDE, 240442 age 25, Enlisted East Dereham, Died of wounds 19 April 1917. Son of John Claude and Lily Burn, of Cam Villa, Gaywood. Gaza War Cemetery, Israel.

BURNETT, Private, THOMAS HENRY, 242538 age 24. Born Trunch, enlisted Cromer. Husband of Ida Burnett, of Brick Kiln Rd., Trunch, North Walsham. Jerusalem Memorial, Israel.

BURRELL, Private, ERNEST, 240871. Enlisted Great Yarmouth. Son of William and Sarah Burrell of 32 Southgates Road, Great Yarmouth. Gaza War Cemetery, Israel.

BUSBY, Private, BENJAMIN J, 240159. Born and enlisted Wells. Son of John and Maria Busby of Freeman Street, Wells. GAZA WAR CEMETERY, Israel.

BUTCHER, Private, CHARLES EDWARD, 240677 age 19. Enlisted East Dereham. Son of George and Alice Mary Butcher, of West Rudham, King's Lynn. Gaza War Cemetery, Israel.

CALLAGHAN, Private, DANIEL, 242449. Born and enlisted Warrington, Lancs. Jerusalem Memorial, Israel.

CASH, Private, VICTOR JAMES, 241064, MM. Born Walsall, Staffs. Enlisted Great Yarmouth. Son of Mary Ann Cash of 61, Exmouth Road, Great Yarmouth. Jerusalem Memorial, Israel.

CATCHPOLE, Lance Serjeant, ALBERT ALFRED, 240186. Born Great Yarmouth. Enlisted Great Yarmouth 4 August 1914. Resided 8, Belfort Place, Great Yarmouth. Jerusalem Memorial, Israel.

CATOR, Private, HARRY, 241196. Born Caston, enlisted Norwich. Son of James and Ann Cator of Caston. Jerusalem Memorial, Israel.

CATTON, Private, GEORGE FREDERICK, 240964 age 19. Born Worthing, Norfolk, enlisted East Dereham. Gaza War Cemetery, Israel.

CHANNELL, Corporal, HARRY, 240390 age 22. Enlisted Great Yarmouth. Son of Mr J.G.D. and Rebecca Channell, of 8, Albemarle Rd., Gorleston. Jerusalem Memorial, Israel.

CHAPMAN, Private, ROBERT JOHN, 241183. Enlisted Norwich. Husband of Dorothy Chapman. Jerusalem Memorial, Israel.

CLARKE, Serjeant, PERCY, 240108 age 22. Born Gimingham, enlisted Mundesley. Son of John and Marie Clarke, of White House, Gimingham, North Walsham. Jerusalem Memorial, Israel.

CLETHEROE, Private, ARTHUR WILLIAM RICHARD, 240202 age 21. Born Bodham, educated at Baconsthorpe. Enlisted Sheringham 5 August 1914. Son of Arthur Edward and Alice Ann Cletheroe of Baconsthorpe Hall, Norfolk. Gaza War Cemetery, Israel.

CORLEY, Private, JOHN, 241024 age 25. Enlisted East Dereham. Husband of Mrs Florence Corley, of Wisbech Rd., Downham West. Jerusalem Memorial, Israel.

COSSEY, Private, JAMES, 241178. Enlisted Cromer. Son of William Cossey of The Old Post Office, Roughton. Jerusalem Memorial, Israel.

CREASEY, Private, CHARLES ROBERT, 240196, C Coy. age 21. Born Little Melton, enlisted Cromer. Son of Henry and Barbara Creasey, of 'Wembley', West Runton, Cromer. Jerusalem Memorial, Israel.

CREASEY, Lance Corporal, THOMAS JAMES, 240197, C Coy. age 20. Born Little Melton, enlisted Cromer. Son of Henry and Barbara Creasey, of 'Wembley', West Runton, Cromer. Jerusalem Memorial, Israel.

CROWN, Private, WILLIAM, 240161 age 24. Born and enlisted Hunstanton. Son of Levina Crown, of 8, Church St., Hunstanton. Jerusalem Memorial, Israel.

CUBITT, Private, GEORGE PHILIP, 242488, C Coy. age 21. Born North Walsham. Son of Herbert and Blanche Cubitt of The Corner, Scottow. Gaza War Cemetery, Israel.

CURSON, Private, BERTIE, 240350. Enlisted East Dereham. Son of Edmund Curzon of Norwich Road, Yaxham. Gaza War Cemetery, Israel.

CURSON, Private, STANLEY, 241173. Enlisted Norwich. Son of John and Sarah Ann Curzon of Mill Road, Great Ryburgh. Gaza War Cemetery, Israel.

CURSON, Lance Corporal, WALTER, 240105. Born Fakenham, enlisted East Dereham. Jerusalem Memorial, Israel.

CUTTING, Private, WALTER JOHN, 240506 age 25. Enlisted Dereham. Son of Samuel and Louisa Cutting, of Lessingham. Gaza War Cemetery, Israel.

DANN, Private, SIDNEY, 240394 age 21. Enlisted East Dereham. Son of Mr E. Dann, of Eastgate St., Elmham. Gaza War Cemetery, Israel.

DAWS, Private, JOHN, 240035. Born Shipdam, enlisted Swaffham. Son of George and Emma Daws of Pales Green, Castle Acre. Jerusalem Memorial, Israel.

DAY, Private, JOHN WILLIAM, 240949 age 37. Born Downham Market, enlisted East Dereham June 1916. Husband of Adelaide Day of 1 Horsley Court, Southgate Street, King's Lynn. Jerusalem Memorial, Israel.

DEWING, Private, JOHN, 240233 age 19. Born Briston, enlisted Melton Constable. Son of John and Annie Dewing, of Briston. Jerusalem Memorial, Israel.

DIX, Private, ROBERT GEORGE, 241048. Enlisted East Dereham. Son of Reuben and Honor Dix of Upper Street, Southrepps. Gaza War Cemetery, Israel.

DIXON, Private, HENRY DANIEL, 242544 age 21. Born St Giles, Norwich, enlisted Norwich. Husband of Mary Dixon of 11, Back City Road, Norwich. Jerusalem Memorial, Israel.

DUNTHORNE, Private, ROBERT WILLIAM, 242336 age 22. Born Shipdam. Enlisted Norwich. Son of William and Julia Dunthorne of Brick Barn Cottage, Whittlingham. Gaza War Cemetery, Israel.

EAGLE, Private, SIDNEY ELIJAH, 240505 age 22. Enlisted East Dereham. Son of William and Maria Eagle of 2, New Cottage, Holme Hale. Gaza War Cemetery, Israel.

EDGELEY, Private, VICTOR, 240025. Born Attleborough, enlisted Fakenham. Son of Mrs Gertrude Edgeley, of Wells Rd., Fakenham. Gaza War Cemetery, Israel.

EDWARDS, Private, ERNEST ROBERT, 240592 age 26. Enlisted Great Yarmouth 11 September 1914. Husband of Maria Deynie Sales (formerly Edwards) of 60, Walpole Rd., Newtown, Great Yarmouth. Jerusalem Memorial, Israel.

EGLINGTON, Private, E J, 240793 age 24. Enlisted East Dereham. Son of Walter Robert and Sarah Arm Eglington, of Wood Dalling. Gaza War Cemetery, Israel.

EKE, Private, FREDERICK JOHN, 240792 age 20. Enlisted East Dereham. Son of Edward and Emily Eke of Mill Rd., Whitwell, Reepham. Jerusalem Memorial, Israel.

ELLIS, Private, WALTER, 240172 age 23. Born Winfarthing, enlisted Stalham. Son of George and Eliza Ellis, of Markshall. Gaza War Cemetery, Israel.

ENGLISH, Private, SYDNEY HERBERT, 240451, B Coy. age 25. Enlisted Sept. 1914 at East Dereham. Son of Richard Herbert and Agnes English, of Wootton Rd., Gaywood. Jerusalem Memorial, Israel.

EVERITT, Private, HUBERT, 203406. Born West Lynn. Enlisted East Dereham. Son of William and Sarah Everitt of Chapel Yard, West Lynn. Gaza War Cemetery, Israel.

FICKLING, Serjeant, ALFRED, 240022. Born St Margaret's, Norwich. Enlisted King's Lynn. Husband of Lucy Fickling of 9 St James Place, Kings Lynn. Gaza War Cemetery, Israel.

FISHER, Serjeant, EDGAR HIPPERSON, 240310 age 28. Born East Tuddenham, enlisted East Dereham. Son of Joseph and Elizabeth Fisher, Grange Farm, Honingham. Gaza War Cemetery, Israel.

FISHER, Serjeant, JOSEPH, 240304 age 25. Born East Tuddenham, enlisted East Dereham. Son of Joseph and Elizabeth Fisher, Grange Farm, Honingham. Gaza War Cemetery, Israel.

FLERTEY, Private, HENRY, 240641 age 29. Enlisted Great Yarmouth September 1914. Husband of Ellen Maud Flertey, of No.7 Row, 10, Church Plain, Great Yarmouth. Jerusalem Memorial, Israel.

FOYSTER, Private, THOMAS ANDREW, 242339. Born St. George's Norwich, enlisted Norwich. Son of William and Elizabeth Foyster. Husband of Ethel Foyster of 21, Russell Street, Heigham, Norwich. Gaza War Cemetery, Israel.

FREEZER, Private, ERNEST JAMES, 240146, A Coy. age 27. Born and enlisted Gressenhall. Son of Louisa Green (formerly Freezer), of Gressenhall. Jerusalem Memorial, Israel.

FUNNELL, Lance Corporal, EDWIN THOMAS, 240569. Born Terrington St Clements. Enlisted East Dereham. Son of Roland and Sarah Funnell of Terrington St Clements. Jerusalem Memorial, Israel.

FURZE, Private, SIDNEY HENRY, 242491 age 26. Born Heigham, Norwich, enlisted Norwich. Son of Harry and Elizabeth Furze, of 43, Pattison Rd., Aylsham Rd., Norwich. Jerusalem Memorial, Israel.

GIBSON, Private, SIDNEY, 240942 age 31. Enlisted Great Yarmouth. Husband of Elizabeth Underwood (formerly Gibson), of No.16, Row 139, South Quay, Great Yarmouth. Jerusalem Memorial, Israel.

GILLINGS, Corporal, ARTHUR WILLIAM, 240018. Born and enlisted Great Yarmouth. One of the seven children of Arthur and Martha Gillings of 19, Gordon Road, Southtown, Great Yarmouth. Gaza War Cemetery, Israel.

GOOCH, Private, ALFRED, 242312 age 28. Born Hethel, enlisted Wrenningham. Son of Mr and Mrs R. Gooch, of Ketteringham. Jerusalem Memorial, Israel.

GOODSON, Private, FREDERICK JAMES, 242549. Born St. Nicholas, enlisted King's Lynn. Son of Joseph and Emily Goodson of 12, Pilot Street, King's Lynn. Jerusalem Memorial, Israel.

GREEN, Private, LIONEL WALTER, 240961, A Coy. age 20. Enlisted East Dereham. Son of George and Sarah Ann Green, of Cranworth Common, Shipdham, Thetford, Norfolk. Gaza War Cemetery, Israel.

GRIEF, Corporal, EDWARD HUGH, 240816. Enlisted East Dereham, August 1914. Husband of Mrs Callaby (formerly Grief), of The Buildings, Tilney St. Lawrence, King's Lynn. Gaza War Cemetery, Israel.

GRIFFIN, Private, WILLIAM, 240457 age 23. Enlisted East Dereham. Son of Joshua and Elizabeth Griffin, of Booth Square, Helhoughton. Jerusalem Memorial, Israel.

GRIMES, Private, THOMAS, 240354. Born Congham. Enlisted East Dereham. Son of William and Georgiana Grimes of Flitcham. Jerusalem Memorial, Israel.

GROOM, Private, WILLIAM, 240047. Born St Nicholas, Great Yarmouth, enlisted Great Yarmouth. Son of Eliza Groom of Cobbs Place, Great Yarmouth. Jerusalem Memorial, Israel.

HALL, Private, ROBERT WILLIAM, 240850 age 19. Enlisted East Dereham. Son of Mrs Flora Rose, of Fern Cottage, Lake Rd., King's Lynn. Jerusalem Memorial, Israel.

HARDEN, Private, EDWIN GEORGE, 241043 age 20. Enlisted East Dereham. Son of Louisa Mary Hall (formerly Harden), of New Road Cottage, Whitwell Common, Reepham, Norwich. Jerusalem Memorial, Israel.

HARMER, Private, EDWIN, 241090 age 25. Enlisted Cromer. Son of Robert and Elizabeth Harmer, of Park Lodge, Upper Sheringham. Jerusalem Memorial, Israel.

HARPER, Private, THOMAS, 242485 age 42. Born Tidgate, Cambs., enlisted Norwich. Son of Thomas William Harper and the late Elizabeth Harper of Congham. Jerusalem Memorial, Israel.

HARRISON, Lance Corporal, GEORGE, 240459. Enlisted East Dereham. Jerusalem Memorial, Israel.

HARRISON, Private, REGINALD, 240626. Enlisted Great Yarmouth. Son of Emma Harrison. Jerusalem Memorial, Israel.

HASTINGS, Serjeant, ARCHIBALD 'Archie', 240038 age 28. Born and enlisted Cromer. Son of Herbert and Mary Ann Hastings, husband of Florence Grace Hastings. His daughter Constance Albinia was born just a few days before he was killed. Jerusalem Memorial, Israel.

HASTINGS, Private, BERTIE, 240043 age 26. Born and enlisted Cromer. Son of Herbert and Mary Ann Hastings. Jerusalem Memorial, Israel. His brother Archie also fell on the same day.

HENDRY, Private, FRANK, 240460 age 21. Enlisted East Dereham. Son of George and Henrietta Hendry of West Acre. Gaza War Cemetery, Israel.

HENSBY, Private, FREDERICK, 242519 age 33. Born Thetford, enlisted Norwich. Husband of Harriet Kent (formerly Hensby), of Aerodrome Cottages, Feltwell. Jerusalem Memorial, Israel.

HORSLEY, Private, ROBERT ARCHIE, 241148. Born and enlisted King's Lynn. Son of Matthew and Jemima Horsley. Jerusalem Memorial, Israel.

HOWARD, Private, ALFRED ERNEST, 240947. Enlisted East Dereham. Son of Ernest and Virtue Howard of Mill Road, Banningham Common. Gaza War Cemetery, Israel.

HOWARD, Private, JESSE JOHN, 240083 age 24. Born and enlisted East Dereham. Son of William and Adelaide Howard, of 59, Baxter Row, East Dereham. Jerusalem Memorial, Israel.

HOWELL, Private, JAMES, 241092 age 20. Enlisted King's Lynn, May 1916. Died of wounds 19 April 1917. Son of George and Elizabeth Howell, of 5, Manor Rd., Dersingham, King's Lynn. Gaza War Cemetery, Israel.

HOWES, Private, ARTHUR WILLIAM, 240319 age 25. Born Gorleston, resided 69 Nelson Road. Enlisted Great Yarmouth. Son of Alfred and Charlotte Howes, of Gorleston. Jerusalem Memorial, Israel.

HOWMAN, Private, BERTIE JOHN, 240504 age 21. Born Bethel Street, Norwich. Enlisted East Dereham, August 1914. Son of James John and Florence Beatrice Howman of 157, Beaconsfield Rd., Norwich. Jerusalem Memorial, Israel.

HUDSON, Private, ALBERT EDWARD, 242462 age 22. Born Surlingham, enlisted Norwich 1914. Son of Mr Henry and Mary Ann Hudson, of Surlingham, Gaza War Cemetery, Israel.

JACKSON, Private, HAZEL RENWICK, 241108. Enlisted Cromer. Son of Mrs Jackson, of Woodmaston, Pembridge, Herefordshire. Gaza War Cemetery, Israel.

JARVIS, Private, ROBERT, 240557. Enlisted East Dereham. Son of Robert Jarvis. Jerusalem Memorial, Israel.

JONAS, Private, ROBERT WILLIAM, 240916 age 25. Enlisted Great Yarmouth. Husband of Ada Elizabeth Chalmers (formerly Jonas), of 39, Winsor Terrace, Beckton, London. Jerusalem Memorial, Israel.

JORDAN, Private, WILLIAM, 240356 age 23. Born Starton, Lincs, enlisted East Dereham. Son of Thomas and Ruth Jordan, of Stourton, Lincoln. Gaza War Cemetery, Israel.

KENT, Private, FREDERICK ARTHUR, 241027. Enlisted East Dereham. Gaza War Cemetery, Israel.

KENT, Private, WALTER, 240853. Enlisted East Dereham. Jerusalem Memorial, Israel.

KING, Private, AARON GEORGE, 240587. Born and enlisted Great Yarmouth 5 September 1914. Resided 44 England's Lane, Gorleston. Wounded 19 April 1917, Died of wounds while Prisoner of War 9 June 1917. Damascus Commonwealth War Cemetery, Syria.

KNIGHTS, Private, GEORGE ROBERT, 242506 age 33. Born Bunwell, enlisted Norwich. Son of Horace Knights; husband of May Agnes Knights, of Diss Rd., Tibenham. Gaza War Cemetery, Israel.

LAKE, Private, ARTHUR ROBERT, 241066. Enlisted East Dereham. Killed in action 19 April 1917. Husband of Violet Lake. Gaza War Cemetery, Israel.

LAMBERT, Private, ERNEST STEPHEN, 241062. Enlisted East Dereham. Son of Mrs Lambert, of Primrose Cottage, Kerdistone. Gaza War Cemetery, Israel.

LAND, Corporal, CHARLES EDWARD, 240803 age 29. Enlisted East Dereham 1914. Husband of Hilda C. Land, of 28, Kent Square, Great Yarmouth. Gaza War Cemetery, Israel.

LARGE, Private, ARTHUR GEORGE, 240312. Born and enlisted East Dereham. Son of Ernest and Elizabeth Large of Clifton Terrace, South End, East Dereham. Jerusalem Memorial, Israel.

LEEDER, Private, NORMAN ROBERT, 240195 age 20. Born Marsham, enlisted Stalham. Son of Robert John and Ellen Margaret Leeder, of High House, Happisburgh. Jerusalem Memorial, Israel.

LEWIS, Corporal, AUSTIN, 240163 age 19. Born and enlisted King's Lynn. Son of John H. and Ethelburga Lewis, of 6, Bridge St., King's Lynn. Jerusalem Memorial, Israel.

LINES, Private, FREDERICK AUGUSTUS, 240132. Born Felbrigg. Enlisted East Runton. Son of Frederick and Harriett Lines of 'Cliffside' West Runton. Gaza War Cemetery, Israel.

LOWN, Private, ERNEST ALBERT HUMPHREY, 240741, D Coy. age 21. Enlisted East Dereham. Son of Nellie Le Roi Harwood (formerly Lown), of Wyckford House, Mare Hill, Pulborough, Sussex. Jerusalem Memorial, Israel.

LYST, Private, ARTHUR ALBERT, 242345 age 19. Enlisted Norwich. Son of George Ambrose Lyst and Ellen Sarah Lyst, of 1, Home St., North Heigham, Norwich. Jerusalem Memorial, Israel.

MAYCRAFT, Private, GEORGE EDGAR, 241081 age 19. Enlisted East Dereham. Son of Charles and Emily Maycraft of Ferry Road, Clenchwarton. Gaza War Cemetery, Israel.

MAYES, Private, FRANCIS, 'Frank' 240470 age 20. Enlisted East Dereham. Taken Prisoner of War Second Gaza 19 April 1917. Died of wounds at hospital in Constantinople while in captivity 22 May 1917. Son of Francis and Rose Mayes, 6 Union Place, King's Lynn. Haifa War Cemetery, Israel.

McNICHOLAS, Private, PETER, 242451 age 34. Born and enlisted Ulverston, Lancs. Killed in action 19 April 1917. Gaza War Cemetery, Israel.

MERRISON, Lance Corporal, PERCY WILLIAM, 240695 age 22. Enlisted East Dereham. Son of James and Mary A. Merrison, of 35, Mount Pleasant Rd., Wisbech. Jerusalem Memorial, Israel.

MINDHAM, Private, WALTER WILLIAM, 240053. Born Snettisham, enlisted Flitcham. Son of Henry and Harriet Mindham of 7 Abbey Road, Flitcham. Gaza War Cemetery, Israel.

MITCHELL, Corporal, HERBERT JAMES, 240188 age 24. Born Thornham, enlisted Hunstanton. Son of Mr H.J. and Louisa Mitchell, of High St., Thornham. Jerusalem Memorial, Israel.

MOORE, Private, ERNEST ROBERT, 240084. Born St Nicholas, Great Yarmouth, resided 10 Adam and Eve's Garden, Great Yarmouth, enlisted Great Yarmouth 4 August 1914. Jerusalem Memorial, Israel.

MOORE, Lance Corporal, WALTER JAMES CHARLES, 240322. Born Bradwell, enlisted Great Yarmouth. Son of Oliver Moore. Jerusalem Memorial, Israel.

MOY, Private, FREDERICK, 240040. Born Aylsham. Son of Jacob and Benina Moy of Town Lane, Aylsham. Gaza War Cemetery, Israel.

MYERS, Private, Charles, 240855 age 21. Enlisted East Dereham. Died of wounds 19 April 1917. Son of the late Mr C. Myers 2, Union Place, King's Lynn. Gaza War Cemetery, Israel.

NEWELL, Private, WILLIAM, 241012. Born East Winch, enlisted East Dereham. Son of William Newell. Jerusalem Memorial, Israel.

NEWSON, Private, WILLIAM JAMES RICHARD, 240658 age 21. Born at Gorleston, resided 4 Avenue Road, enlisted Great Yarmouth 1915. Son of Richard and Alice Newson of Great Yarmouth. Gaza War Cemetery, Israel.

NEWSTEAD, Private, ALFRED BASIL, 240513 age 22. Enlisted East Dereham. Son of James and Catherine Newstead of Hunstanton. Jerusalem Memorial, Israel.

OGILVY, Company Quartermaster Serjeant, ALEXANDER GEORGE, 240473 age 22. Enlisted East Dereham. Son of James Alexander Ogilvy and Jessie Morrison Ogilvy, of Cromer Rd., North Walsham. Jerusalem Memorial, Israel.

OXBOROUGH, Private, GEORGE, 241091 age 19. Born Sporle. Enlisted Cromer. Son of John and Anna Maria Oxborough of Sporle Road Cottages, Swaffham. Gaza War Cemetery, Israel.

PARKER, Private, ERNEST GEORGE, 240878. Enlisted Great Yarmouth. Resided at 13, Palgrave Road, Great Yarmouth. Jerusalem Memorial, Israel.

PERRY, Private, JOSEPH, 242470 age 28. Born and enlisted Colchester. Son of the late Mr and Mrs J. Perry. Jerusalem Memorial, Israel.

PINCHEN, Corporal, JOHN, 240309 age 25. Born Corpusty, enlisted East Dereham. Son of Emily Arthurton (formerly Pinchen), of Little Witchingham Hall, Norwich. Jerusalem Memorial, Israel.

PITCHER, Private, CHARLES, 240717. Born Shernbourne. Enlisted East Dereham. Son of John and Caroline Pitcher of Shernbourne. Jerusalem Memorial, Israel.

PITCHER, Private, ROBERT, 241067. Born Shernbourne. Enlisted East Dereham. Killed in action 19 April 1917. Son of John and Caroline Pitcher of Shernbourne. Gaza War Cemetery, Israel.

PITCHER, Private, WILFRED, 240948. Born Aldborough. Enlisted East Dereham. Son of Elliott and Alice Pitcher of 38, Waldeck Road, Norwich. Gaza War Cemetery, Israel.

PLAICE, Private, ARTHUR EDWARD, 240900 age 20. Enlisted East Dereham. Son of Robert and Mary Elizabeth Plaice, of Westgate St., Shouldham. Gaza War Cemetery, Israel.

PLATTEN, Private, JOHN, 240219 age 26. Born Northrepps, enlisted Mundesley. Son of Thomas and Sarah Platten of Sea View Cottage, Mundesley. Gaza War Cemetery, Israel.

PORTER, Private, BERTIE WILLIAM, 240857 age 21. Enlisted East Dereham. Son of Robert and Harriett Porter, of Well Cottage, Harpley. Jerusalem Memorial, Israel.

POSTLE, Private, ERNEST CHARLES, 240383 age 19. Resided No.28, Row 99. Enlisted Great Yarmouth, September 1914. Son of Charles and Elizabeth Postle, of Row 101, 4, King St., Great Yarmouth. Gaza War Cemetery, Israel.

PROUDFOOT, Private, SAMUEL EDWARD, 241122 age 25. Enlisted King's Lynn. Son of Robert and Jane Proudfoot, of Brancaster. Gaza War Cemetery, Israel.

RAMM, Private, WILLIAM, 240981. Enlisted East Dereham. Son of Mary A. Cason. Jerusalem Memorial, Israel.

RASBERRY, Private, ROBERT WILLIAM, 241007 age 20. Born and enlisted King's Lynn. Son of Sarah Rasberry, 17 Coronation Square, King's Lynn. Jerusalem Memorial, Israel.

REEVE, Private, CECIL ARTHUR, 240613 age 20. Enlisted East Dereham. Son of Herbert and Marie Reeve, of Hope House Yard, Hindolvestone. Jerusalem Memorial, Israel.

REYNOLDS, Private, JAMES EDWARD, 240694. Born Dillington. Enlisted East Dereham. Son of Edward and Georgina Reynolds, workers on the Dillington Hall Estate, East Dereham. Gaza War Cemetery, Israel.

ROBINSON, Serjeant, JAMES WILLIAM, 240585. Resided 4 Paston Place, St. George's Road, Great Yarmouth. Enlisted Great Yarmouth 11 September 1914. Gaza War Cemetery, Israel.

ROY, Private, BERTIE, 240432. Enlisted East Dereham. Son of Mrs Roy, of 11, Church St., East Dereham. Gaza War Cemetery, Israel.

RUDD, Private, LESLIE WILLIAM, 242323. Born Norwich. Enlisted Norwich, August 1914. Taken prisoner 19 April 1917, died 19 October 1917. Son of William Rudd. Gaza War Cemetery, Israel.

RUDMAN, Private, WILLIAM, 203315. Born Barking. Enlisted Birmingham. Husband of Jane Rudman. Jerusalem Memorial, Israel.

RUDRAM, Private, AUSTIN GEORGE, 240220 age 32. Born and enlisted Mundesley. Son of James and Sophia Rudram of 5 Town's End Cottages, Mundesley. Jerusalem Memorial, Israel. His brother Charles fell on the same day.

RUDRAM, Private, CHARLES JAMES, 240107 age 26. Born and enlisted Mundesley. Son of James and Sophia Rudram of Mundesley. Gaza War Cemetery, Israel. His brother Austin fell on the same day.

RUSTED, Private, ALBERT, 240607 age 21. Born Metfield, Suffolk. Enlisted East Dereham. Son of the late Richard and Sarah Rusted. Jerusalem Memorial, Israel.

SADLER, Private, JOHN, 240091. Born Tichwell, enlisted Thornham. Son of Robert Sadler. Gaza War Cemetery, Israel.

SEALS, Private, RICHARD WILLIAM, 240789 age 21. Enlisted East Dereham. Son of Charles Seals, of 27, High Terrace, Fakenham. Jerusalem Memorial, Israel.

SMALLS, Private, IVO, 240652 age 40. Born Snettisham, enlisted East Dereham. Son of Frederick and Elizabeth Smalls, of Snettisham. Gaza War Cemetery, Israel.

SMITH, Private, HERBERT, 242326, D Coy. age 28. Born at Fakenham, Norfolk, enlisted Norwich. Son of Henry and Elizabeth Smith; husband of Mrs M.B. Smith of 9, Castle Row, Castle St., Thetford. Gaza War Cemetery, Israel.

SMITH, Private, SIDNEY, 240424 age 21. Enlisted East Dereham. Son of James and Sarah Smith, of 24, Lincoln Terrace, Becclesgate, East Dereham. Jerusalem Memorial, Israel.

SMITH, Lance Corporal, THOMAS JAMES, 240530. Enlisted East Dereham. Jerusalem Memorial, Israel.

SMITH, Private, WILLIAM, 241150. Enlisted East Dereham. Jerusalem Memorial, Israel.

SNELLING, Private, HENRY WILLIAM, 240267, D Coy. age 19. Born Great Yarmouth. Enlisted Great Yarmouth, August 1914. Son of Herbert William and Margaret Snelling of No.4, Row 137, Great Yarmouth. Gaza War Cemetery, Israel.

SOUTHGATE, Serjeant, HERBERT WILLIAM LEONARD, 240701, A Coy. age 28. Enlisted East Dereham. Son of Herbert William and Hannah Southgate, of East Raynham. Gaza War Cemetery, Israel.

SPARKES, Private, ERNEST WALTER, 240433 age 30. Enlisted East Dereham. Son of George and Ellen Sparkes, of Worthing, North Elmham. Jerusalem Memorial, Israel.

SPOONER, Private, CLARENCE, 240781 age 21. Enlisted East Dereham. Son of William and Deborah Spooner, of Fring, Docking. Jerusalem Memorial, Israel.

SPURGEON, Private, FRANK BASIL, 240881 age 18. Enlisted Great Yarmouth 1914. Son of Mrs Clara Lurkins, of 214, High St., Gorleston. Jerusalem Memorial, Israel.

STAFF, Private, FRANK HENRY, 242509. Born Hackney Middx., enlisted Norwich. Gaza War Cemetery, Israel.

STANNARD, Private, SIDNEY ERNEST, 241009. Born King's Lynn. Enlisted King's Lynn June 1915. Taken Prisoner of War 19 April 1917, died while in captivity 30 September 1918 age 22. Son of William and Susan Stannard, of 4, Elsdens Houses, Friars St., King's Lynn. Baghdad (North Gate) War Cemetery, Iraq.

STEARMAN, Private, MARSHALL THOMAS, 240698 age 20. Enlisted East Dereham. Son of James and Sarah Seeley Stearman, of 26, Salle St., Reepham. Jerusalem Memorial, Israel.

STEGGLES, Private, ALFRED CHARLES, 240748 age 22. Enlisted East Dereham. Son of Alfred and Kezia Steggles, of Little Dunham. Jerusalem Memorial, Israel.

STONE, Private, GEORGE ERNEST ROBERT, 240882 age 20. Enlisted Great Yarmouth, March 1915. Son of George I.R. and Hannah Louisa Stone, of 36, Waveney Rd., Southtown, Great Yarmouth. Jerusalem Memorial, Israel.

STRANGLEMAN, Private, CECIL, 240807 age 22. Enlisted East Dereham. Son of John and Amelia Strangleman, of East Rudham, King's Lynn. Gaza War Cemetery, Israel.

SUSSUMS, Private, HAROLD, 242319 age 24. Born Scoulton, enlisted Watton. Son of William and Elizabeth Sussums, of Scoulton, Attleborough. Jerusalem Memorial, Israel.

TEE, Private, JOSEPH, 242563 age 35. Born Peterborough, enlisted Cromer. Husband of Blanche Tee. Jerusalem Memorial, Israel.

THOMPSON, Private, HARRY ROBERT, 240861 age 26. Enlisted East Dereham. Son of William and Elizabeth Thompson, of Gonville Terrace, Terrington St. Clement's, King's Lynn. Jerusalem Memorial, Israel.

TIPTOD, Lance Corporal, ROBERT, 240662 age 26. Born St Nicholas, Great Yarmouth. Enlisted Great Yarmouth. Son of Robert and Emily Tiptod. Gaza War Cemetery, Israel.

TODD, Serjeant, LEONARD ROSS, 241029. Born Wickham Market, Suffolk, enlisted East Dereham. Son of Mrs Todd, of 1, Paddow Rd., Chelmsford. Gaza War Cemetery, Israel.

TOOKE, Private, ALBERT EDWARD, 240685, A Coy. age 21. Enlisted East Dereham. Son of Mr and Mrs Frederick Tooke, of 91, King's Rd., East Dereham. Gaza War Cemetery, Israel.

TUCK, Private, CHARLES JOHN, 241154 age 23. Born Bessingham, enlisted at Norwich January 1916. Only son of John and Mary Ann Tuck of Bessingham. Gaza War Cemetery, Israel.

TUDDENHAM, Serjeant, WALTER SIDNEY, 240150. Born Whitwell, enlisted Downham Market. Gaza War Cemetery, Israel.

TULLETT, Lance Corporal, ARTHUR WILLIAM, 241564 age 30. Born and enlisted King's Lynn. Son of Walter William and Rebecca Tullett of 4, Clough Lane, King's Lynn. Jerusalem Memorial, Israel.

TURNER, Private, REGINALD ARTHUR, 241089 age 19. Enlisted Cromer. Son of Mrs. Ellen Turner, of 'Hazelbank', Beeston End, Sheringham. Jerusalem Memorial, Israel.

VURLEY, Private, FREDERICK JAMES, 240742 age 21. Enlisted East Dereham. Son of James and Ann Mary Vurley, of Hempton Green, Fakenham. Gaza War Cemetery, Israel.

WARD, Private, HARRY, 241063. Enlisted East Dereham. Jerusalem Memorial, Israel.

WARD, Private, REGINALD HERBERT 'REGGIE', 242317. Born and enlisted Harleston. Son of Herbert and Lucy Ward of Jays Green, Harleston. Jerusalem Memorial, Israel.

WARDALE, Private, JAMES WILLIAM, 240768age 20. Enlisted East Dereham. Son of Florence Wardale, of St. Peter's Rd., St. Germans, King's Lynn, and the late James Wardale. Jerusalem Memorial, Israel.

WARNER, Private, WILLIAM FREDERICK, 241177, D Coy. age 22 Enlisted Cromer. Son of John and Maria Warner, of Martello Lodge, Golf Rd., Felixstowe. Gaza War Cemetery, Israel.

WATKINS, Lance Serjeant, JAMES ARTHUR, 242498. Born Tottenhill, enlisted King's Lynn. Son of John Watkins. Gaza War Cemetery, Israel.

WATSON, Private, EDWIN, 240221. Born and enlisted Mundesley. Son of Sophia Watson of 3 Town's End Cottages, Mundesley. Jerusalem Memorial, Israel.

WATTS, Private, WILLIAM, 240542 age 19. Enlisted East Dereham. Son of Mrs Elizabeth Watts, of No.8, Row 43, Great Yarmouth. Gaza War Cemetery, Israel.

WEBSTER, Private, CHARLES REGINALD, 240543, A Coy. age 20. Enlisted East Dereham. Died of wounds while a Prisoner of War 10 May 1917. Son of Charles and Elizabeth Webster, of 4, Station Terrace, Swaffham, Norfolk. Haifa War Cemetery, Israel.

WEIR, Private, JOHN, 240042. Born Norwich, enlisted Great Yarmouth. Nephew of Maud Grey of 15 Row 47, North Quay, Great Yarmouth. Jerusalem Memorial, Israel.

WELHAM, Company Serjeant Major, BENJAMIN, 240493 age 26. Born Gayton Thorpe. Enlisted East Dereham. Son of Charles and Emily Welham of Old Farm Cottages, Gayton Thorpe. Husband of Gladys Welham. Gaza War Cemetery, Israel.

WHITE, Private, JAMES, 242480. Born Corpusty, enlisted Norwich. Son of Oscar and Esther White employed on Dairy Farm, Weston Lonville. Gaza War Cemetery, Israel.

WIER, Private, GEORGE WRIGHT, 240821 age 21. Born North Tuddenham. Enlisted East Dereham. Son of George and Gertrude Wier of Low Street, North Tuddenham. Husband of Elsie Wier. Jerusalem Memorial, Israel.

WOODCOCK, Private, FRANCIS HENRY, 242511. Enlisted Norwich. Son of Mrs Woodcock, of The Green Kimberley, Norfolk. Gaza War Cemetery, Israel.

WOODS, Private, ERNEST JOHN, 240378 age 22. Enlisted Great Yarmouth. Son of Walter and Harriett Woods of Riverside, Potter Heigham Gaza War Cemetery, Israel.

WOODS, Private, SIDNEY SAMUEL, 240050. Born and enlisted East Dereham. Son of Robert and Elizabeth Woods, of 2, Rose Hill Cottages, Swaffham Rd., East Dereham. Gaza War Cemetery, Israel.

WRIGHT, Private, CECIL ASHTON, 241020 age 18. Enlisted East Dereham. Son of Mrs Sarah Wright, of 61, Chapel Rd. Jerusalem Memorial, Israel.

WRIGHT, Private, ROBERT CHARLES, 241093 age 27. Enlisted at King's Lynn in August 1914. Son of Robert and Eliza Wright of 2, Providence St., King's Lynn. Jerusalem Memorial, Israel.

WRIGHT, Private, ROBERT WILLIAM, 240497 age 27. Enlisted East Dereham. Son of Robert and Jessie Wright of 2, Providence Street, King's Lynn. Jerusalem Memorial, Israel.

YOUNGE, Private, HORACE, 240096 age 23. Born St Nicholas, King's Lynn and enlisted King's Lynn. Wounded and taken prisoner of war on 19 April 1917 he died while in captivity on 19 October 1917. Son of Osborne and Harriett Younge of 14 Valingers Place, King's Lynn. Jerusalem Memorial, Israel.

1/4th Battalion wounded at Gaza and died shortly after

BALAAM, Private, CHARLES HENRY, 200181 age 22. Born Hardingham, enlisted Hingham. Died of wounds 20 April 1917. Son of James and Mary Ann Balaam, of

Hackford Rd., Hardingham, Attleborough, Norfolk. Deir El Belah War Cemetery, Israel.

BALLS, Lance Corporal, GEORGE ALFRED, 200008, DCM age 44. Born Strumpshaw, enlisted Thorpe St. Andrews. Died of wounds 24 April 1917. Husband of Alice Balls, of 38, School Terrace, Lingwood, Norwich. Deir El Belah War Cemetery, Israel.

BARBER, Private, ARTHUR LYSETT, 201016. Born King's Lynn, enlisted Norwich. Died of wounds 21 April 1917. Son of Edward and Louisa Barber of Hilgay Norfolk. Deir El Belah War Cemetery, Israel.

CARTER, Private, WILLIAM, 202859 age 39. Born Clitheroe, enlisted Preston Lancs. Died of wounds 20 April 1917. Son of John and Ellen Carter, of Clitheroe; husband of Alice Ann Carter, of 19, Victoria St., Clitheroe, Lancs. Deir El Belah War Cemetery, Israel.

FOX, Private, ALBERT, 200949, A Coy. Age 19. Born St Mary's, Norwich, enlisted Norwich. Died of wounds 21 April 1917. Son of Fred and Ellen Fox, of Norwich; husband of Mabel Longbone (formerly Fox), of 93, Aylsham Rd., Norwich. Deir El Belah War Cemetery, Israel.

HILL, Private, HARRY, 200953 age 33. Born North Heigham, enlisted Norwich. Died of wounds 24 April 1917. Son of Mrs A. Hill, of 20a, St. Swithin's Alley, Westwick St., Norwich. Kantara War Memorial Cemetery, Egypt.

SAUNDERS, Private, JOHN, 201142 age 25. Enlisted Norwich. Died of wounds 20 April 1917. Son of John and Annie Saunders, of Wicklewood, Norfolk. Gaza War Cemetery, Israel.

SEWELL, Private, WILLIAM JAMES, 201374 age 36. Waresley, Hunts, enlisted Waresley Park. Died of wounds 20 April 1917. Son of George and Fanny Sewell; husband of Theresa Elizabeth Sewell, of Waresley, Sandy, Beds. Gaza War Cemetery, Israel.

1/5th Battalion Wounded at Gaza and died shortly after

BIRD, Private, ARTHUR, 240766, C Coy. age 33. Enlisted East Dereham. Died on 25 April 1917 from the wounds he received at Gaza. Son of Arthur and Amanda Bird, of Garden Cottage, East Runton, Norfolk. Alexandria (Hadra) War Memorial Cemetery, Egypt. His brothers Horace and Clifford fell on 19 April 1917.

CAUSTON, Private, ERNEST EDGAR, 240960 age 22. Born London, enlisted East Dereham. Died of wounds 20 April 1917. Son of Mrs Alice Causton, of 3, Garden Row, Highgate, King's Lynn. Deir El Belah War Cemetery, Israel.

CLARKE, Private, GEORGE, 242334. Enlisted Norwich. Died of wounds 25 April 1917. Port Said War Memorial Cemetery, Egypt.

CURSON, Lance Corporal, WILLIAM, 240302 age 29. Born East Tuddenham, enlisted East Dereham. Died of wounds 20 April 1917. Son of Mr H. Curson of Honingham, Norfolk. Deir El Belah War Cemetery, Israel.

DIX, Private, GEORGE, 240975. Enlisted East Dereham. Died of wounds 27 April 1917 age 19. Son of William and Susannah Dix, of West Bilney, King's Lynn. Cairo War Memorial Cemetery, Egypt.

ETHERIDGE, Private, HORACE, 242455 age 21. Enlisted Norwich. Died of wounds 22 April 1917. Son of James and Martha Etheridge, of 54, Rackheath, Norwich. Kantara War Memorial Cemetery, Egypt.

HALL, Corporal, HARRY, 241025 age 35. Enlisted King's Lynn. Died of wounds 20 April 1917. Husband of Ada Hall, of 18, King St., Sutton Bridge, Lincs. Gaza War Cemetery, Israel.

HOWARD, Serjeant, FRANK EDWARD, 240306 age 31. Born West Acre, enlisted East Dereham. Died of wounds 25 April 1917. Son of Charles Abram and Emma E. Howard, of 2, Post Office Terrace, Lynn St., Swaffham, Norfolk. Port Said War Memorial Cemetery, Egypt.

HOWLETT, Private, JAMES, 241124. Enlisted East Dereham. Died of wounds 23 April 1917. Deir El Belah War Cemetery, Israel.

READ, Private, LEOPOLD ARCHIE, 241008, B Coy. Age 19. Born Norwich, enlisted King's Lynn. Died of wounds 20 April 1917. Son of Richard and Alice Read, of 15, Newmarket St., Brunswick Rd., Norwich. Deir El Belah War Cemetery, Israel.

RYE, Private, ERNEST EDWARD, 242494. Born Middleton, enlisted King's Lynn. Died of wounds 21 April 1917. Deir El Belah War Cemetery, Israel.

THOMPSON, Private, HUBERT WILLIAM, 240488 Age 21. Enlisted East Dereham. Died of wounds 20 April 1917. Son of Mr W.H. Thompson, of Prince of Wales Rd., Swaffham. Deir El Belah War Cemetery, Israel.

WICKS, Private, GEORGE, 242481 age 34. Born Ickworth, enlisted Norwich. Died of wounds 22 April 1917. Son of George Wicks; husband of Beatrice May Wicks, of 9, Town St., Old Brandon, Suffolk. Gaza War Cemetery, Israel.

Select Bibliography and Sources

Aspinall-Oglander, Brig-Gen Cecil, *Official History of the War, Military Operations, Gallipoli* (vols. 1 and 2, appendices and maps) (London 1929, 1932)

Carlyon, L.A., *Gallipoli* (London 2002)

Chambers, Stephen, *Gallipoli: August Offensive* (Barnsley 2011)

Codling, Eddie, *Coming Home*, (Norfolk 1994)

Davy, Terry, *Dereham in the Great War* (Dereham 1990)

Dutt, William Alfred (intro. By H. Rider Haggard), *The King's Homeland: Sandringham and Northwest Norfolk* (London 1904)

Fair, Captain A. and Wolton, Captain E.D., *The History of 1/5th Battalion: The Suffolk Regiment* (London 1923)

Fuller, J.F.C., *The Decisive Battles of the Western World* (vol. III) (London 1956)

Gallishaw, John *Trenching at Gallipoli* (New York 1916)

Hamilton, Sir Ian, *Ian Hamilton's Final Despatches* (London 1916)

Hamilton, Sir Ian *Gallipoli Diary* (London 1920)

Hayward, James, *Myths and Legends of the First World War* (Stroud 2002)

James, Brigadier E.A., OBE TD, *British Regiments 1914-18*, (London 1993)

Jones, John Philip, *Johnny: The Legend and Tragedy of General Sir Ian Hamilton* (Barnsley 2012)

Kelly's Directory of Norfolk (London 1912)

Lee, John, *A Soldier's Life: General Sir Ian Hamilton 1853-1947* (London 2000)

Marie Louise, Her Highness Princess, *My Memories of Six Reigns* (London 1956)

Matson, John, *Sandringham Days* (Stroud 2015)

McCrery, Nigel, *All the King's Men* (London 1992)

Morris, Captain Joseph, *The German Air Raids on Great Britain 1914-1918*, (London 1969)

Longmate, Norman, *Island Fortress: The Defence of Britain 1603-1945* (London 1991)

Messenger, Charles, *Call-To-Arms: The British Army 1914-18* (London 2005)

North, John, *Gallipoli: The Fading Vision* (London 1966)

Pelly, Arthur Roland (Rollo), *My Masters* (Great Dunmow 1993)

Petre, F. Loraine, OBE, *The History of The Norfolk Regiment 1685-1918*, Vol. II (Norwich 1920)

Ponsonby, Sir Frederick, *Recollections of Three Reigns* (London 1988)

Richards, Walter, *His Majesty's Territorial Army*, (London c1910)

Sellwood, A.V., *The Saturday Night Soldiers* (London 1966)

Storey, Neil R., *The Pride of Norfolk* (Wellington 2009)

Westlake, Ray, *British Regiments at Gallipoli*, (Barnsley 1996)

Westlake, Ray, *The Territorial Battalions*, (Tunbridge Wells 1986)

Williamson, Tom, *The Disappearance of the King's Company (Sandringham) in Gallipoli, The Day the Hills Caught Fire*, (Stockwell 1979)

Windsor, HRH the Duke of, *A King's Story: The Memoirs of HRH the Duke of Windsor* (London 1951)

Newspapers and Periodicals

The Britannia Magazine, The Times, The Graphic, Great Eastern Railway Magazine, Bury Free Press, The War Budget, The Sphere, The War Illustrated, The Illustrated War News, The Lady's Realm, The Manchester Guardian, Norfolk Chronicle, Eastern Daily Press, Eastern Evening News, Yarmouth Mercury, Dereham & Fakenham Times, Lynn News & County Press, Lynn Advertiser, North Walsham Post, North Walsham & District Parish Magazine, Dersingham Parish Magazine.

Official Sources

Commonwealth War Graves Commission, Report 14, Gallipoli, Revd. Charles Pierrepont Edwards (London 1930)

The Dardanelles Commission 1914-16 (HMSO 1917)

War Service Roll of the Members of The Royal Households and Estates of The King and The Queen (HMSO)

War Diaries of 1/4th, 1/5th Battalions, The Norfolk Regiment (T.F.)

War Diary of 1/8th Battalion, Hampshire Regiment (Isle of Wight Rifles) (T.F.)

War Diary of 1/5th Battalion, The Suffolk Regiment (T.F.)

War Diary of 163rd Infantry Brigade

War Diary of 54th Division

Officer's Service Record and Statement regarding circumstances of Capture of 2/Lieut W.G.S. Fawkes, B Company, 1/5th Norfolk Regiment (T.F.), National Archives WO 374/23786

Royal Army Chaplains Department (Code 38(B)): Report of chaplains attached to graves registration unit, Gallipoli, National Archives WO32/5640

Unpublished sources

Diaries and papers of Lieutenant-Colonel T.W. Purdy TD

The scrapbooks of Major A.C.M. Coxon TD

Typed manuscript *A History of the 4th Battalion, The Norfolk Regiment 1859-1921* by Colonel J.R. Harvey DSO, TD

Letters of Captain Frank Beck MVO

Letters of Captain Evelyn Beck MC

Letters from Colonel Arthur Stanley Woodwark CBE CMG RAMC

Letters and telegrams from HM King George V

Letters and telegrams from Sir Dighton Probyn VC, Comptroller to the Household of HM Queen Alexandra

Letters from Miss Charlotte Knollys, Lady of the Bedchamber and Private Secretary to HM Queen Alexandra

Letters, diaries and scrapbooks from numerous members of the Norfolk Regiment Territorial Force Battalion's rank and file and their families.

Acknowledgements

Her Majesty the Queen; The Heritage Lottery Fund; Michael O'Lone, the Queen's Estate Agent, Sandringham; Helen Walch, Sandringham Estate Public Enterprises Manager; Revd. Jonathan Riviere, Rector of Sandringham and West Newton; Sandringham and West Newton School; Alexis Brand; the Beck family; Peter Purdy; Norfolk Libraries and Information Service (Norfolk Heritage Centre, Norwich Millennium Library, Great Yarmouth and King's Lynn libraries); Norfolk Record Office; Kate Thaxton, curator of The Royal Norfolk Regimental Museum, BBC Radio Norfolk; West Mersea Museum, Hilary Venn, Burnham-on-Sea Baptist Church, Arthur Coxon, Jane Chater; Raymond Rogers; Geoffrey Woollard; Margaret Keeler; Paul Pearce; Carol Claxton; Ellee Seymour; Peter Whitby; John Stevens; Pamela Weal; Joyce Stevenson; Philip Theobald; Hannah Jackson; Allen Prior; John Crowe; Rob Carman; Tim Rose; my partner Fiona for her additional research, love and support; my Mother Diane and the many descendants of the members of the 4th and 5th Battalions, The Norfolk Regiment who have supported and encouraged my research over the years.

Index